ILLEGITIMATE AUTHORITY

ILLEGITIMATE
AUTHORITY

FACING THE CHALLENGES OF OUR TIME

NOAM CHOMSKY

EDITED BY C. J. POLYCHRONIOU

A TRUTHOUT COLLECTION

HAYMARKET BOOKS
CHICAGO, ILLINOIS

Published in 2023 by
Haymarket Books
P.O. Box 180165
Chicago, IL 60618
773-583-7884
www.haymarketbooks.org
info@haymarketbooks.org

ISBN: 978-1-64259-905-3

Distributed to the trade in the US through Consortium Book Sales
and Distribution (www.cbsd.com) and internationally through Ingram
Publisher Services International (www.ingramcontent.com).

This book was published with the generous support of Lannan Foundation and Wallace Action Fund.

Special discounts are available for bulk purchases by organizations and
institutions. Please email info@haymarketbooks.org for more information.

Cover photograph by Kelly Sikkema.
Cover design by Rachel Cohen.

Printed in Canada by union labor.

Library of Congress Cataloging-in-Publication data is available.

10 9 8 7 6 5 4 3 2 1

CONTENTS

PREFACE

We live in dangerous and disconcerting times. The world is fraught with aggression and tension and the Russian invasion of Ukraine on February 24, 2022, brought war back to Europe. Climate change is accelerating, with the extreme effects of global warming having become a frightening new normal, while the continued existence of nuclear weapons poses a unique threat to the environment and human survival. International cooperation for tackling the global challenges is sorely missing.

On domestic politics, the situation is hardly less distressing. Most people around the world, especially in the developed countries, believe that their society is more divided than ever before. Neoliberalism has destroyed the social fabric by unleashing destructive social and economic trends and paved the way for the rise of authoritarian populism.

However, no other country in the industrialized world is more divided than the United States. In no other country in the Western world are the forces of reaction as powerful and destructive as they are in the US. The Republican Party, a reactionary political force virtually from the early twentieth century onward, has dropped the mask and has become a full-fledged "proto-fascist" political organization. The highest court in the federal judiciary of the United States is dominated by an ultraconservative wing, a bunch of "partisan hacks." The Supreme Court's decision on June 24, 2022, to overturn the constitutional right to abortion is a huge setback for women's rights and outraged the world. The five justices who overturned *Roe v. Wade* were nominated by Republican presidents. A day earlier, the "partisan hacks" struck down a New York hand-gun licensing law (an "obnoxious law," according to the National Rifle Association) which required people to show proper cause to carry concealed handguns in public.

In a country plagued with gun violence, the Supreme Court justices decided that people should be allowed to carry concealed guns in public for "self-defense." Indeed, as Noam Chomsky points out in some of the interviews included in this volume, the US is a global outlier on multiple fronts: gun ownership and gun violence, religious fundamentalism, health care, inequality, global warming, and now abortion has been added to the list.

The interviews included in this volume began with what seemed to be the start of a new era in US and even world affairs as the "worst criminal in human history," according to Noam Chomsky, had joined history's club of one-term presidents. The election of Joe Biden offered hope that US democracy (or what's left of it) might be saved, that a much-needed progressive economic agenda would be implemented, and that the climate crisis would receive its due attention after four years not simply of complete neglect by the Trump administration but by the pursuit of policies that severely damaged the environment and accelerated global warming. Hence why Noam Chomsky had called Trump the worst criminal in history. No exaggeration at all when we consider what was at stake under Trump's policies.

To be sure, with Trump out and Biden in, things looked rather promising, but the forces of reaction had other plans in mind. Republicans and a handful of so-called "moderate Democrats" blocked Biden's economic agenda. Biden himself betrayed his climate promises and the activists who had supported him by siding with Big Oil. And his foreign policy became barely distinguishable from that of Donald Trump.

Scores of interviews assembled here address and analyze the social, economic, and political conditions in the United States in the post-Trump era. The US is still the only superpower in the world, and what is happening in the country tends to have global ramifications. The present-day Republican Party, with its "proto-fascist" ideological orientation and strong bonds to the fossil fuel industry, is capable of destroying the country and dragging down the world with it.

Of course, nothing is predetermined. "Human agency is not finished," as Noam Chomsky tends to point out. The US is not devoid of people and organizations dedicated to the causes of social and economic justice, peace, and sustainability. On the contrary, progressive forces in the US are at the forefront of the struggle for a new socioeconomic order and a carbon-free future. Fighting under highly adverse political and cultural conditions, progressive and radical forces in the US have managed to make a democratic-socialist agenda appealing to the younger generation of Americans. Progressive political economists, like those assembled at the Political Economy Research Institute at the University of Massachusetts–Amherst, are leading the way to a green economy.

However, even disappointment with Biden's policies took a back seat following the Russian invasion of Ukraine, which Noam Chomsky has characterized as "a major war crime, ranking alongside the US invasion of Iraq and the Hitler-Stalin invasion of Poland in September 1939." Putin's criminal action has far-reaching consequences beyond Ukraine. The invasion, while causing immeasurable suffering and destruction and creating a humanitarian crisis, also triggered a global food crisis, revitalized NATO, and put climate action on the back burner.

Western countries also imposed unprecedented sanctions on Russia over its invasion of Ukraine. But, in a typical display of hypocrisy, to which they are so much accustomed, Western governments and mainstream media alike kept silent about the provocative role of NATO (the US) in the tragic and shocking Russian-Ukrainian conflict. In scores of interviews assembled here, Noam Chomsky dissects with surgical precision the root cause of the war in Ukraine, the risks associated with the escalation of the conflict, and delves into the making of the new international order.

Illegitimate Authority: Facing the Challenges of Our Time is the third volume of collected interviews with Noam Chomsky, the world's greatest public intellectual, regarded by millions as a national and international treasure. The interviews were conducted between late March 2021 and the end of June 2022 and originally appeared in *Truthout*, a nonprofit progressive news organization dedicated to providing an independent alternative to mainstream, corporate organizations and aiming to spark action by revealing systemic injustice and crimes against humanity.

The collaboration with Noam Chomsky, extensive and uninterrupted for a quarter of a century, is an extraordinary honor and privilege for me. It has also been, needless to say, a most stimulating experience. As such, there are no adequate words to express my gratitude to him or fully describe all the feelings I have for him.

I also want to express my deepest thanks to Maya Schenwar, Alana Price, and Britney Schultz for working closely with me over many years and for publishing these interviews as stand-alone pieces in *Truthout*. They have made a huge contribution in helping to introduce the views and ideas of Noam Chomsky to a new generation of readers and activists.

Finally, heartfelt thanks to Robert Pollin and Gerald Epstein, two brilliant economists of the left, codirectors of the Political Economy Research Institute (PERI) at the University of Massachusetts at Amherst, whose work is paving the way for a decent life for all and a sustainable future. I am grateful for their support.

The struggle continues.

—C. J. Polychroniou, July 2022

BIDEN'S EARLY AGENDA GIVES HOPE, BUT ACTIVIST PRESSURE MUST NOT CEASE

March 20, 2021

C. J. Polychroniou: *President Joe Biden has been in office for approximately two months now, in the course of which he has signed scores of executive orders meant to reverse the policies of Donald Trump. But he has also managed to pass a huge and ambitious stimulus bill unlike anything seen during peacetime. What's your assessment of Biden's actions so far to deal with the most pressing issues facing US society, namely, the coronavirus pandemic and the pain caused to millions of Americans on account of the pandemic?*

Noam Chomsky: Better than I'd anticipated. Considerably so.

The stimulus bill has its flaws, but considering the circumstances, it's an impressive achievement. The circumstances are a highly disciplined opposition party dedicated to the principle announced years ago by its maximal leader, Mitch McConnell: *If we are not in power, we must render the country ungovernable and block government legislative efforts, however beneficial they might be. Then the consequences can be blamed on the party in power, and we can take over.* It worked well for Republicans in 2009—with plenty of help from Obama. By 2010, the Democrats lost Congress, and the way was cleared to the 2016 debacle.

There's every reason to suppose that the strategy will be renewed—this time under more complex circumstances. The voting

1

base in the hands of Trump, who shares the objective but differs from McConnell on who will pick up the pieces: McConnell and the donor class, or Trump and the voting base he mobilized, almost half of whom worship him as the messenger God sent to save the country from . . . we can fill in our favorite fantasies, but should not overlook the fact that what may sound [ridiculous] has roots in the lives of the victims of the neoliberal globalization of the past forty years—extended by Trump, apart from some rhetorical flourishes.

In those circumstances, passing a stimulus bill was a major accomplishment. Republicans who favor it, and know that their constituents do, nevertheless voted against it, in lockstep obedience to what the Central Committee determines. Some Democrats insisted on watering it down. But what finally passed has valuable elements, which could be a basis for moving on.

There are huge gaps. The bill surely should have contained an increase in the miserable minimum wage, an utter scandal. But that would have been very difficult in the face of total Republican opposition, along with a few Democrats. And there are other crucial features that are missing. Nevertheless, if the short-term measures on child poverty, income support, medical insurance, and other basic needs can be extended, it would be a substantial step toward fulfilling the promise envisioned by such careful observers as Roosevelt Institute president Felicia Wong, who reflected that, "As I see it, both the scale and the direction of the American Rescue Plan break the neoliberal, deficits-and-inflation-come-first mold that has hollowed out our economy for a generation." We haven't seen anything that could elicit such hopes for a long time.

There is also hope in appointments on economic issues. Who would have imagined that a regular contributor to radical economics journals would be appointed to the Council of Economic Advisers (Heather Boushey), joined by the senior economic adviser of the labor-oriented Economic Policy Institute (Jared Bernstein)?

Biden's strong support for Amazon workers, and unions generally, is a welcome shift. Nothing like it has been heard from the chambers of power in many years. In a sharp reversal of Trump legislation, the tax changes raise incomes mostly for the poor, not the rich. Economic Policy Institute president Thea Lee summarizes the package by saying that it "will provide crucial support to millions of working families; dramatically reduce the race, gender, and income inequalities that were exacerbated by the crisis; and create the conditions for a truly robust recovery once the virus is under control and people are able to resume normal economic activity." Optimistic, but within reach.

House Democrats have passed other important legislation. H.R. 1 protects voting rights, a critical matter now, with Republicans working overtime to try to block the votes of [people of color] and the poor, recognizing that this is the only way a minority party dedicated to wealth and corporate power can remain viable.

On the labor front, the House passed the Protecting the Right to Organize (PRO) Act, "a critical step toward restoring workers' right to organize and bargain collectively," the Economic Policy Institute reports, a fundamental right that "has been eroded for decades as employers exploited weaknesses in the current law." It'll probably be killed by the Senate. Even apart from party loyalty, there is little sympathy for working people in Republican ranks.

But even so, it's a basis for organizing and education. It can be a step toward revitalizing the labor movement, a prime target of the neoliberal project since [Ronald] Reagan and [Margaret] Thatcher, who understood well that working people must be deprived of means to defend themselves from the assault.

Decline of union membership is by now recognized, even in the mainstream, to be a major factor in rising inequality—a phrase that translates to "robbery of the general public by a tiny fraction of super-rich." The Economic Policy Institute has reviewed the facts regularly, most recently in a chart that graphically demonstrates the remarkable correlation between rising/falling union membership and falling/rising inequality.

More generally, there is a good opportunity to overcome the baleful legacy of Trump's bitterly anti-labor Labor Department, headed by corporate lawyer Eugene Scalia, who used his term in office to eviscerate worker rights, notoriously during the pandemic. Scalia was perfectly chosen for the transformation of the Republicans to a "working-class party," as hailed by Marco Rubio and Josh Hawley in a triumph of propaganda, or maybe sheer chutzpah.

Michael Regan's appointment as Environmental Protection Agency administrator should replace corporate greed by science and human welfare in this essential agency, a move toward human decency that in this case is a prerequisite for survival.

It's easy to find serious omissions and deficiencies in Biden's programs on the domestic front, but there are signs of hope for emerging from the Trump nightmare and moving on to what really should, what really must be done. The hopes are, however, conditional. The temporary measures of the stimulus on child poverty and many other issues must be made permanent, and improved. Crucially, activist pressure must not cease. The masters of the universe pursue their class war relentlessly, and can only be countered by an aroused public opposition that is no less dedicated to the common good.

What do you think of Biden's refusal to cancel $50,000 in student loans?

A bad decision. What the realistic options were, I don't frankly know. Higher education at a high level should be recognized to be a basic right, freely available, as it is elsewhere: in our Mexican neighbor, in rich developed countries like Germany, France, the Nordic countries, and a great many others, with at most nominal fees. As it substantially was in the US when it was a much poorer country than it is today. The postwar GI Bill of Rights provided free education for great numbers of white males who would never have gone to college otherwise. There is no reason why young people of any race should be denied the privilege today.

In light of the January 6 attack on the US Capitol, Biden has vowed to fight domestic terrorism by passing a new law "that respects free speech and civil liberties." Does the US need a new domestic terrorism agenda?

A prior question is whether we should retain the current domestic terrorism agenda. There are strong reasons to question that. And any

expansion should be a matter of serious concern. That aside, white supremacist violence is no laughing matter. Through the Trump years, the
FBI and other monitors report steadily increasing white supremacist
terror, by now covering almost all recorded terror. Armed militias are
rampant—Trump's "tough guys" as he's admiringly called them. The
problems can't be overlooked, but have to be handled with great caution and a close eye on the temptations for abuse.

*Biden has proposed a plan to strengthen the middle class by encouraging
unionization and collective bargaining, and his recent affirmation of the
rights of workers to unionize, which was widely interpreted as support for
Amazon workers' rights to organize in Alabama, has spread considerable
enthusiasm among progressives. Indeed, Biden's support for unions is in
pace with the highly favorable ratings that unions have been receiving in the
last couple of years. What's behind the support for unions in the present era?*

One reason is objective reality. The sharp rise in inequality is a growing curse, with extremely harmful effects across the society. As mentioned earlier, it closely tracks decline of unions, for reasons that are
well understood. Historically, labor unions have been in the forefront
of struggles for justice and rights. They also pioneered the environmental movement, as we've discussed before. Workers' organizations are
changing in character with the growth of service and knowledge-based
economies. They have shared interests, and foster the values of solidarity and mutual aid on which the hope for a decent future rest. Many
unions retain the world "international" in their names. It should not
just be a symbol or a dream. The dire challenges we face have no borders. Global heating, pandemics, disarmament will be dealt with internationally, if at all. The same is true of labor rights and human rights
more generally. At every level, associations of working people should
once again be prominent, if not leading the way, toward a better world.

BIDEN'S FOREIGN POLICY IS LARGELY INDISTINGUISHABLE FROM TRUMP'S

March 29, 2021

C. J. Polychroniou: *Noam, two months after being in the White House, Biden's foreign policy agenda is beginning to take shape. What are the signs so far of how the Biden administration intends to address the challenges to US hegemony posed by its primary geopolitical rivals, namely Russia and China?*

Noam Chomsky: The challenge to US hegemony posed by Russia and particularly China has been a major theme of foreign policy discourse for some time, with persistent agreement on the severity of the threat.

The matter is plainly complex. It's a good rule of thumb to cast a skeptical eye when there is general agreement on some complex issue. This is no exception.

What we generally find, I think, is that Russia and China sometimes deter US actions to enforce its global hegemony in regions on their periphery that are of particular concern to them. One can ask whether they are justified in seeking to limit overwhelming US power in this way, but that is a long distance from the way the challenge is commonly understood: as an effort to displace the US global role in sustaining a liberal rule-based international order by new centers of hegemonic power.

Do Russia and China actually challenge US hegemony in the ways commonly understood?

Russia is not a major actor in the world scene, apart from the military force that is a (very dangerous) residue of its earlier status as a second superpower. It does not begin to compare with the US in outreach and influence.

China has undergone spectacular economic growth, but it is still far from approaching US power in just about any dimension. It remains a relatively poor country, ranked eighty-fifth in the UN Human Development Index, between Brazil and Ecuador. The US, while not ranked near the top because of its poor social welfare record, is far above China. In military strength and global outreach (bases, forces in active combat), there is no comparison. US-based multinationals have about half of world wealth and are first (sometimes second) in just about every category. China is far behind. China also faces serious internal problems (ecological, demographic, political). The US, in contrast, has internal and security advantages unmatched anywhere.

Take sanctions, a major instrument of world power for one country on Earth: the US. They are, furthermore, third-party sanctions. Disobey them, and you're out of luck. You can be tossed out of the world financial system, or worse. It's pretty much the same wherever we look.

If we look at history, we find regular echoes of Senator Arthur Vandenberg's 1947 advice to the president that he should "scare hell out of the American people" if he wanted to whip them up to a frenzy of fear over the Russian threat to take over the world. It would be necessary to be "clearer than truth," as explained by Dean Acheson, one of the creators of the postwar order. He was referring to NSC-68 of 1950, a founding document of the Cold War, declassified decades later. Its rhetoric continues to resound in one or another form, again today about China.

NSC-68 called for a huge military buildup and imposition of discipline on our dangerously free society so that we can defend ourselves from the "slave state" with its "implacable purpose . . . to eliminate the challenge of freedom" everywhere, establishing "total power over all men [and] absolute authority over the rest of the world." And so on, in an impressive flow.

China does confront US power—in the South China Sea, not the Atlantic or Pacific. There is an economic challenge as well. In some areas, China is a world leader, notably renewable energy, where it is far ahead of other countries in both scale and quality. It is also the world's manufacturing base, though profits go mostly elsewhere, to managers like Taiwan's Foxconn or investors in Apple, which is increasingly reliant on intellectual property rights—the exorbitant patent rights that are a core part of the highly protectionist "free trade" agreements.

China's global influence is surely expanding in investment, commerce, takeover of facilities (such as management of Israel's major port). That influence is likely to expand if it moves forward with provision of vaccines virtually at cost in comparison with the West's hoarding of vaccines and its impeding of distribution of a "People's Vaccine" so as to protect corporate patents and profits. China is also advancing substantially in high technology, much to the consternation of the US, which is seeking to impede its development.

It is rather odd to regard all of this as a challenge to US hegemony.

US policy might help create a more serious challenge by confrontational and hostile acts that drive Russia and China closer together in reaction. That has, in fact, been happening, under Trump and in Biden's first days—though Biden did respond to Russia's call for renewing the New START Treaty on limiting nuclear weapons at the last minute, salvaging the one major element of the arms-control regime that had escaped Trump's wrecking ball.

Clearly what is needed is diplomacy and negotiations on contested matters, and real cooperation on such crucial issues as global warming, arms control, future pandemics—all very severe crises that know no borders. Whether Biden's hawkish foreign policy team will have the wisdom to move in these directions is, for now, at best unclear—at worst, frightening. Absent significant popular pressures, prospects do not look good.

Another issue that calls for popular attention and activism is the policy of protecting hegemony by seeking to harm potential rivals, very publicly in the case of China, but elsewhere too, sometimes in ways that are sometimes hard to believe.

A remarkable example is buried in the Annual Report for 2020 of the Department of Health and Human Services, proudly presented by Secretary Alex Azar. Under the subheading "Combatting malign influences in the Americas," the report discusses the efforts of the Department's Office of Global Affairs (OGA)

> to mitigate efforts by states, including Cuba, Venezuela and Russia, who are working to increase their influence in the region to the detriment of U.S. safety and security. OGA coordinated with other U.S. government agencies to strengthen diplomatic ties and offer technical and humanitarian assistance to dissuade countries in the region from accepting aid from these ill-intentioned states. Examples include *using OGA's Health Attaché office to persuade Brazil to reject the Russian COVID-19 vaccine, and offering CDC technical assistance in lieu of Panama accepting an offer of Cuban doctors.* [Emphasis mine]

In the midst of a raging pandemic, according to this report, we must block malignant initiatives to help miserable victims.

Under President Jair Bolsonaro's grotesque mismanagement, Brazil has become the global horror story of failure to deal with the pandemic, despite its outstanding health institutes and fine past record in vaccination and treatment. It is suffering from a severe shortage of vaccines, so the US takes pride in its efforts to prevent it from using the Russian vaccine, which Western authorities recognize to be comparable to the Moderna and Pfizer vaccines used here.

Even more astonishing, as the author of this article in the EU-based *Brasil Wire* comments, is "that the US dissuaded Panama from accepting Cuban doctors, who have been on the global front line against the pandemic, working in over 40 countries." We must protect Panama from the "malign influence" of the one country in the world to exhibit the kind of internationalism that is needed to save the world from disaster, a crime that must be stopped by the global hegemon.

Washington's hysterical dedication to crush Cuba from almost the first days of its independence in 1959 is one of the most extraordinary phenomena of modern history, but still, the level of petty sadism is a constant surprise.

With regards to Iran, also there do not seem to be signs of hope as the Biden administration has named Richard Nephew, an architect of sadistic sanctions against Iran under Barack Obama, as its deputy Iran envoy. Right or wrong?

Biden adopted Trump's Iran program with virtually no change, even in rhetoric. It is worthwhile to recall the facts.

Trump withdrew US participation in the JCPOA (the nuclear agreement), in violation of UN Security Council Resolution 2331, which obligates all states to abide by the JCPOA, and in violation to the wishes of all other signers. In an impressive display of hegemonic power, when the UN Security Council members insisted on abiding by 2331 and not extending UN sanctions, Secretary of State Mike Pompeo told them to get lost: You are renewing the sanctions. Trump imposed extremely harsh new sanctions to which others are obliged to conform, with the goal of causing maximum pain to Iranians so that perhaps the government might relent and accept his demand that the JCPOA be replaced by a new agreement that imposes much harsher restrictions on Iran. The pandemic offered new opportunities to torture Iranians by depriving them of desperately needed relief.

Furthermore, it is Iran's responsibility to take the first steps toward negotiations to capitulate to the demands, by terminating actions it took in reaction to Trump's criminality.

As we've discussed before, there is merit in Trump's demand that the JCPOA can be improved. A far better solution is to establish a nuclear weapons–free zone (or WMD-free zone) in the Middle East. There is only one barrier: the US will not permit it, and vetoes the proposal when it arises in international forums, most recently seen by President Obama. The reason is well understood: It's necessary to protect Israel's major nuclear arsenal from inspection. The US does not even formally acknowledge its existence. To do so would prejudice the vast flood of US aid to Israel, arguably in violation of US law, a door that neither political party wants to open. It's another topic that will not even be discussed unless popular pressure makes suppression impossible.

In US discourse, Trump is criticized because his policy of torturing Iranians didn't succeed in bringing the government to capitulate. The stance is reminiscent of Obama's highly praised moves toward limited relations with Cuba, because, as he explained, we need new tactics after our efforts to bring democracy to Cuba had failed—namely, a vicious terrorist war that led almost to extinction in the 1962 missile crisis and sanctions of unparalleled cruelty that are unanimously condemned by the UN General Assembly (Israel excepted). Similarly, our wars in Indochina, the worst crimes since World War II, are criticized as a "failure," as is the invasion of Iraq, a textbook example of the "supreme international crime" for which Nazi war criminals were hanged.

These are among the prerogatives of a true hegemon, immune to the cackles of foreigners and confident in the support of those whom an acerbic critic [Harold Rosenberg] once called "the herd of independent minds," the bulk of the educated classes and the political class.

Biden took over the entire Trump program, without any change. And to twist the knife further, he appointed Richard Nephew as deputy Iran envoy. Nephew has explained his views in his book *Art of Sanctions*, where he outlines the proper "strategy to carefully, methodically, and efficiently increase pain on areas that are vulnerabilities while avoiding those that are not." Just the right choice for the policy of torturing Iranians because the government that most of them despise will not bend to Washington's demands.

US government policy toward Cuba and Iran provides very valuable insight into how the world works under the domination of imperial power.

Cuba since independence in 1959 has been the target of unremitting US violence and torture, reaching truly sadistic levels—with scarcely a word of protest in elite sectors. The US, fortunately, is an unusually free country, so we have access to declassified records explaining the ferocity of the efforts to punish Cubans. Fidel Castro's crime, the State Department explained in the early years, is its "successful defiance" of US policy since the Monroe Doctrine of 1823, which declared Washington's right to control the hemisphere. Plainly harsh measures are required to stifle such efforts, as any Mafia don would understand—and the analogy of world order to the Mafia has considerable merit.

Much the same is true of Iran since 1979, when a popular uprising overthrew the tyrant installed by the US in a military coup that rid the country of its parliamentary regime. Israel had enjoyed very close relations with Iran during the years of the Shah's tyranny and extreme human rights violations, and like the US, was appalled by his overthrow. Israel's de facto ambassador to Iran, Uri Lubrani, expressed his "strong" belief that the uprising could be suppressed, and the Shah restored "by a very relatively small force, determined, ruthless, cruel. I mean the men who would lead that force will have to be emotionally geared to the possibility that they would have to kill ten thousand people."

US authorities pretty much agreed. President Carter sent NATO general Robert E. Huyser to Iran to try to convince the Iranian military to undertake the task—a surmise confirmed by recently released internal documents. They refused, considering it hopeless. Shortly after, Saddam Hussein invaded Iran—an attack that killed hundreds of thousands of Iranians, with full support from the Reagan administration, even when Saddam resorted to chemical weapons, first against Iranians, then against Iraqi Kurds in the Halabja atrocities. Reagan protected his friend Hussein by attributing the crimes to Iran and blocking congressional censure. He then turned to direct military support for Hussein with naval forces in the Gulf. One vessel, the USS *Vincennes*, shot down an Iranian civilian airliner in a clearly marked commercial airspace, killing 290 people, returning to a royal welcome at its home base where the commander and flight officer who had directed the destruction of the airliner were rewarded with Medals of Honor.

Recognizing that it could not fight the US, Iran effectively capitulated. Washington then to turned harsh sanctions against Iran, while rewarding Hussein in ways that sharply increased threats to Iran, which was then just emerging from a devastating war. President Bush I invited Iraqi nuclear engineers to the US for advanced training in nuclear weapons production, no small matter for Iran. He pushed through agricultural aid that Hussein badly needed after having destroyed rich agricultural areas with his chemical weapons attack against Iraqi Kurds. He sent a high-level mission to Iraq headed by the Republican Senate leader Bob Dole, later presidential candidate, to deliver his respects to Hussein, to assure him that critical comment about him would be curbed on Voice of America, and to advise Hussein that he should ignore critical comment in the press, which the US government can't prevent.

This was April 1990. A few months later, Hussein disobeyed (or misunderstood) orders and invaded Kuwait. Then everything changed.

Almost everything. Punishment of Iran for its "successful defiance" continued, with harsh sanctions, and new initiatives by President Bill Clinton, who issued executive orders and signed congressional legislation sanctioning investment in Iran's oil sector, the basis of its economy. Europe objected, but had no way to avoid US extraterritorial sanctions.

US firms suffered too. Princeton University Middle East specialist Seyed Hossein Mousavian, former spokesman for Iran nuclear negotiators, reports that Iran had offered a billion-dollar contract to the US energy firm Conoco. Clinton's intervention, blocking the deal, closed off an opportunity for reconciliation, one of many cases that Mousavian reviews.

Clinton's action was part of a general pattern, an unusual one. Ordinarily, particularly on energy-related issues, policy conforms to Adam Smith's comments on eighteenth-century England, where the "masters of mankind" who own the private economy are the "principal architects" of government policy, and act to ensure that their own interests are foremost, however "grievous" the effect on others, including the people of England. Exceptions are rare, and instructive.

Two striking exceptions are Cuba and Iran. Major business interests (pharmaceuticals, energy, agribusiness, aircraft, and others) have been eager to break into Cuban and Iranian markets and to establish relations with domestic enterprises. State power bars any such moves, overruling parochial interests of the "masters of mankind" in favor of the transcendent goal of punishing successful defiance.

There's a good deal to say about these exceptions to the rule, but it would take us too far afield.

The release of the Jamal Khashoggi murder report disappointed almost everyone, save Saudi Arabia. Why is the Biden administration taking such a soft approach toward Saudi Arabia, and Crown Prince Mohammed bin Salman in particular, which prompted New York Times columnist Nicholas Kristof to write that "Biden . . . let the murderer walk"?

Not hard to guess. Who wants to offend the close ally and regional power that the State Department described during World War II as "a stupendous source of strategic power, and one of the greatest material prizes in world history . . . probably the richest economic prize in the world in the field of foreign investment." The world has changed in many ways since, but the basic reasoning remains.

Biden had promised that, if elected, he would scale back Trump's nuclear weapons spending, and that the US would not rely on nuclear weapons for defense. Are we likely to see a dramatic shift in US nuclear strategy under the Biden administration whereby the use of these weapons will be far less likely?

For reasons of cost alone, it is a goal that should be high on the agenda of anyone who wants to see the kinds of domestic programs the country badly needs. But the reasons go far beyond. Current nuclear strategy calls for preparation for war—meaning terminal nuclear war—with China and Russia.

We should also remember an observation of Daniel Ellsberg's: Nuclear weapons are constantly used, much in the way a gun is used by a robber who aims his gun at a storekeeper and says, "Your money or your life." The principle in fact is enshrined in policy, in the important 1995 document "Essentials of Post-Cold War Deterrence" issued by Clinton's Strategic Command (STRATCOM). The study concludes that nuclear weapons are indispensable because of their incomparable destructive power, but even if not used, "nuclear weapons always cast a shadow over any crisis or conflict," enabling us to gain our ends through intimidation; Ellsberg's point. The study goes on to authorize "preemptive" use of nuclear weapons and provides advice for planners, who should not "portray ourselves as too fully rational and cool-headed." Rather, the "national persona we project" should be "that the US may become irrational and vindictive if its vital interests are attacked and that "some elements may appear to be potentially 'out of control.'"

Richard Nixon's "madman theory," but this time not from reports by associates but from the designers of nuclear strategy.

Two months ago, the UN Treaty on the Prohibition of Nuclear Weapons went into effect. The nuclear powers refused to sign, and still violate their legal responsibility under the Non-Proliferation of Nuclear Weapons to undertake "effective measures" to eliminate nuclear weapons. That stance is not carved in stone, and popular activism could induce significant moves in that direction, a necessity for survival.

Regrettably, that level of civilization still seems beyond the range of the most powerful states, which are careening in the opposite direction, upgrading and enhancing the means to terminate organized human life on Earth.

Even junior partners are joining in the race to destruction. Just a few days ago, British prime minister Boris Johnson "announced a 40 per cent increase in UK's stockpile of nuclear warheads. His review . . . recognised 'the evolving security environment,' identifying Russia as Britain's 'most acute threat.'"

Lots of work to do.

NOAM CHOMSKY AND ROBERT POLLIN

GREEN NEW DEAL IS ESSENTIAL FOR HUMAN SURVIVAL

April 22, 2021

C. J. Polychroniou: *The theme of Earth Day 2021, which first took place in 1970 with the emergence of environmental consciousness in the US during the late 1960s, is "Restore Our Earth." Noam, how would you assess the rate of progress to save the environment since the first Earth Day?*

Noam Chomsky: There is some progress, but by no means enough, almost anywhere. Evidence unfortunately abounds. The drift toward disaster proceeds on its inexorable course, more rapidly than rise in general awareness of the severity of the crisis.

To pick an example of the drift toward disaster almost at random from the scientific literature, a study that appeared a few days ago from the *Conversation* reports that "marine life is fleeing the equator to cooler waters—this could trigger a mass extinction event," an eventuality with potentially horrendous consequences.

It's all too easy to document the lack of awareness. One striking illustration, too little noticed, is the dog that didn't bark. There is no end to the denunciations of Trump's misdeeds, but virtual silence about the worst crime in human history: his dedicated race to the abyss of environmental catastrophe, with his party in tow.

They couldn't refrain from administering a last blow just before being driven from office (barely, and perhaps not for long). The final act in August 2020 was to roll back the last of the far-too-limited Obama-era regulations to have escaped the wrecking ball, "effectively freeing oil and gas companies from the need to detect and repair methane leaks—even as new research shows that far more of the potent greenhouse gas is seeping into the atmosphere than previously known . . . a gift to many beleaguered oil and gas companies." It is imperative to serve the prime constituency, great wealth and corporate power, damn the consequences.

Indications are that with the rise of oil prices, fracking is reviving, adhering to Trump's deregulation so as to improve profit margins, while again placing a foot on the accelerator to drive humanity over the cliff. An instructive contribution to impending crisis, minor in context.

Even though we know what must and can be done, the gap between willingness to undertake the task and severity of the crisis ahead is large, and there is not much time to remedy this deep malady of contemporary intellectual and moral culture.

Like the other urgent problems we face today, heating the planet knows no boundaries. The phrase "internationalism or extinction" is not hyperbole. There have been international initiatives, notably the 2015 Paris Agreement and its successors. The announced goals have not been met. They are also insufficient and toothless. The goal in Paris was to reach a treaty. That was impossible for the usual reason: the Republican Party. It would never agree to a treaty, even if it had not become a party of rigid deniers.

Accordingly, there was only a voluntary agreement. So it has remained. Worse still, in pursuit of his goal of wrecking everything in reach, the hallmark of his administration, Trump withdrew from the agreement. Without US participation, in fact leadership, nothing is going to happen. President Joe Biden has rejoined. What that means will depend on popular efforts.

I said "had not become" for a reason. The Republican Party was not always dedicated rigidly to destruction of organized human life on

Earth; apologies for telling the truth, and not mincing words. In 2008, John McCain ran for president on a ticket that included some concern for destruction of the environment, and congressional Republicans were considering similar ideas. The huge Koch brothers energy consortium had been laboring for years to prevent any such heresy, and moved quickly to cut it off at the pass. Under the leadership of the late David Koch, they launched a juggernaut to keep the party on course. It quickly succumbed, and since then has tolerated only rare deviation.

The capitulation, of course, has a major effect on legislative options, but also on the voting base, amplified by the media echo chamber to which most limit themselves. "Climate change"—the euphemism for destruction of organized human life on Earth—ranks low in concern among Republicans, frighteningly low in fact. In the most recent Pew poll, just days ago, respondents were asked to rank fifteen major problems. Among Republicans, climate change was ranked last, alongside of sexism, far below the front-runners, the federal deficit and illegal immigration. Fourteen percent of Republicans think that the most severe threat in human history is a major problem (though concerns seem to be somewhat higher among younger ones, an encouraging sign). This must change.

Turning elsewhere, the picture varies but is not very bright anywhere. China is a mixed story. Though far below the US, Australia, and Canada in per-capita emissions—the relevant figure—it nevertheless is poisoning the planet at much too high a level and is still building coal plants. China is far ahead of the rest of the world in renewable energy, both in scale and quality, and has pledged to reach net-zero emissions by 2060—difficult to imagine at the present pace, but China has had a good record in reaching announced goals. In Canada, the parties have just released their current plans: some commitment but nowhere near enough. That's aside from the terrible record of Canadian mining companies throughout the world. Europe is a mixed story.

The Global South cannot deal with the crisis on its own. To provide substantial assistance is an obligation for the rich, not simply out of concern for their own survival but also a moral obligation, considering an ugly history that we need not review.

Can the wealthy and privileged rise to that moral level? Can they even rise to the level of concern for self-preservation if it means some minor sacrifice now? The fate of human society—and much of the rest of life on Earth—depends on the answer to that question. An answer that will come soon, or not at all.

Bob, in hosting the Earth Day 2021 summit, Biden hopes to persuade the largest emitters to step up their pledges to combat the climate crisis. However, the truth of the matter is that most countries are not hitting the Paris climate targets and the decline in emissions in 2020 was mostly driven by the COVID-19 lockdowns and the ensuing economic recession. So, how do we move from rhetoric to accelerated action, and, in your own view, what are the priority actions that the Biden administration should focus on in order to initiate a clean energy revolution?

Robert Pollin: In terms of moving from rhetoric to accelerated action, it will be useful to be clear about what was accomplished with the 2015 Paris Climate Agreement. Noam described the Paris Agreement and its successors as "insufficient and toothless." Just how insufficient and toothless becomes evident in considering the energy consumption and CO_2 emissions projections generated by the International Energy Agency (IEA), whose global energy and emissions model is the most detailed and widely cited work of its kind. In the most recent 2020 edition of its World Energy Outlook, the IEA estimates that, if all signatory countries to the Paris Agreement fulfilled all of their "Nationally Determined Contributions" set out at Paris, global CO_2 emissions will not fall at all as of 2040.

It's true that, according to the IEA's model, emissions level will not increase any further from now until 2040. But this should be cold comfort, given that, according to the Intergovernmental Panel on Climate Change (IPCC), CO_2 emissions need to fall by 45 percent as of 2030 and hit net-zero emissions by 2050 in order for there to be at least a decent chance of stabilizing the global average temperature at 1.5 degrees Celsius above preindustrial levels. In other words, soaring rhetoric and photo opportunities aside, the Paris Agreement accomplishes next to nothing if we are serious about hitting the IPCC emissions reduction targets.

The "American Jobs Plan" that the Biden administration introduced at the end of March does give serious attention to many of the main areas in which immediate dramatic action needs to occur. It sets out a range of measures to move the US economy onto a climate stabilization path, including large-scale investments in energy efficiency measures, such as retrofitting buildings and expanding public transportation, along with investments to dramatically expand the supply of clean energy sources to supplant our current fossil-fuel-dominant energy system. Burning oil, coal, and natural gas to produce energy is now responsible for about 70 percent of all CO_2 emissions globally.

The Biden proposal also emphasizes the opportunity to create good job opportunities and expand union organizing through these investments in energy efficiency and clean energy. It also recognizes the need for just transition for workers and communities that are now dependent on the fossil fuel industry. These are important positive steps. They resulted because of years of dedicated and effective organizing by many labor and environmental groups, such as the Green New Deal Network and the Labor Network for Sustainability.

I also have serious concerns about the Biden proposal. The first is that the scale of spending is too small. This is despite the constant barrage of press stories claiming that the spending levels are astronomical. During the presidential campaign, Biden's "Build Back Better" proposal was budgeted at $2 trillion over four years—that is, $500 billion per year. His current proposal is at $2.3 trillion over eight years—that is, somewhat less than $300 billion per year. So, on a year-by-year basis, Biden's current proposal is already 40 percent less than what he had proposed as a candidate.

This overall program also includes lots of investment areas other than those dealing with the climate crisis, such as traditional infrastructure spending on roads, bridges, and water systems; expanding broadband access; and supporting the care economy, including child and elder care. Many of these other measures are highly worthy. But we need to recognize that they will not contribute to driving down emissions. I would say a generous assessment of the Biden plan is that 30 percent of the spending will contribute to driving down emissions. We now are at a total annual budget of perhaps $100 billion. That is equal to 0.5 percent of current US GDP.

It is conceivable that this level of federal spending could be in the range of barely adequate. But that would be only if state and local governments, and even more so, private investors—including small-scale cooperatives and community-owned enterprises—commit major resources to clean energy investments. By my own estimates, the US will need to spend in the range of $600 billion per year in total through 2050 to create a zero-emissions economy. That will be equal to nearly 3 percent of US GDP per year.

But the private sector will not come up with the additional $400–$500 billion per year unless they are forced to do so. That will entail, for example, stringent regulations requiring the phaseout of fossil fuels as energy sources. As one case in point, utilities could be required to reduce their consumption of coal, natural gas, and oil by, say, 5 percent per year. Their CEOs would then be [held responsible] if they fail to meet that requirement.

At the same time, the Federal Reserve can easily leverage federal spending programs by establishing Green Bond purchasing programs at scale, such as in the range of $300 billion per year to finance clean energy investments by both state and local governments as well as private investors. Right now, a significant number of Green Bond programs do already exist at state and local government levels, including through Green Banks. These are all worthy, but are operating at too small a scale relative to the need.

Beyond all this, those of us living in high-income countries need to commit to paying for most of the clean energy transformations in low-income countries. This needs to be recognized as a minimal ethical requirement, since high-income countries are almost entirely responsible for having created the climate crisis in the first place. In addition, even if we don't care about such ethical matters, it is simply a fact that, unless the low-income countries also undergo clean energy transformations, there will be no way to achieve a zero-emissions global economy, and therefore no solution to the climate crisis, in the US, Europe, or anyplace else. The Biden proposal to date includes nothing about supporting climate programs in developing economies. This must change.

Noam, when surveying reactions to whatever environmental gains have been made over the past fifty years, one observes a rather unsurprising pattern, which is, namely, that the right assigns virtually all credit to businessmen and to capitalism, while the left to environmental activists, and contends that the only hope for a greener tomorrow mandates the rejection of capitalist logic. Is capitalism saving or killing the planet?

Chomsky: It's close to a truism that "capitalist logic will kill the planet." That's one of the many reasons why business has always rejected the suicidal doctrines that are piously preached. Rather, the business world demands that a powerful state, under its control, intervene constantly to protect private power from the ravages of an unconstrained market and to sustain the system of public subsidy, private profit that has been a cornerstone of the economy from the early days of industrial state capitalism. . . .

The only way to answer the question posed is to look at examples. Let's pick a central one: a Green New Deal. In one or another form, such a program is essential for survival. A few years ago, the idea was ignored or ridiculed. Now it is at least on the legislative agenda. How did the transition occur? Overwhelmingly, thanks to wide-ranging activism taking many forms, culminating in the occupation of congressional offices by activists of Sunrise Movement. They received support from representatives swept into office on the Sanders wave of popular activism, notably Representative Alexandria Ocasio-Cortez, joined by senior Senator Ed Markey, who had long been concerned with environmental issues.

There's a long way to go from legislative agenda to implementation, but we can be confident that steady and dedicated activism will be a prime factor in carrying the project forward; to be concrete, in pressing Biden's program, itself a product of sustained activism, toward the kinds of policies that are necessary to reach such goals as net-zero emissions by mid-century. The example breaks no new ground. It is, in fact, the norm.

The protestations of the right are, however, not without merit. Given the right structure of benefits and threats, private capital, driven by profit and market share, can be enlisted in pursuing the goal of species survival. That covers contingencies ranging from incentives to invest in solar power to imposing what the private sector calls "reputational risks," the polite term for the fear that the peasants are coming with the pitchforks.

There is an impact. We see it in the current rage for ESG investment (environmental and social factors in corporate government)—all, of course, in service of the bottom line. We also see it in the solemn pledges of corporate executives and business groups to reverse their self-serving course of recent years and to become responsible citizens dedicated to the common good—to become what used to be called "soulful corporations" in an earlier phase of this recurrent performance—which may, on occasion, have an element of sincerity, though always subject to institutional constraints.

Such impacts of popular activism should not be dismissed—while always regarded with due caution. They may induce the search for private gain to veer in a constructive direction—though far too slowly, and only in limited ways. Like it or not, there is no alternative now to large-scale governmental projects. The reference to the New Deal is not out of place.

Whatever the source, the outcome should be welcomed. It's of no slight importance when "more than 300 corporate leaders are asking the Biden administration to nearly double the emission-reduction targets set by the Obama administration," including big boys like Google, McDonald's, Walmart.

The choice is not popular activism or managerial decisions, but both. However, a little reflection on time scales, and on the urgency of the crisis, suffices to show that the critical problems must be addressed within the general framework of existing state capitalist institutions. These can and should be radically changed. At the very least, serious moves should be made to escape the grip of predatory financial capital and the rentier economy that impedes the right mixture of growth/degrowth: growth in what is needed, like renewable energy, efficient mass transportation, education, health, research and development, and much more; degrowth where imperative, as in fossil fuel production. But overall, substantial social change, however important for decent survival, is a long-term project.

Bob, certain studies seem to indicate that the climate crisis won't be stopped even if we reduced greenhouse gas emissions to zero. I am compelled therefore to ask you this: Is the climate crisis a race we can actually win?

Pollin: I am not a climate scientist, so I am not qualified to answer the question at the first, most critical level of climate science itself. But I can at least comment on some related points.

First, we do know what the IPCC has said about what is needed to have a reasonable chance at climate stabilization—that is, first of all, to cut global CO_2 emissions by 45 percent as of 2030 and to reach net-zero emissions by 2050 in order to stabilize the global average temperature at 1.5 degrees Celsius above preindustrial levels. How are we doing in terms of meeting those goals? The only fair assessment is that, to date, the record is dismal.

I would add here one additional set of observations beyond what we have already described. That is, climate scientists have known about the phenomenon of global warming since the late nineteenth century. But, as a steady pattern, the average global temperature only began rising above the preindustrial level in the late 1970s. By the mid-1990s, the average temperature was 0.5 degrees Celsius above the preindustrial level. As of 2020, we are nearly at 1 degree above the preindustrial level. If we follow the pattern of the past twenty years, we will therefore breach the 1.5 degrees threshold by roughly 2040.

What happens if we do breach the 1.5 degrees threshold? I claim no expertise on this, and I think it is fair to say that nobody knows for certain. But we do at least know that the patterns we are already seeing at our current level of warming will only intensify. Thus, the

World Meteorological Organization's provisional 2020 report, "State of the Global Climate," finds that

> heavy rain and extensive flooding occurred over large parts of Africa and Asia in 2020. Heavy rain and flooding affected much of the Sahel, the Greater Horn of Africa, the India subcontinent and neighboring areas, China, Korea and Japan, and parts of southeast Asia at various times of the year. Severe drought affected many parts of interior South America in 2020, with the worst-affected areas being northern Argentina, Paraguay and western border areas of Brazil. . . . Climate and weather events have triggered significant population movements and have severely affected vulnerable people on the move, including in the Pacific region and Central America.

We also know that poor people and poor countries have already borne the greatest costs of the climate crisis, and that this pattern will continue as global average temperatures increase. As the economist James Boyce has written, poor people "are less able to invest in air conditioners, sea walls and other adaptations. They live closer to the edge . . . and the places that climate models show will be hit hardest by global warming—including drought-prone regions of sub-Saharan Africa and typhoon-vulnerable South and South East Asia—are home to some of the world's poorest people."

It therefore seems clear that we are obligated to act now on the premise that the climate crisis is a race that we can still win, even if we don't know for certain whether that is true. But in addition, it is important to also recognize that advancing a global Green New Deal is fundamentally a no-lose proposition, as long as it includes generous transition support for fossil-fuel-dependent workers and communities. This is because, first, the global clean energy transformation will be a major source of job creation in all regions of the world as well as creating a viable path to building a zero-emissions global economy. It will also significantly improve public health by reducing air pollution, lower energy costs across the board, and create opportunities to deliver electricity to rural areas of low-income countries for the first time.

All of these impacts will also help break the grip that neoliberalism has maintained over the global economy over the past forty years. If we do end up building a viable clean energy system through a global Green New Deal, we will therefore also succeed in advancing democracy and egalitarianism.

WITHOUT US AID, ISRAEL WOULDN'T BE KILLING PALESTINIANS EN MASSE

May 12, 2021

C. J. Polychroniou: *Noam, I want to start by asking you to put into context the Israeli attack against Palestinians at the Al-Aqsa Mosque amid eviction protests, and then the latest air raid attacks in Gaza. What's new, what's old, and to what extent is this latest round of neocolonial Israeli violence related to Trump's move of the US embassy to Jerusalem?*

Noam Chomsky: There are always new twists, but in essentials it is an old story, tracing back a century, taking new forms after Israel's 1967 conquests and the decision fifty years ago, by both major political groupings, to choose expansion over security and diplomatic settlement—anticipating (and receiving) crucial US material and diplomatic support all the way.

For what became the dominant tendency in the Zionist movement, there has been a fixed long-term goal. Put crudely, the goal is to rid the country of Palestinians and replace them with Jewish settlers cast as the "rightful owners of the land" returning home after millennia of exile.

At the outset, the British, then in charge, generally regarded this project as just. Lord Balfour, author of the declaration granting Jews a "national home" in Palestine, captured Western elite ethical judgment fairly well by declaring that "Zionism, be it right or wrong, good or bad, is rooted in age-long tradition, in present needs, in future hopes, of far profounder import than the desires and prejudices of the 700,000 Arabs who now inhabit that ancient land."

The sentiments are not unfamiliar.

Zionist policies since have been opportunistic. When possible, the Israeli government—and indeed the entire Zionist movement—adopts strategies of terror and expulsion. When circumstances don't allow that, it uses softer means. A century ago, the device was to quietly set up a watchtower and a fence, and soon it will turn into a settlement, facts on the ground. The counterpart today is the Israeli state expelling even more Palestinian families from the homes where they have been living for generations—with a gesture toward legality to salve the conscience of those derided in Israel as "beautiful souls." Of course, the mostly absurd legalistic pretenses for expelling Palestinians (Ottoman land laws and the like) are 100 percent racist. There is no thought of granting Palestinians rights to return to homes from which they've been expelled, even rights to build on what's left to them.

Israel's 1967 conquests made it possible to extend similar measures to the conquered territories, in this case in gross violation of international law, as Israeli leaders were informed right away by their highest legal authorities. The new projects were facilitated by the radical change in US-Israeli relations. Pre-1967 relations had been generally warm but ambiguous. After the war they reached unprecedented heights of support for a client state.

The Israeli victory was a great gift to the US government. A proxy war had been underway between radical Islam (based in Saudi Arabia) and secular nationalism ([Gamal Abdel] Nasser's Egypt). Like Britain before it, the US tended to prefer radical Islam, which it considered less threatening to US imperial domination. Israel smashed Arab secular nationalism.

Israel's military prowess had already impressed the US military command in 1948, and the '67 victory made it very clear that a militarized Israeli state could be a solid base for US power in the region—also providing important secondary services in support of US imperial goals beyond. US regional dominance came to rest on three pillars: Israel, Saudi Arabia, Iran (then under the Shah). Technically, they were all at war, but in reality, the alliance was very close, particularly between Israel and the murderous Iranian tyranny.

Within that international framework, Israel was free to pursue the policies that persist today, always with massive US support, despite occasional clucks of discontent. The Israeli government's immediate policy goal is to construct a "Greater Israel," including a vastly expanded "Jerusalem" encompassing surrounding Arab villages; the Jordan valley, a large part of the West Bank with much of its arable land; and major towns deep inside the West Bank, along with Jews-only infrastructure projects integrating them into Israel. The project bypasses Palestinian population concentrations, like Nablus, so as to fend off what Israeli leaders describe as the dread "demographic problem": too many non-Jews in the projected "democratic Jewish state" of "Greater Israel"—an oxymoron more difficult to mouth with each passing year. Palestinians within "Greater Israel" are confined to 165 enclaves, separated from their lands and olive groves by a hostile military, subjected to constant attack by violent Jewish gangs ("hilltop youths") protected by the Israeli army.

Meanwhile Israel settled and annexed the Golan Heights in violation of UN Security Council orders (as it did in Jerusalem). The Gaza horror story is too complex to recount here. It is one of the worst of contemporary crimes, shrouded in a dense network of deceit and apologetics for atrocities.

Trump went beyond his predecessors in providing free rein for Israeli crimes. One major contribution was orchestrating the Abraham Accords, which formalized long-standing tacit agreements between Israel and several Arab dictatorships. That relieved limited Arab restraints on Israeli violence and expansion.

The accords were a key component of the Trump geostrategic vision: to construct a reactionary alliance of brutal and repressive states, run from Washington, including [Jair] Bolsonaro's Brazil, [Narendra] Modi's India, [Viktor] Orbán's Hungary, and eventually others like them. The Middle East–North Africa component is based on [Abdel Fattah] al-Sisi's hideous Egyptian tyranny, and now under the accords, also family dictatorships from Morocco to the UAE and Bahrain. Israel provides the military muscle, with the US in the immediate background.

The Abraham Accords fulfill another Trump objective: bringing under Washington's umbrella the major resource areas needed to accelerate the race toward environmental cataclysm, the cause to which Trump and associates dedicated themselves with impressive fervor. That includes Morocco, which has a near monopoly of the phosphates needed for the industrialized agriculture that is destroying soils and poisoning the atmosphere. To enhance the Moroccan near-monopoly, Trump officially recognized and affirmed Morocco's brutal and illegal occupation of Western Sahara, which also has phosphate deposits.

It is of some interest that the formalization of the alliance of some of the world's most violent, repressive, and reactionary states has been greatly applauded across a broad spectrum of opinion.

So far, Biden has taken over these programs. He has rescinded the gratuitous brutality of Trumpism, such as withdrawing the fragile lifeline for Gaza because, as Trump explained, Palestinians had not been grateful enough for his demolition of their just aspirations. Otherwise, the Trump-Kushner criminal edifice remains intact, though some specialists on the region think it might totter with repeated Israeli attacks on Palestinian worshippers in the Al-Aqsa Mosque and other exercises of Israel's effective monopoly of violence.

Israel's settlements have no legal validity, so why is the US continuing to provide aid to Israel in violation of US law, and why isn't the progressive community focusing on this illegality?

Israel has been a highly valued client since the demonstration of its mastery of violence in 1967. Law is no impediment. US governments have always had a cavalier attitude to US law, adhering to standard imperial practice. Take what is arguably the major example: The US Constitution declares that treaties entered into by the US government are the "supreme law of the land." The major postwar treaty is the UN

Charter, which bars "the threat or use of force" in international affairs (with exceptions that are not relevant in real cases). Can you think of a president who hasn't violated this provision of the supreme law of the land with abandon? For example, by proclaiming that all options are open if Iran disobeys US orders—let alone such textbook examples of the "supreme international crime" (the Nuremberg judgment) as the invasion of Iraq.

The substantial Israeli nuclear arsenal should, under US law, raise serious questions about the legality of military and economic aid to Israel. That difficulty is overcome by not recognizing its existence, an unconcealed farce, and a highly consequential one, as we've discussed elsewhere. US military aid to Israel also violates the Leahy Law, which bans military aid to units engaged in systematic human rights violations. The Israeli armed forces provide many candidates.

Congresswoman Betty McCollum has taken the lead in pursuing this initiative. Carrying it further should be a prime commitment for those concerned with US support for the terrible Israeli crimes against Palestinians. Even a threat to the huge flow of aid could have a dramatic impact.

REPUBLICANS ARE WILLING TO DESTROY DEMOCRACY TO RETAKE POWER

June 16, 2021

C. J. Polychroniou: *Over the course of the past few decades, the Republican Party has gone through a series of ideological transformations—from traditional conservatism to reactionism and finally to what we may define as "protofascism," where the irrational has become the driving force. How do we explain what has happened to the GOP?*

Noam Chomsky: Your term "neoliberal protofascism" seems to me quite an accurate characterization of the current Republican organization—I'm hesitant to call them a "party" because that might suggest that they have some interest in participating honestly in normal parliamentary politics. More fitting, I think, is the judgment of American Enterprise Institute political analysts Thomas Mann and Norman Ornstein that the modern Republican Party has transformed to a "radical insurgency" with disdain for democratic participation. That was before the Trump-McConnell hammer blows of the past few years, which drove the conclusion home more forcefully.

The term "neoliberal protofascism" captures well both the features of the current party and the distinction from the fascism of the past. The commitment to the most brutal form of neoliberalism is apparent in the legislative record, crucially the subordination of the party to private capital, the inverse of classic fascism. But the fascist symptoms are there, including extreme racism, violence, worship of

32

the leader (sent by God, according to former secretary of state Mike Pompeo), immersion in a world of "alternative facts," and a frenzy of irrationality. Also in other ways, such as the extraordinary efforts in Republican-run states to suppress teaching in schools that doesn't conform to their white supremacist doctrines. Legislation is being enacted to ban instruction in "critical race theory," the new demon, replacing communism and Islamic terror as the plague of the modern age. "Critical race theory" is the scare-phrase used for the study of the systematic structural and cultural factors in the hideous four-hundred-year history of slavery and enduring racist repression. Proper indoctrination in schools and universities must ban this heresy. What actually happened for four hundred years and is very much alive today must be presented to students as a deviation from the real America, pure and innocent, much as in well-run totalitarian states.

What's missing from "protofascism" is the ideology: state control of the social order, including the business classes, and party control of the state with the maximal leader in charge. That could change. German industry and finance at first thought they could use the Nazis as their instrument in beating down labor and the left while remaining in charge. They learned otherwise. The current split between the more traditional corporate leadership and the Trump-led party is suggestive of something similar, but only remotely. We are far from the conditions that led to Mussolini, Hitler, and their cohorts.

On the driving force of irrationality, the facts are inescapable and should be of deep concern. Though we can't credit Trump entirely with the achievement, he certainly has shown great skill in carrying out a challenging assignment: implementing policies for the benefit of his primary constituency of great wealth and corporate power while conning the victims into worshipping him as their savior. That's no mean achievement, and inducing an atmosphere of utter irrationality has been a primary instrument, a virtual prerequisite.

We should distinguish the voting base, now pretty much owned by Trump, from the political echelon (Congress)—and distinguish both from a more shadowy elite that really runs the party, McConnell and associates.

Attitudes among the voting base are truly ominous. Put aside the fact that a large majority of Trump voters believe that the elections were stolen. A majority also believe that "the traditional American way of life is disappearing so fast that we may have to use force to save it," and 40 percent take a stronger stand: "If elected leaders will not protect America, the people must do it themselves, even if it requires violent actions." Not surprising, perhaps, when a quarter of Republicans are reported to believe that "the government, media, and financial worlds in the US are controlled by a group of Satan-worshipping pedophiles who run a global child sex trafficking operation."

In the background are more realistic concerns about the disappearance of "the traditional American way of life": a Christian and white supremacist world where Black people "know their place" and there are no infections from "deviants" who call for gay rights and other such obscenities. That traditional way of life indeed is disappearing.

There are also elements of realism in the various "great replacement" theories that seem to consume much of the Trump base. Putting aside absurdities about immigration and elite plotting, a simple look at distribution of births suffices to show that white domination is declining.

It's also worth remembering the deep roots of these concerns. Among the founders, there were two distinguished figures of the Enlightenment, one of whom hoped that the new country would be free of "blot or mixture," red or black (Jefferson), while the other felt that Germans and Swedes should perhaps be barred entry because they are too "swarthy" (Franklin). Myths of Anglo-Saxon origin were prevalent through the nineteenth century. All of this is apart from the virulent racism and its horrifying manifestations.

Concerns about satanic cults are dangerous enough, but other deeply irrational beliefs are far more consequential. One of the most threatening revelations of recent days was a scarcely noticed observation in the latest report of a Yale University group that monitors attitudes on climate change—the euphemism for the heating of the planet that will end organized human life on Earth unless soon brought under control. The report found that "over the past year, there has been a sharp decline in the percentages of both liberal/moderate Republicans and conservative Republicans who think developing sources of clean energy should be a priority for the president and Congress. The current numbers are all-time lows since we first asked the question in 2010."

Meanwhile every day's news provides information about new potential disasters—for example, the June 11 release of studies reporting the accelerated collapse of a huge Antarctic glacier that might raise sea levels by a foot and a half—along with reminders by the scientists reporting the warning that "the future is still open to change—if people do what is needed to change it."

They won't, as long as the reported attitudes prevail. Unless overcome, they might be a kiss of death if the current strategy of the Republican Party succeeds in putting the wreckers back in power. The strategy is plain enough: no matter what the harm to the country, and to their own voting base, ensure that the Biden administration can do nothing to remedy severe domestic problems, and ram through Jim Crow–style legislation to block voting of people of color and the poor, counting on the acquiescence of the reactionary judiciary that McConnell-Trump have succeeded in installing.

The party is not a lost cause. The Democrats have helped by failing to provide a constructive alternative that answers to the needs and just aspirations of many of those who have flocked to the Trump banner. That can change. Furthermore, attitudes are shifting among younger Republicans, even among younger Evangelicals, a core part of the Republican base since the '70s.

Nothing is irremediable.

With regard to the political echelon, there is little to say. With fringe exceptions, they have abandoned any semblance of integrity. Current votes are a clear indication: total Republican opposition to measures that they know are favored by their constituents in order to ensure that the Biden administration can achieve nothing.

The most abject capitulation of the political echelon was on global warming. In 2008, Republican presidential candidate John McCain had a limited climate plank in his program, and congressional Republicans were considering related legislation. The Koch energy conglomerate responded in force, and any spark of independence was extinguished. That much was evident in the last Republican primaries in 2016, pre-Trump: 100 percent denial that what is happening is happening, or worse, saying maybe it is but we're going to race toward disaster without apologizing (as said John Kasich, who was honored for his integrity by being invited to speak at the 2020 Democratic convention).

I can't raise any objections whatsoever to what you say, but I am a bit baffled by Biden's insistence in trying to reach out to Republicans on some of the major issues confronting the country. Isn't bipartisanship a pipe dream?

Not entirely. Democratic majority leader Chuck Schumer did manage a triumph of bipartisanship. Abandoning a prior commitment to legislation on global warming, Schumer teamed up with Republican Todd Young to conceal a limited industrial policy program within a "hate China" bill that appealed to shared jingoist sentiments. Republicans ensured that such significant components as funding for the National Science Foundation would be whittled down. Young celebrated the triumph by declaring that "when future generations of Americans cast their gaze toward new frontiers," they won't see "a red flag planted" there, but our own red, white, and blue. What better reason could there be to try to revive domestic manufacturing while trying to undermine the Chinese economy—at a moment when cooperation is a prerequisite for survival.

Meanwhile Biden's Department of Defense is reorienting resources and planning to war with China, a form of madness barely receiving attention, analyzed in detail in issue #1 of the Committee for a Sane US-China Policy, June 11, 2021.

Trump has transformed the Republican Party into a cult of personality. Is this why Republican leaders blocked the creation of a commission to investigate the January 6 attack on the Capitol?

Trump has captured the voting base, but the political echelon faces a quandary. For a long time, the party elite has been a rich man's club, pandering to business power even more than the Democrats, even after the Democrats abandoned the working class in the '70s, becoming a party of Wall Street and affluent professionals. The business world was willing to tolerate Trump's antics as long as he was loyally serving them—with some distaste, since he tarnished the image they project of "soulful corporations." But for major sectors, January 6 was too much.

The McConnell types who run the party are caught between a raging voting base in thrall to Trump and the masters of the economy whom they serve. A commission of inquiry, if at all honest, would have deepened this rift, which they have to find a way to paper over if the party, such as it is, is to survive. Best then to cancel it.

Lies, propaganda, and restricting voting rights have become the governing principles of today's GOP. To what extent will the new voting restrictions work to the advantage of the Republican Party, and how will they impact on the current political climate in general and the future of whatever is left of democracy in the United States in particular?

Trump's highly effective strategy of legitimizing "alternative facts" was based on an endless flood of lies, but a few true statements floated in the debris. One was his comment that Republicans can never win a fair election. That's a real problem for the rich man's club. It's hard to garner votes with the slogan "I want to rob you. Vote for me." That leaves only a few options. One is to prevent the "wrong people" from voting. Another is to shape the party program so that policy is concealed by appeals to "cultural issues." Both have been actively pursued. Trump gave the practices a particularly vulgar twist in his usual style, but he didn't invent them.

The current wave of Republican Jim Crow–style legislation is understandable: Trump's observation is accurate, and is likely to be more so in the future with demographic changes and the tendency of younger voters to favor social justice and human rights, among Republicans as well. The efforts have become more feasible after the

Roberts Court gutted the Voting Rights Act in the *Shelby* decision in 2013, which "set the stage for a new era of white hegemony," as Vann Newkirk rightly observed.

Displacement of policy by "cultural issues" traces back to Nixon's Southern Strategy. With Democrats beginning to support mild civil rights legislation, Nixon and his advisers recognized that they could switch the Southern vote to Republican by racist appeals, barely disguised.

Under Reagan there was little disguise; racist rhetoric and practices came naturally to him. Meanwhile, the Republican Christian nationalist strategist Paul Weyrich easily convinced the political leadership that by abandoning their former "pro-choice" stands and pretending to oppose abortion, they could pick up the Northern Catholic and newly politicized Evangelical vote. Gun loving was soon added to the mix, by now reaching such weird absurdities as the recent [US District Court judge Roger] Benitez decision overturning California's ban on assault rifles, which are, after all, hardly different from Swiss army knives [according to Benitez]. Trump added more to the mix. Like his fellow demagogues in Europe, he understood well that refugees can be used to whip up xenophobic passions and fears. His racist appeals also went beyond the norm.

Trump has exhibited a certain genius in tapping poisons that run not far below the surface of American society and culture. By such means, he managed to capture the Republican voting base. The party leadership is dedicated to the obstructionist strategy of sacrificing the interests of the country in order to regain power. That leaves the country with one functioning political party, itself torn between the neoliberal leadership and a younger social-democratic voting base.

Your phrase "whatever is left of American democracy" is to the point. However progressive it might have been in the eighteenth century—and there is much to say about that—by today's standards American democracy is deeply flawed in ways that were already becoming clear to the leading framer, James Madison, by 1791, when he wrote to Jefferson deploring "the daring depravity of the times," as the "stockjobbers will become the pretorian band of the government—

at once its tools and its tyrant; bribed by its largesses, and overawing it by clamors and combinations."

That could well be a description of recent years, particularly as the neoliberal assault achieved its entirely predictable consequence of placing government even more at the command of concentrations of private power than before. The "largesses" are too familiar to review. Ample research in mainstream political science has shown that the "clamors and combinations" have left the majority of voters unrepresented, as their own representatives heed the voices of the super-rich, wealthy donors and corporate lobbyists.

The most recent study, using sophisticated AI techniques, dispels "notions that anyone's opinion about public policy outside of the top 10 percent of affluent Americans independently helps to explain policy." Thomas Ferguson, the leading academic scholar of the power of the "tools and tyrants" of government, concludes, "Knowing the policy area, the preferences of the top 10 percent, and the views of a handful of interest groups suffice to explain policy changes with impressive accuracy."

But some vestiges of democracy remain, even after the neoliberal assault. Probably not for long if neoliberal "protofascism" extends its sway.

But the fate of democracy won't actually matter much if the "protofascists" regain power. The environment that sustains life cannot long endure the wreckers of the Trump era of decline. Little else will matter if irreversible tipping points are passed.

TO RETAIN POWER, DEMOCRATS MUST STOP ABANDONING THE WORKING CLASS

July 8, 2021

C. J. Polychroniou: *In our last interview, you analyzed the political identity of today's Republican Party and dissected its strategy for returning to power. Here, I am interested in your thoughts on the current shape of the Democratic Party and, more specifically, on whether it is in the midst of loosening its embrace of neoliberalism to such an extent that an ideological metamorphosis may in fact be underway.*

Noam Chomsky: The short answer is: maybe. There is much uncertainty.

With all of the major differences, the current situation is somewhat reminiscent of the early 1930s, which I'm old enough to remember, if hazily. We may recall Antonio Gramsci's famous observation from Mussolini's prison in 1930, applicable to the state of the world at the time, whatever exactly he may have had in mind: "The crisis consists precisely in the fact that the old is dying and the new cannot be born; in this interregnum a great variety of morbid symptoms appear."

Today, the foundations of the neoliberal doctrines that have had such a brutal effect on the population and the society are tottering, and might collapse. And there is no shortage of morbid symptoms.

In the years that followed Gramsci's comment, two paths emerged to deal with the deep crisis of the 1930s: social democracy, pioneered by the New Deal in the US, and fascism. We have not reached that state, but symptoms of both paths are apparent, in no small measure on party lines.

To assess the current state of the political system, it is useful to go back a little. In the 1970s, the highly class-conscious business community sharply escalated its efforts to dismantle New Deal social democracy and the "regimented capitalism" that prevailed through the postwar period—the fastest growth period of American state capitalism, egalitarian, with financial institutions under control so there were none of the crises that punctuate the neoliberal years and no "bailout economy" of the kind that has prevailed through these years, as Robert Pollin and Gerald Epstein very effectively review.

The business attack begins in the late 1930s with experiments in what later became a major industry of "scientific methods of strike-breaking." It was on hold during the war and took off immediately afterwards, but it was relatively limited until the 1970s. The political parties pretty much followed suit; more accurately perhaps, the two factions of the business party that share government in the US one-party state.

By the '70s, beginning with Nixon's overtly racist Southern Strategy, the Republicans began their journey off the political spectrum, culminating (so far) in the McConnell-Trump era of contempt for democracy as an impediment to holding uncontested power. Meanwhile, the Democrats abandoned the working class, handing working people over to their class enemy. The Democrats transitioned to a party of affluent professionals and Wall Street, becoming "cool" under Obama in a kind of replay of the infatuation of liberal intellectuals with the Camelot image contrived in the Kennedy years.

The last gasp of real Democratic concern for working people was the 1978 Humphrey-Hawkins Full Employment Act. President Carter, who seemed to have had little interest in workers' rights and needs, didn't veto the bill but watered it down so that it had no teeth. In the same year, UAW president Doug Fraser withdrew from Carter's Labor-Management committee, condemning business leaders—belatedly—for having "chosen to wage a one-sided class war . . . against working people, the unemployed, the poor, the minorities, the very young and the very old, and even many in the middle class of our society."

The one-sided class war took off in force under Ronald Reagan. Like his accomplice Margaret Thatcher in England, Reagan understood that the first step should be to eliminate the enemy's means of defense by harsh attack on unions, opening the door for the corporate world to follow, with the Democrats largely indifferent or participating in their own ways—matters we've discussed before.

The tragicomic effects are being played out in Washington right now. Biden attempted to pass badly needed support for working people who have suffered a terrible blow during the pandemic (while billionaires profited handsomely and the stock market boomed). He ran into a solid wall of implacable Republican opposition. A major issue was how to pay for it. Republicans indicated some willingness to agree to the relief efforts if the costs were borne by unemployed workers by reducing the pittance of compensation. But they imposed an unbreachable Red Line: not a penny from the very rich.

Nothing can touch Trump's major legislative achievement, the 2017 tax scam that enriches the super-rich and corporate sector at the expense of everyone else—the bill that Joseph Stiglitz termed the "US Donor Relief Act of 2017," which "embodies all that is wrong with the Republican Party, and to some extent, the debased state of American democracy."

Meanwhile, Republicans claim to be the party of the working class, thanks to their advocacy of lots of guns for everyone, Christian nationalism, and white supremacy—our "traditional way of life."

To Biden's credit, he has made moves to reverse the abandonment of working people by his party, but in the "debased state" of what remains of American democracy, it's a tough call.

The Democrats are meanwhile split between the management of the affluent professional/Wall Street–linked party, still holding most of the reins, and a large and energetic segment of the popular base that has been pressing for social-democratic initiatives to deal with the ravages of the forty-year bipartisan neoliberal assault—and among some of the popular base, a lot more.

The internal conflict has been sharp for years, particularly as the highly successful Sanders campaign began to threaten absolute control by the Clinton-Obama party managers, who tried in every way to sabotage his candidacy. We see that playing out again right now in the intense efforts to block promising left candidates in Buffalo and the Cleveland area in northeast Ohio.

We should bear in mind the peculiarities of political discourse in the US. Elsewhere, "socialist" is about as controversial as "Democrat" is here, and policies described as "maybe good but too radical for Americans" are conventional. That's true, for example, of the two main programs that Bernie Sanders championed: universal health care and free higher education. The economics columnist and associate editor of the London *Financial Times*, Rana Foroohar, hardly exaggerated when she wrote that while Sanders is considered the spokesperson of the radical left here, "in terms of his policies, he's probably pretty close to your average German Christian Democrat," the German conservative party in a generally conservative political system.

On issues, the split between the party managers and progressive sectors of the voting base is pretty much across the board. It is not limited to the relics of social welfare but to a range of other crucial matters, among them, the most important issue that has ever arisen in human history, along with nuclear weapons: the destruction of the environment that sustains life, proceeding apace.

We might tarry a moment to think about this. The most recent general assessment of where we stand comes from a leaked draft of the forthcoming IPCC study on the state of the environment. According to the report of the study, it "concludes that climate change will fundamentally reshape life on Earth in the coming decades, even if humans can tame planet-warming greenhouse gas emissions. Species extinction, more widespread disease, unlivable heat, ecosystem collapse, cities menaced by rising seas—these and other devastating climate impacts are accelerating and bound to become painfully obvious before a child born today turns 30. . . . On current trends, we're heading for three degrees Celsius at best."

Thanks to activist efforts, notably of the Sunrise Movement, Representative Alexandria Ocasio-Cortez and Senator Ed Markey have been able to introduce a congressional resolution on a Green New

Deal that spells out quite carefully what can and must be done. Further popular pressures could move it toward proposed legislation. It is likely to meet an iron wall of resistance from the denialist party, which increasingly is dedicated to the principle enunciated in 1936 by Francisco Franco's companion, the fascist general [José] Millán-Astray: "*¡Abajo la inteligencia! ¡Viva la muerte!*": "Down with intelligence! Viva death!"

As of now, the Democratic response would be mixed. The president refuses to support a Green New Deal, a prerequisite for decent survival. Many in Congress, too. That can change, and must. A lot will depend on the coming election.

While all of this is going on here, OPEC is meeting, and is riven by conflicts over how much to increase oil production, with the White House pressuring for increased production to lower prices and Saudi Arabia worrying that if prices rise it "would accelerate the shift toward renewable energy"—that is, toward saving human society from catastrophe, a triviality not mentioned in the news report, as usual.

Going back to the crisis of ninety years ago, as the neoliberal assault faces increasingly angry resistance, we see signs of something like the two paths taken then: a drift toward protofascism or creation of genuine social democracy. Each tendency can of course proceed further, reawakening Rosa Luxemburg's warning "Socialism or Barbarism."

It is useful to recall that the primary intellectual forces behind the neoliberal assault have a long history of support for fascism. Just a few years before the assault was launched, they had conducted an experiment in neoliberal socioeconomic management under the aegis of the Pinochet dictatorship, which prepared the ground by destroying labor and dispatching critics to hideous torture chambers or instant death. Under near-perfect experimental conditions, they managed to crash the economy in a few years, but no matter. On to greater heights: imposing the doctrine on the world.

In earlier years, their guru, Ludwig von Mises, was overjoyed by the triumph of fascism, which he claimed had "saved European civilization," exulting, "The merit that Fascism has thereby won for itself will live on eternally in history." Mussolini's "achievement" was much like Pinochet's: destroying labor and independent thought so that "sound economics" could proceed unencumbered by sentimental concerns about human rights and justice.

In defense of von Mises, we may recall that he was far from alone in admiring Mussolini's achievements, though few sank to his depths of adulation. In his case, on principled grounds. All worth recalling when we consider the possible responses to the neoliberal disaster.

How do we explain the rise of the progressive left in the Democratic Party?

It's only necessary to review the effects of the forty-year neoliberal assault, as we have done elsewhere. It's hardly surprising that the victims—the large majority of the population—are rebelling, sometimes in ominous ways, sometimes in ways that can forge a path to a much better future.

Democrats may need to expand their base in order to keep the House in 2022. How do they do that, especially with the presence of so many different wings within the party?

The best way is by designing and implementing policies that will help people and benefit the country. Biden's programs so far move in that direction—not enough, but significantly. Such efforts would show that under decent leadership, impelled by popular pressure, reform can improve lives, alleviate distress, satisfy some human needs. That would expand the Democratic base, just as social-democratic New Deal–style measures have done in the past.

The Republican leadership understands that very well. That is why they will fight tooth and nail against any measures to improve life, with strict party discipline. We have been witnessing this for years. One of many illustrations is the dedication to block the very limited improvement of the scandalous US health care system in the Affordable Care Act—"Obamacare." Another is the sheer cruelty of Republican governors who refuse federal aid to provide desperate people with even meager Medicaid assistance.

That's one way to expand the base, which could have large effects if it can break through Republican opposition and the reluctance of the more right-wing sectors of the Democratic Party (termed "moderate" in media discourse). It could bring back to the Democratic fold the working-class voters who left in disgust with Obama's betrayals, and further back, with the Democrats' abandonment of working people since the reshaping of the party from the '70s.

There are other opportunities. Working people and communities that depend on the fossil fuel economy can be reached by taking seriously their concerns and working with them to develop transitional programs that will provide them with better jobs and better lives with renewable energy. That's no idle dream. Such initiatives have had substantial success in coal-mining and oil-producing states, thanks in considerable measure to Bob Pollin's grassroots work.

There is no mystery about how to extend the base: pursue policies that serve peoples' interests, not the preferences of the donor class.

I worry about reports about some immigrant neighborhoods showing increased enthusiasm for the ideals and values expressed by the Republican Party of Donald Trump. Do you have any insights?

The evidence that this is happening seems slim. There was a slight shift in the last election, but the results don't seem to depart significantly from the historical norm. Latino communities varied. Where there had been serious Latino organizing, as in Arizona and Nevada, there was no drift to Trump. Where Mexican American communities were ignored, as in South Texas, Trump broke records in Latino support. There seem to be several reasons. People resented being taken for granted by the Democratic Party ("You're Latino, so you're in our pocket"). There was no effort to provide the constructive alternative to the Republican claim that global warming is a liberal hoax and the Democrats want to take your jobs away. The communities are often attracted by the Republican pretense of "defending religion" from secular attack. It's necessary to explore these matters with some care.

Many Democrats wish to eliminate the filibuster—another Jim Crow relic—because with the wafer-thin majority that they hold it is impossible to pass into law landmark pieces of legislation. However, given today's political climate, and with the possibility looming on the horizon that Trumpist Republicans will retake the House in 2022, aren't there risks in abolishing the filibuster?

It's a concern, and it would have some weight in a functioning democracy. But a long series of Republican attacks on the integrity of Congress, culminating in McConnell's machinations, have seriously undermined the Senate's claim to be part of a democratic polity. If Democrats were to resort to filibuster, McConnell, who is no fool, might well find ways to use illegal procedures to ram through acts that would establish more firmly the rule of the far right, whatever the population might prefer. We saw that illustrated recently in his shenanigans with the Garland-Gorsuch Supreme Court appointments, but it goes far back.

Political analyst Michael Tomasky argued recently, quite seriously, that the Senate should be abolished, converted to something like the British House of Lords, with a peripheral role in governance. There has always been an argument for that, and with the evisceration of remaining shreds of democracy under Republican leadership, it is an idea whose time may have come, at least as a goal for the future.

When all is said and done, the US does not have a functional democratic system, and it is probably best defined as a plutocracy. With that in mind, what do you consider to be the issues of paramount importance that progressives, both activists and lawmakers, must work on in order to bring about meaningful reform that would improve average people's lives, as well as enhance the prospects of a democratic future?

For good reason, the gold standard in scholarship on the Constitutional Convention, by Michael Klarman, is entitled *The Framers' Coup*—meaning, the coup against democracy by a distinguished group of wealthy, white, (mostly) slave owners. There were a few dissidents—Benjamin Franklin and Thomas Jefferson (who did not take part in the

Convention). But the rest were pretty much in agreement that democracy was a threat that had to be avoided. The Constitution was carefully designed to undercut the threat.

The call for plutocracy was not concealed. Madison's vision, largely enacted, was that the new government should "protect the minority of the opulent against the majority." Many devices were introduced to ensure this outcome. Primary power was placed in the (unelected) Senate, with long terms to insulate senators from public pressure.

"The senate ought to come from and represent the wealth of the nation," Madison held, backed by his colleagues. These are the "more capable set of men," who sympathize with property owners and their rights. In simple words, "those who own the country ought to govern it," as explained by John Jay, first justice of the Supreme Court. In short, plutocracy.

In Madison's defense, it should be recalled that his mentality was precapitalist. Scholarship recognizes that Madison "was—to depths that we today are barely able to imagine—an eighteenth century gentleman of honor," in the words of Lance Banning. It is the "enlightened Statesman" and "benevolent philosopher" who were to exercise power. They would be "men of intelligence, patriotism, property and independent circumstances," and "pure and noble" like the Romans of the imagination of the time; men "whose wisdom may best discern the true interests of their country, and whose patriotism and love of justice will be least likely to sacrifice it to temporary or partial considerations." They would thus "refine" and "enlarge" the "public views," Banning continues, guarding the public interest against the "mischiefs" of democratic majorities.

The picture is richly confirmed in the fascinating debates of the convention. It has ample resonance to the present, quite strikingly in the most respected liberal democratic theory.

Madison himself was soon disabused of these myths. In a 1791 letter to Jefferson, he deplored "the daring depravity of the times" as the "stockjobbers will become the pretorian band of the government—at once its tools and its tyrant; bribed by its largesses, and overawing it by clamors and combinations." Not a bad picture of America today.

The contours have been sharpened by forty years of bipartisan neoliberalism, now challenged by the progressive base that Democratic Party managers are working to subdue.

With all its antidemocratic features, by eighteenth-century standards, the American constitutional system was a significant step toward freedom and democracy, enough so as to seriously frighten European statesmen who perceived the potential domino effect of subversive republicanism. The world has changed. The plutocracy remains in place, a terrain of struggle.

Over time, popular struggles have expanded the realm of freedom, justice, and democratic participation, not without regression. There are many barriers that remain to be demolished in the political system and the general social order: bought elections, the "bailout economy," structural racism and other attacks on basic rights, suppression of labor.

It is all too easy to extend the list and to spell out more radical goals that should be guidelines for the future, all overshadowed by the imminent threats to survival.

BOLSONARO IS SPREADING TRUMP-LIKE FEAR OF "ELECTION FRAUD" IN BRAZIL

July 16, 2021

C. J. Polychroniou: *Jair Bolsonaro—an apologist for torture and dictatorship and part of the global trend toward authoritarianism that brought us Donald Trump—was sworn in as president of Brazil on January 1, 2019. Since that day, his administration has been pushing an agenda with disastrous consequences for democracy and the environment. I want to start by asking you of the conditions in Brazil that brought Bolsonaro to power, a development which coincided with the end of the "pink tide" that had swept across Latin America in the early 2000s.*

Noam Chomsky: A lot is uncertain and documentation is slim, but the way it looks to me is basically like this.

With the fall of commodity prices a few years after Lula da Silva left office in 2010, the Brazilian right wing—with US encouragement, if not direct support—recognized an opportunity to return the country to their hands and to reverse the welfare and inclusiveness programs they despised. They proceeded to carry out a systematic "soft coup." One step was impeaching Lula's successor, Dilma Rousseff, in utterly corrupt and fraudulent proceedings. The next was to imprison Lula on corruption charges, preventing him from running in (and almost surely winning) the 2018 presidential election. That set the stage for Bolsonaro to be elected on a wave of an incredible campaign of lies, slanders, and deceit that flooded the internet sites that most Brazilians use as a main source of "information." There's reason to suspect a significant US hand.

The charges against Lula were withdrawn by the courts after they were completely discredited by Glenn Greenwald's exposure of the shenanigans of the prosecution in connivance with "anti-corruption" (Car Wash) investigator Sergio Moro. Before the exposures, Moro had been appointed minister of justice and public security by Bolsonaro, perhaps a reward for his contributions to his election. Moro has largely disappeared from sight with the collapse of his image as the intrepid white knight who would save Brazil from corruption—while, probably not coincidentally, destroying major Brazilian businesses that were competitors to US corporations (which are not exactly famous for their purity).

Though Moro's targets were selective, much of what he revealed is credible—and not difficult to find in Latin America, where corruption is practically a way of life in the political and economic worlds. One can, however, debate whether it attains the level that is familiar in the West, where major financial institutions have been fined tens of billions of dollars, usually in settlements that avoid individual liability. One indication of what the scale might be was given by the London *Economist*, which found over two thousand corporate convictions from 2000 to 2014. That's just "corporate America," which has plenty of company elsewhere. Furthermore, the notion of "corruption" is deeply tainted by ideology. Much of the worst corruption is "legal," as the legal system is designed under the heavy hand of private power.

Despite Moro's own corruption, much of what he unearthed was real and had been for a long time. His main target, Lula's Workers Party (PT), it appears, did not break this pattern. Partly for this reason, the PT lost an opportunity to introduce the kinds of lasting progressive changes that are badly needed to undermine the rule of Brazil's rapacious and deeply racist traditional ruling classes.

Lula's programs were designed so as not to infringe seriously on elite power, but they were nonetheless barely tolerated in these circles. Their flaw was that they were oriented toward the needs of those suffering bitterly in this highly inegalitarian society. The basic character of Lula's programs was captured in a 2016 World Bank study of Brazil, which described his time in office as a "golden decade" in Brazil's history. The Bank praised Lula's "success in reducing poverty and inequality and its ability to create jobs. Innovative and effective policies to reduce poverty and ensure the inclusion of previously excluded groups have lifted millions of people out of poverty." Furthermore,

> Brazil has also been assuming global responsibilities. It has been successful in pursuing economic prosperity while protecting its unique natural patrimony. Brazil has become one of the most important emerging new donors, with extensive engagements particularly in Sub-Saharan Africa, and a leading player in international climate negotiations. Brazil's development path over the past decade has shown that growth with shared prosperity, but balanced with respect for the environment, is possible. Brazilians are rightly proud of these internationally recognized achievements.

Some Brazilians. Not those who consider it their right to wield power in their own interest.

Brazil became an effective voice for the Global South in international affairs, not a welcome development in the eyes of Western leaders, and a particular irritant to the Obama-Biden-Clinton administration when Brazil's foreign minister Celso Amorim came close to negotiating a settlement on Iran's nuclear programs, undercutting Washington's intent to run the show on its own terms.

The bank report also concluded that with proper policies, the "golden decade" could have persisted after the collapse of commodity prices. That was not to be, however, as the soft coup proceeded. Some analysts have suggested that a crucial turning point was when Dilma announced that profits from newly discovered offshore oil reserves would be directed to education and welfare instead of the eager hands of international investors.

The PT had failed to sink social roots, to such an extent that beneficiaries of its policies were often unaware of their source, attributing the benefits to God or to luck. The corruption, failure of mobilization, and lack of structural reform all contributed to Bolsonaro's electoral victory.

Bolsonaro's victory was welcomed with enthusiasm by international capital and finance. They were particularly impressed by Bolsonaro's economic czar, ultra-loyal Chicago economist Paulo Guedes. His program was very simple: in his words, "privatize everything," a bonanza for foreign investors. They were, however, disillusioned as Brazil collapsed during the Bolsonaro years and Guedes's promises remained unfulfilled.

Let's talk now specifically about some of Bolsonaro's policies, which have been denounced by activists, economists, and organizations such as Human Rights Watch, as well as by Indigenous leaders. And how would you compare his policies to those of Donald Trump?

The analogy is apt. Trump was Bolsonaro's unconcealed model, though not the only one. In casting his vote to impeach Dilma, he dedicated it to her torturer during the military dictatorship. That's a level of depravity that even his hero Trump didn't reach. His admiration for the dictatorship is also unconcealed, though he does have some criticisms of the military. His prime complaint is that they were too mild. They should have killed thirty thousand people as the military did in Argentina next door. He has also criticized the behavior of the military in earlier years. They should have imitated the US cavalry, which virtually eliminated the Native population. Instead, the Brazilian military left remnants in the Amazon. But Bolsonaro has made it quite clear that he intends to overcome that problem.

Like Trump, Bolsonaro's most important policy commitments, by far, are to destroy the prospects for organized human life in the interest of short-term profits for his friends—in his case, mining, agribusiness, and illegal logging that have sharply accelerated the destruction of the Amazon forests. Scientists had anticipated, pre-Bolsonaro, that in a few decades, the Amazon would shift from one of the world's greatest carbon sinks to a carbon source, as it transitions from tropical forest to savannah. Thanks to Bolsonaro, that point may already be approaching. For Brazil, the effects will be devastating. Rainfall will sharply decline, with much of the rich agricultural land turning to desert. The world as a whole will suffer a severe blow, a wound that might prove to be lethal. For the Indigenous inhabitants of the forest, the outcome is genocidal.

As elsewhere in the world, the Indigenous in Brazil have been in the forefront for years in trying to protect human society from the depredations of "advanced civilization." But time is growing short, and if the Trumps and Bolsonaros of the world are granted free rein, chances of decent survival are slim.

Again, as in the case of Trump, Bolsonaro's malevolence is not exhausted by his commitment to destroy organized human society— along with the innumerable species that we are quickly driving to extinction. Like Trump, he can claim personal responsibility for tens (if not hundreds) of thousands of COVID deaths, to mention one salient contribution to the welfare of his country. Police killings, overwhelmingly with Black victims, have long been a plague, mounting under Bolsonaro. A particularly shocking recent incident of military assault on a Rio favela reached international headlines.

All too easy to continue.

What is the likelihood that Bolsonaro could face charges in The Hague over the Amazon?

Virtually none. His contributions to global suicide may be particularly severe, but once that door is opened . . .

Who is going to allow that?

Brazilians took to the streets recently, demanding the removal of Bolsonaro over his handling of the pandemic. Indeed, it seems that public opinion has finally turned overwhelmingly against Bolsonaro, and Lula is expected to trounce him in the 2022 elections. However, in a rather unsurprising manner, and reminiscent of his idol Trump, Bolsonaro announced just a few days ago that he may not accept the results of the 2022 election under the current voting system. How likely is the chance that the generals, on whom Bolsonaro has relied on from the first day he got into power, will stay the course and support an attempt of his to stay in power even if he loses next year's presidential election?

Since 2018, Bolsonaro has been claiming that the only way he can be defeated in an election is by fraud. He's even claimed (of course, without evidence) that Dilma actually lost the 2014 election, which she won handily by over three million votes, mostly on sharp class lines, by historical standards a slim margin. He's now stepped up the rhetoric, preemptively charging the 2022 election with attempted fraud by his political enemies and telling a crowd of supporters a few weeks ago that "elections next year will be clean. Either we have clean elections in Brazil or we don't have elections" (*Jornal do Brasil,* 7-8-21).

Not exactly unfamiliar.

Right now, Lula is well ahead in the polls, just as in 2018, when measures were taken to bar his candidacy. There are legitimate concerns of a recurrence.

Parliamentary inquiries into the devastating mishandling of the pandemic by Bolsonaro's government are now reportedly reaching the military. The three branches of the armed services recently released a statement declaring that no inquiry that impugns the honor of the military will be tolerated.

There have been reports of steps that might be preparation for a military coup, perhaps modeled on the 1964 coup that installed the first of the vicious "National Security States" that terrorized the hemisphere for twenty years.

The pretext for overthrowing the mildly reformist [João] Goulart government in 1964 was the ritual appeal to save the country from "Communism." Something similar could be concocted today.

How would Washington react? There are precedents that suggest an answer. One is 1964. The military coup that overthrew the parliamentary government was lauded by Kennedy-Johnson ambassador to Brazil Lincoln Gordon as "the most decisive victory for freedom in the mid-twentieth century." As I discuss in *Year 501*, it was a "democratic rebellion" that would help in "restraining left-wing excesses" and should "create a greatly improved climate for private investment" in the hands of the "democratic forces" now in charge. After twenty-one years of rule, Latin America scholar Stephen Rabe comments in *The Most Dangerous Area in the World*, the "democratic forces" left the country in "the same category as the less developed African or Asian countries when it came to social welfare indices" (malnutrition, infant mortality, etc.), with conditions of inequality and suffering rarely matched elsewhere, but a grand success for foreign investors and domestic privilege.

That's putting aside the "systematic use of torture" and other crimes of state documented by the Church-run Truth Commission during the dictatorship's last days.

We should also recall that the reaction to the Brazil coup—and possible involvement in it—was no exception. Rather, it was the norm after 1962, when JFK changed the mission of the Latin American military from anachronistic "hemispheric defense" to very live "internal security." The predictable results were described by Charles Maechling, who led US counterinsurgency and internal defense planning from 1961 to 1966. Kennedy's 1962 decision, he wrote, shifted the US stand from toleration "of the rapacity and cruelty of the Latin American military" to "direct complicity" in their crimes, to US support for "the methods of Heinrich Himmler's extermination squads."

Those who might innocently believe that things have changed can turn to the Obama-Clinton reaction to the military coup in Honduras in 2009, overthrowing the mildly reformist [Manuel] Zelaya government. Their support for the coup, almost alone, helped turn Honduras into one of the murder capitals of the world, stimulating a flood of terrified refugees now cruelly and illegally turned back at the US border, if they can make it that far through the barriers imposed by US clients.

The rich and ugly record might suggest something about Washington's possible reaction to actions by the Brazilian military to "save the country from Communism."

Peruvians elected as their president last month Pedro Castillo, a teacher and labor union leader, but the far-right opponent Keiko Fujimori and her supporters are refusing to accept the outcome by crying fraud, allegations which have been rejected by international observers and while both the European Union and the United States praised the conduct of the election. But in places like Chile and Colombia, the right is also under pressure by citizens fed up with neoliberalism. Is another "pink tide" in the making across South America?

In Chile, a remarkable popular uprising is seeking to free the country at last from the clutches of the Pinochet dictatorship, a criminal enterprise backed even more strongly than usual by the US, with particular enthusiasm by the "libertarians" who then turned to launching the global neoliberal assault of the past forty years. Colombia is being subjected to yet another renewal of the state and paramilitary violence escalated by Kennedy in 1962, when his military mission to Colombia, led by marine general William Yarborough, recommended "paramilitary sabotage and/or terrorist activities against known communist proponents," which "should be backed by the United States"—as it has been through many horrifying years, recently Clinton's Plan Colombia.

There is turmoil and uncertainty throughout the hemisphere, including "the colossus of the North." What happens here will, as always, have enormous impact.

WE NEED GENUINE INTERNATIONAL COOPERATION TO TACKLE THE CLIMATE CRISIS

July 29, 2021

C. J. Polychroniou: *Climate emergency facts are piling up almost on a daily basis—extreme heat waves in various parts of the US and Canada, with temperatures rising even above 49 degrees Celsius (over 120 degrees Fahrenheit); deadly floods in western Europe, with close to two hundred dead and hundreds remaining unaccounted for in the flooding; and Moscow experienced its second-hottest June. In fact, the extreme weather conditions even have climate scientists surprised, and they are now wondering about the accuracy of prediction models. What are your thoughts on these matters? It appears that the world is losing the war against global warming.*

Noam Chomsky: You probably remember that three years ago, Oxford physicist Raymond Pierrehumbert, a lead author of the just-released Intergovernmental Panel on Climate Change (IPCC) report, wrote that "it's time to panic. . . . We are in deep trouble."

What has been learned since only intensifies that warning. An IPCC draft report leaked to *Agence France-Presse* in June 2021 listed irreversible tipping points that are ominously close, warning of "progressively serious, centuries-long and, in some cases, irreversible consequences."

Last November 3 was a narrow escape from what might well have been indescribable disaster. Another four years of Trump's passionate racing to the abyss might have reached those tipping points. And if the denialist party returns to power, it may be too late to panic. We are indeed in deep trouble.

The leaked IPCC draft was from before the extreme weather events of summer 2021, which shocked climate scientists. Heating of the planet "is pretty much in line with climate model predictions from decades ago," climate scientist Michael Mann observed, but "the rise in extreme weather is exceeding the predictions." The reason seems to be an effect of heating of the atmosphere that had not been considered in climate studies: wobbling of the jet stream, which is causing the extreme events that have plagued much of the world in the past few weeks.

The frightening news has a good side. It may awaken global leaders to recognition of the horrors that they are creating. It's conceivable that seeing what's happening before their eyes might induce even the GOP and its Fox News echo chamber to indulge in a glimpse of reality.

We have seen signs of that in the COVID crisis. After years of immersion in their world of "alternative facts," some Republican governors who have been mocking precautions are taking notice, now that the plague is striking their own states because of lack of preventive measures and vaccine refusal. As Florida took the lead nationwide in cases and deaths, Governon Ron DeSantis backed away (only partially) from his ridicule—eliciting charges of selling out to the enemy from party stalwarts and perhaps endangering his presidential aspirations. A shift which might, however, be too late to influence the loyal party base that has been subjected to a stream of disinformation.

Possibly the sight of cities drowning and burning up may also dent GOP-Fox loyalty to the slogan "Death to intelligence! Viva death!" borrowed from the annals of fascism.

The denialism of environmental destruction naturally has an impact on public opinion. According to the most recent polls, for 58 percent of Republicans, climate change is "not an important concern." A little over 40 percent deny that humans make a significant contribution to this impending catastrophe. And 44 percent think that "climate scientists have too much influence on climate policy debates."

If there ever is a historical reckoning of this critical moment in history—possibly by some alien intelligence after humans have wrecked this planet—and if a Museum of Evil is established in memory of the crime, the GOP-Fox dyad will have a special room in their honor.

Responsibility is far broader, however. There is no space to review the dismal record, but one small item gives the general picture. The indispensable media analysis organization FAIR reports a study comparing coverage on morning TV of the climate crisis with Jeff Bezos's space launch: 267 minutes in all of 2020 on the most important issue in human history, 212 minutes on a single day for Bezos's silly PR exercise.

Returning to your question, humanity is quite clearly losing the war, but it is far from over. A better world is possible, we know how to achieve it, and many good people are actively engaged in the struggle. The crucial message is to panic now, but not to despair.

One of the most worrisome developments regarding the climate crisis is that while virtually all of the published climate science shows the impacts of global warming are increasingly irreversible, climate skepticism and inactivism remain quite widespread. In your view, is climate crisis denial motivated by cultural and economic factors alone, or is there possibly something else also at work? Specifically, I am wondering if there is a connection between postmodern attacks on science and objectivity and climate science denial and inactivism.

There was a skeptical crisis in the seventeenth century. It was real, a significant moment in intellectual history. It led to a much better understanding of the nature of empirical inquiry. I'm not convinced that the postmodern critique has improved on this.

With regard to your question, I doubt that the postmodern critique has had much of an impact, if any, outside of rather narrow educated circles. The major sources of climate science denial—in fact much broader rejection of science—seem to me to lie elsewhere, deep in the culture.

I was a student seventy-five years ago. If evolution was brought up in class, it was preceded by what's now called a trigger warning: "You don't have to believe this, but you should know what some people believe." This was in an Ivy League college.

Today, for large parts of the population, deeply held religious commitments conflict with the results of scientific inquiry. Therefore, science must be wrong, a cult of liberal intellectuals in urban dens of iniquity infected by people who are not "true Americans" (no need to spell out who they are). All of this has been inflamed by the very effective use of irrationality in the Trump era, including his skillful resort to constant fabrication, eroding the distinction between truth and falsehood. For a showman with deeply authoritarian instincts, and few principles beyond self-glorification and abject service to the welfare of the ultrarich, there's no better slogan than: "Believe me, not your lying eyes."

The organization that Trump now owns, which years ago was an authentic political party, had already moved on a path that provided a generous welcome to such a figure. We've discussed previously how the brief Republican flirtation with reality on environmental destruction during the McCain campaign was quickly terminated by the Koch brothers' campaign of intimidation. The last time Republican leaders spoke freely without obeisance to Trump, in the 2016 primaries, all were loyal climate denialists, or worse.

Scientists are human. They're not above criticism, nor their institutions. One can find error, dishonesty, childish feuds, all of the normal human flaws. But to be critical of *science* as such is to condemn the human quest to understand the world in which we live. And truly to abandon hope.

Many discussions on the climate crisis revolve around "equity" and "justice." Leaving aside the question of "climate equity vs. climate justice," especially in the context of the Paris Agreement, how much importance should we assign to these debates in the context of the overall goal of decarbonizing the global economy, which is obviously the only way to tackle the existential crisis of global warming?

It shouldn't be overlooked that it is the small, very affluent minority, most of them in the rich countries, who have overwhelming responsibility for the environmental crisis, in the past and right now. Decarbonizing and concern for equity and justice, therefore, considerably overlap. Beyond that, even on narrow, pragmatic grounds, putting aside moral responsibility, the major socioeconomic changes required for the necessary scale of decarbonization must enlist committed mass popular support, and that will not be achieved without a substantial measure of justice.

Robert Pollin has been making the case for a Global Green New Deal as the only effective way to tackle global warming, and the two of you are coauthors of the recently published work, Climate Crisis and the Global Green New Deal: The Political Economy of Saving the Planet. *No doubt, we need internationalism in the fight against climate breakdown because, as you have so aptly put it yourself, it is either "extinction or internationalism." My question to you is twofold: First, how do you understand "internationalism" in the current historical juncture where, in spite of all of the globalizing processes under way in the course of the past forty or fifty years, the nation-state remains the central agency? And, secondly, what system changes are required to give "internationalism" a real fighting chance in the war against the apocalyptic consequences of global warming which are already knocking at humanity's door?*

There are many forms of internationalism. It's worthwhile to think about them. They carry lessons.

One form of internationalism is the specific kind of "globalization" that has been imposed during the neoliberal years through a series of investor-rights agreements masquerading as free trade. It constitutes a form of class war.

Another form of internationalism is the Axis alliance that brought us World War II. A pale reflection is Trump's sole geostrategic program: construction of an alliance of reactionary states run from Washington, including as one core component the Middle East Abraham Accords and its side agreements with the Egyptian and Saudi dictatorships, taken over by Biden.

Still another form of internationalism has been championed on occasion by workers' movements, in the US by the "Wobblies," the Industrial Workers of the World (IWW). Other unions, too, have the term "international" in their names, a relic of commitment to true internationalism.

In Europe, the most eloquent spokesperson for this form of internationalism was Rosa Luxemburg. The conflict between internationalism and chauvinism came to a head with the outbreak of World War I. Chauvinism conquered. The Socialist International collapsed. In Luxemburg's acidic words, the slogan "Proletarians of all countries united" was abandoned in favor of "Proletarians of all countries cut each other's throat."

Luxemburg held true to the internationalist vision, a rare stance. In all countries, intellectuals across the political spectrum rallied enthusiastically to the chauvinist cause. Those who did not were likely to find their way to prison, like Luxemburg: Karl Liebknecht, Bertrand Russell, Eugene Debs. The IWW was crushed by state-capital violence.

Turning to the present, we find other manifestations of internationalism. When the COVID pandemic broke out in early 2020, the rich countries of central Europe at first managed to get it more or less under control, a success that collapsed when Europeans chose not to forego their summer vacations.

While Germany and Austria were still in fairly good shape in early 2020, there was, however, a severe pandemic in northern Italy a few miles to their south, within the European Union. Italy did benefit from true internationalism—not on the part of its rich neighbors. Rather, from the world's one country with internationalist commitments: Cuba, which sent doctors to help, as it did elsewhere, extending a record that goes far back. Among others, Panama received assistance from Cuba, but the US took care of that. In its final 2020 report, Trump's Department of Health and Human Services proudly announced that it had successfully pressured Panama to expel Cuban doctors to protect the hemisphere from Cuba's "malign" influence.

The malign influence, spelled out in the early days of Cuban independence in 1959, was that Cuba might infect Latin America with its "successful defiance" of US policies since the Monroe Doctrine of 1823. To prevent this threat, the US launched a major campaign of terror and economic strangulation, following the logic spelled out at the State Department in 1960 by Lester Mallory. He recognized, as US intelligence knew, that the "majority of Cubans support Castro," and that the "only foreseeable means of alienating internal support is through disenchantment and disaffection based on economic dissatisfaction and hardship." Therefore, "it follows that every possible means should be undertaken promptly to weaken the economic life of Cuba . . . to bring about hunger, desperation and overthrow of government."

The policy has been rigorously followed with bipartisan fervor in the face of unanimous world opposition (Israel excepted). The days of "decent respect for the opinions of mankind" have long faded to oblivion, along with such frivolities as the UN Charter and the rule of law. It is astonishing that Cuba has survived the relentless assault.

The successes of the policy of strangulation and torture are reported with no little exuberance, an unusual exhibition of sadistic cowardice. Among the many popular protests underway in Latin America, one is front-page news: in Cuba, giving Biden an opportunity to slap even more sanctions on the "villain" for its resort to abusive measures to suppress the demonstrations, which appear to be mostly about "economic dissatisfaction and hardship," and failures of the authoritarian government to respond in timely and effective fashion.

Cuba's unique internationalism is also undermined, freeing the world from any departure from the norm of self-interest, rarely breached in more than the most limited ways.

That must change. It is by now broadly understood that hoarding of vaccines by the rich countries is not only morally obscene but also self-destructive. The virus will mutate in countries with nondominant economies, and among those refusing vaccination in the rich countries, posing severe dangers to everyone on Earth, the rich included. Much more seriously, heating of the planet also knows no borders. There will be nowhere to hide for long. The same is true of the growing threat of nuclear war among major powers: the end.

Rosa Luxemburg and the Wobblies sketched the kinds of "system changes" toward which humanity should strive, in one or another way. Short of the goals they envisioned, steps must be taken toward engaging an informed and concerned public in international institutions of solidarity and mutual aid, eroding borders, recognizing our shared fate, committing ourselves to working together for the common good instead of "cutting each other's throats."

BIDEN'S "RADICAL" PROPOSALS ARE MINIMUM MEASURES TO AVOID CATASTROPHE

August 12, 2021

C. J. Polychroniou: *It's been said by far too many, including myself, that we live in dark times. And for good reasons. We live in an era where the rich get richer and the poor get poorer, authoritarianism is a global political phenomenon, and life on Earth is entering a state of collapse. From that perspective, human civilization is on an inexorable course of decline and nothing but a radical overhaul of the way humans conduct themselves will save us from a return to barbarism. Yet, there are at the same time signs of progress on numerous fronts, which are hard to overlook. Societies are becoming increasingly multicultural and also more aware of and sensitive to patterns of racism and discrimination. In the light of all this, do we see the glass half empty or half full? Moreover, is it possible to evaluate the qualities of decline and progress scientifically, or do we have to rely purely on normative evaluations and value judgments?*

Noam Chomsky: There are attempts to measure the contents of the glass. The best-known is the Doomsday Clock of the Bulletin of the Atomic Scientists, with the hands placed a certain distance from midnight: the end. Each year that Trump was in office, the minute hand was moved closer to midnight, soon reaching the closest it had ever been, then going beyond. The analysts finally abandoned minutes and turned to seconds: 100 seconds to midnight, where the clock now stands. That seems to me a fair assessment.

The analysts identify three major crises: nuclear war, environmental destruction, and the deterioration of rational discourse. As we've often discussed, Trump has made a signal contribution to each, and the party he now owns is carrying his legacy forward. They are also currently hard at work to regain power by overcoming the dread danger of a government of the people, with plenty of far-right big money at hand. If the project succeeds, emptying of the glass will be accelerated.

There has indeed been progress on many fronts. It is startling to look back and see what was regarded as proper behavior and acceptable attitudes not many years ago, even written into law. While substantial, the progress has not, however, been sufficient to contain and reverse the continuing assault on the social order, the natural world, and the climate of rational discourse.

Without disparaging the great activist achievements, it's hard sometimes to suppress memory of an ironic slogan of the '60s: They may win the battles, but we have all the best songs.

The glass that is before our eyes is not an encouraging sight, to put it mildly. Take the state of the three major crises identified in the setting of the clock.

The major nuclear powers are obligated by the Nuclear Non-Proliferation Treaty "to pursue negotiations in good faith on effective measures relating to cessation of the nuclear arms race at an early date and to nuclear disarmament, and on a treaty on general and complete disarmament under strict and effective international control."

They are pursuing the opposite course.

In its latest annual survey, the prime monitor of global armament, the Stockholm International Peace Research Institute, reports that "the growth in total spending in 2020 was largely influenced by expenditure patterns in the United States and China. The USA increased its military spending for the third straight year to reach $778 billion in 2020," as compared with China's increase to $252 billion. In fourth place, below India, is the second US adversary, Russia: $61.7 billion.

The figures are instructive, but misleading. The US is alone in facing no credible security threats. The threats that are invoked in the calls for even more military spending are at the borders of adversaries, which are ringed with US nuclear-armed missiles in some of the eight hundred US military bases around the world (China has one, Djibouti).

Further threats, in this case quite real, are the development of new and more dangerous weapons systems. They could be banned by treaties, which were effective, until they were mostly dismantled by Bush II and Trump.

The current mythology concocted to justify escalation of this suicidal enterprise is carefully dismantled by nuclear physicist Lawrence Krauss, who for many years had the responsibility to present publicly the setting of the clock. He also reminds us that "the US and Russia have both come within seconds of launching nuclear weapons due to software or human errors that erroneously indicated an incoming nuclear missile strike" and now have "more than 5,000 nuclear weapons each, with more than 1,000 of these on high alert, launch-on-warning status" just waiting for another accident or human decision. That might be by someone well down the chain of command, as we learned from Daniel Ellsberg in his essential book, *The Doomsday Machine*.

The bloated military budget could be sharply cut without harm to authentic security—in fact enhancing genuine security if undertaken as a project of international cooperation, which is not an idle dream as history reveals. That would free up badly needed funds for urgent necessities. But it is not to be. The military budget remains untouchable, the example of the cherished ideal of bipartisanship. For some, it is not enough. Three influential Republican senators have just introduced an amendment to the Bipartisan Infrastructure Bill (BIP) now being debated, calling for another $50 billion for the "undernourished" Pentagon.

One consequence is a substantial contribution to environmental destruction: recent studies show that "the US military is one of the largest polluters in history, consuming more liquid fuels and emitting more climate-changing gases than most medium-sized countries."

That brings us to the one comparable threat to survival of organized human life: environmental destruction. In this case, unlike the nuclear menace, there is at least discussion and sometimes even corrective action, though nowhere near what is urgently needed. For years, scientists have been warning of a "climate emergency." Thousands more are joining the call as the world is swept with disasters intensified by heating the atmosphere. A few weeks ago, we reviewed recent discoveries that show, once again, that the dire predictions of earlier studies were too conservative. Inexorably, the grim tale continues to unfold.

To mention a few more recent examples, new research has found that thawing of permafrost in rapidly heating Siberia may be releasing the "methane time bomb" that scientists have long feared—a rapid release of massive quantities of methane, which is not as long-lasting as carbon dioxide (CO_2) but far more destructive. The main surprise is that the release is from hard rock, not wetlands, as previously anticipated. The lead researcher [Nikolaus Froitzheim] cautions that data are still uncertain; interpreting it correctly, he says, "may make the difference between catastrophe and apocalypse" as the climate crisis worsens.

Those are in fact the likely alternatives on our current course.

An accompanying report calls for a "global state of emergency" as temperatures continue to climb in Siberia and other Arctic regions. "Scientists have been shocked that the warm weather conducive to permafrost thawing is occurring roughly 70 years ahead of model projections," the study warns. "The story is simple," the report concludes. "Climate change is happening faster than anticipated. One consequence—the loss of ice in the polar regions—is also a driver for more rapid global heating and disastrously rapid global sea level rise."

Turning elsewhere, new studies find alarming signs of collapse in major ocean currents that regulate global climates, possibly with an impact on the Gulf Stream, all with incalculable but likely far-reaching effects.

If we return to the topic in a few weeks, there will be more unpleasant news. Meanwhile, political leaders dither, or even act to amplify the threats.

That is the state of threats to survival—threats that could be overcome in a world of rational deliberation and judgment; we know the means.

That brings us to the third factor in the advance of the Doomsday Clock to midnight: the decline of rationality.

Illustrations are so numerous that any small sample will be hopelessly misleading. The most extreme form of irrationality is flat denial of what you don't like. In the case of nuclear weapons and climate, the word "denial" translates as *Doom*, and not in the distant future.

Lesser examples illustrate the depths to which the malady has penetrated.

One example has to do with nuclear weapons in the Middle East, an obsession of the political class and the media for years. Anyone in the vicinity of the real world knows that Israel has a substantial arsenal of nuclear weapons and that there is universal agreement among intelligence agencies that Iran has none.

Trump didn't get his "beautiful wall," but in protection of beliefs from reality, it may not be needed. A University of Maryland Critical Issues poll reveals that "more Americans think Iran possesses nuclear weapons than think Israel does . . . 60.5%, including 70.6% of Republicans and 52.6% of Democrats, say Iran possesses nuclear weapons—compared to 51.7% who say Israel does, including 51.7% of Republicans and 51.9% of Democrats."

We have frequently discussed the obvious solution to the concern that Iran might develop nuclear weapons: a nuclear-weapons-free-zone (NWFZ) in the Middle East. In that case, there would be no constant tensions, no threat of major war, no murderous sanctions that the world must honor or be thrown out of the US-run global financial system. In short, an ideal solution.

A few weeks ago, it seemed that there was finally a convert: the editorial board of the *New York Times*, who concluded that "ideally, the result [of current negotiations] would be a nuclear-weapons-free zone in the Middle East."

The editors acknowledge that there are some problems, not least "Israel's unacknowledged and nonnegotiable possession of nuclear weapons"—also unacknowledged by the US to avoid the embarrassment of opening the question of the status of US military aid to Israel under American law. Unmentioned is that Washington has unilaterally blocked moves toward the "ideal" solution for these reasons (notably Obama). And that the US has some means to pressure Israel when it cares to, wielded by all pre-Obama presidents.

The editorial also states that there is an African NWFZ, failing to mention that it cannot go into effect because of the US military base in Diego Garcia, part of Mauritius in Africa according to the World Court, the United Nations, and the International Tribunal for the Law of the Sea. But not according to the US and its British client, which claims the island in order to provide Washington with the base.

Meanwhile the US-UK righteously proclaim their leadership of the "rules-based international order" challenged by forces of evil.

Defiance of law is no minor matter in this case, not only for the expelled inhabitants and Mauritius, but also for the targets of US bombing in the Middle East and Central Asia.

Nevertheless, at least the "ideal" solution is on the table, though it will plainly be a long struggle to free the public mind from the impressive grip of propaganda.

In a different domain, the gap between prevailing invented reality and old-fashioned reality is illustrated by the fealty of the Republican voting base to, for many of them, their bitter enemy.

Under Trump, the one legislative achievement of the self-declared party of the working man was the tax scam to enrich the very rich and harm the rest that we've already discussed. The practice now extends to the BIP. It has to be funded somehow. "Congressional Republicans objected to tax hikes on the rich or corporations, while also eventually ruling out other measures proposed by the White House, such as stepped-up IRS enforcement on tax cheats. The White House, meanwhile, ruled out higher taxes on Americans earning under $400,000, including a proposed gas tax."

An instructive impasse.

Another illustration of deep loyalty, well reported, is the "stolen election" charade, still upheld by nearly two-thirds of Republicans.

A more subtle, though highly consequential, case is vaccine rejection, persisting in the face of overwhelming evidence of the efficacy of the vaccines and the grave danger of refusal. The danger, of course, is not limited to the refuser. On a sufficient scale, refusal will prevent herd immunity so that the plague will persist, and worse, will expedite mutations that may reach beyond control. Inquiry has identified many factors in refusal. A careful statistical study by Anthony DiMaggio reveals that the culprit, for once, is not Fox News, which has had no statistically significant effect on refusal. Rather, the most salient sector is Republicans confined to social media bubbles, already primed for distrust of science by decades of right-wing propaganda.

Refusal is no small matter. Nearly 60 percent of Republicans say they are unwilling to get vaccinated. Meanwhile, Republican leaders continue to oppose vaccine requirements, arguing that it's up to the individual—whatever the lethal effect on others. The most outspoken is the new heroine of the party, Marjorie Taylor Greene, whose fans cheered when she heralded the low vaccination rate in Alabama, which tossed 65,000 unused doses—badly needed elsewhere—in the midst of another sharp spike in cases.

This is the barest sample. The task of restoring a measure of rationality is daunting, and a responsibility that cannot be shirked.

Should we accept social change as inevitable or is it completely a consequence of collective action? Moreover, given that social change occurs rather slowly in the course of history, in what context is radicalism of better use than pragmatism for achieving progressive social change?

There are some tendencies in history, rooted in the nature of institutions, but it does not follow a predetermined course. Human agency is essential for achieving progressive social change. Almost invariably, it crucially involves collective action. The great historian and activist Howard Zinn dedicated his life's work to "the countless small actions of unknown people" that lie at the roots of "those great moments" that enter the historical record, small actions almost always undertaken in concert. Labor historian Erik Loomis adds the crucial qualification that the labor actions that have commonly been in the forefront of the struggle for a better world have achieved success when a sympathetic administration contained state-business violence.

The usual path to success is a combination of radical goals and pragmatic choice of tactics, but there cannot be a general formula for the proper course.

Looking at the state of the contemporary United States, one is struck by the nearly simultaneous explosion of two highly contradictory phenomena— white supremacist ideology and a new civil rights or social justice movement known as Black Lives Matter, respectively. How do you assess the historical significance of the Black Lives Matter (BLM) movement, and do you see it as a pragmatic or a radical response to the plague of systemic racism?

Black Lives Matter has proven to be a highly significant social movement. The "simultaneous explosion" is real, and not too surprising. BLM is an activist manifestation of a long overdue reckoning with a shameful past and its bitter surviving legacy. Many want that history erased, and its legacy ignored. One salient reason, it seems, is fear of the "Great Replacement."

It's easy to scoff at Great Replacement absurdities, and to condemn the demagogues and cynics who exploit them for their ugly purposes. But it's not hard to see why they appeal to parts of the population—mostly rural, white, Christian, less educated, relatively affluent, often tending toward white supremacist commitments and Christian nationalism. The absurdities resonate because they rest on a core of fact: those who have survived under the jackboot for centuries are demanding basic rights and are receiving more general support. BLM and its broad outreach have significantly advanced this cause. The "traditional way of life" that rests on denying these rights is facing threats, including demographic realities.

It's not necessary here to trace how these conflicts have poisoned American society from its origins. They remain virulent, unpredictable, affecting many aspects of life and the social order.

A noticeable change is also being observed among a growing segment of American citizens, from both political parties, with regard to attitudes toward Israel and the Palestinians. How significant is this shift in public opinion, and how do we explain it?

Highly significant, and unmistakable. The poll I cited earlier on the astonishing perception of Middle East nuclear weapons found that the latest Israeli assault on Gaza "appears to have led to the largest increase to date in the number of Democrats, especially young Democrats, who want the US to lean toward the Palestinians."

Each of the murderous Israeli assaults on Gaza has had that effect. The regular crimes of settlers and the army in the West Bank mostly pass under the radar. But the longtime tendency is very clear. In earlier years, even at moments where there was some recognition of the brutality of Israeli crimes, in the eyes of liberal America, Israel remained "a society in which moral sensitivity is a principle of political life" and which "through its tumultuous history" has been animated by "high moral purpose" (*New York Times*; *Time*, fall 1982, at the peak of condemnation of Israeli crimes after the Sabra-Shatila massacres).

That has changed. Now support for Israel has shifted to Evangelical Christians, right-wing nationalists, and military-security sectors. The shift largely traces the drift to the ultranationalist right within Israel, along with the increasing difficulty of covering up its brutal actions and increased sensibility on a broad scale in the US.

The shift among the population has so far had little impact on policy, in fact runs counter to it. Obama was more supportive of Israel than his predecessors, even if not sufficiently so for the ascendant far right in Israel. Trump pulled out all the stops. Biden, so far, has scarcely modified his extremist stance. If the growing opposition to Israeli crimes crystallizes into an effective solidarity movement, it could bring about significant changes in US policy. That could not fail to have major effects in Israel, which has been dependent on US protection since the 1970s, when the Labor governments made the fateful decision to reject live diplomatic options, choosing instead expansion and construction of Greater Israel in violation of UN Security Council orders and international law.

Environmental activism is growing on a global scale and in various ways. Green political parties are flourishing in Europe, grassroots organizations such as the Sunrise Movement and Extinction Rebellion have emerged as crucial agents in the battle against the climate crisis, and even women in Latin America and the Caribbean have become active in defending the environment and fighting global warming. How do you assess the impacts of environmental movements so far to influence environmental policies and practices of governments and corporations?

There has been a notable impact, but it is nowhere near enough even to keep pace with the race to catastrophe, let alone to act decisively to avert it. There is much more to do, and not much time to do it. We cannot emphasize too strongly the immensity of the stakes.

The so-called radical wing of the Democratic Party, which is most vocally represented by Senator Bernie Sanders and Representative Alexandria Ocasio-Cortez, is coming under rather enigmatic criticism, at least as far as I am concerned, by various left-minded groups and individuals for allegedly not doing enough to push forward a radical agenda of social change, which includes, among other things, Medicare for All. How justified is this criticism, considering that the so-called radical wing of the Democratic Party consists of just a handful of individuals, which means that they obviously lack the power to be movers and shakers in Washington, DC?

Much of the criticism seems to me misguided in two respects: first, it focuses on alleged failures to achieve what is beyond reach under existing circumstances; and second, and more significant, it largely ignores very serious failures to achieve what is well within reach, and crucial for survival.

In the first category, it makes very good sense to strongly advocate for Medicare for All and other measures that would bring the US into the "civilized" world, and enable it to realize its potential to become a leading force for progress, as it was in many ways in the New Deal years.

It is a stunning fact that despite its unique advantages, the United States ranks last among the rich societies in health care. The most recent international study of eleven high-income countries finds that "the United States ranks last overall, despite spending far more of its gross domestic product on health care. The US ranks last on access to care, administrative efficiency, equity, and health care outcomes, but second on measures of care process." This scandal is mirrored in other measures of social justice. And efforts to overcome it are imperative.

Choice of measures to do so has to begin with assessment of social and political reality. The reality is that the levers of power are in the hands of concentrated wealth, the corporate world and their political representatives. The labor movement has been severely weakened by the neoliberal assault, and other popular movements are in no position to challenge concentrated political-economic power even when their goals are backed by a majority of the population. The Republican half of the Senate is opposed, rock solid, to change that impinges on the welfare of their actual constituency of private wealth and corporate power (posturing aside). Simply look at their conditions on funding the BIP. And enough (so-called moderate) Democrats go along with them to block progressive legislation.

Vigorous advocacy should continue, accompanying the educational and organizational work that is needed to overcome dominant reactionary forces. It is idle, however, to direct criticism to a scattered few for failing to do what cannot be done until this foundational work is accomplished. To do that work is the proper task for the critics.

The second category of criticisms, which is largely lacking, should be directed at failures to undertake actions that are within reach and are of immense significance. I have already mentioned one: sharply cutting the Pentagon budget. A related concern is provocative foreign policy stances, dangerous and readily avoided in favor of diplomacy.

Keeping just to the domestic scene, there is a great deal that merits serious critical attention. The major Biden initiative is the BIP. As the business press reports, referring to climate policy, "Most of Biden's plans for radical change can't be found anywhere" in the bill. The "radical" proposals that can't be found are in fact moderate measures that are essential for escape from catastrophe.

The few progressives in Congress, backed by the Sunrise Movement, have said they will not vote for the BIP unless Congress moves on a subsequent legislation that includes the full range of necessary proposals. The fate of the contemplated larger bill is very much in doubt.

While this failure is receiving at least some attention, there is more that is passing in silence and is truly ominous. AP reports that "approvals for companies to drill for oil and gas on US public lands are on pace this year to reach their highest level since George W. Bush was president, underscoring President Joe Biden's reluctance to more forcefully curb petroleum production in the face of industry and Republican resistance." The reference is to reserves already under lease but not authorized.

While there are legal issues about blocking prior leases, there seems to be plenty of room for executive action. Much had been hoped for from Interior Secretary Deb Haaland, who while in Congress had adamantly opposed drilling on federal lands and opposed fracking, and had cosponsored the original Green New Deal. But the signs so far are hardly encouraging—and one can't reiterate often enough that there is not much time.

In this domain, critical commentary is well warranted. And even more so, direct engagement and action.

NOAM CHOMSKY AND ROBERT POLLIN

WE CAN'T RELY ON PRIVATE SECTOR FOR NECESSARY CLIMATE ACTION

August 16, 2021

C. J. Polychroniou: *Noam, the new IPCC climate assessment report, which deals with the physical science basis of global warming, comes in the midst of extreme heat waves and devastating fires taking place both in the US and in many parts of the world. In many ways, it reinforces what we already know about the climate crisis, so I would like to know your own thoughts about its significance and whether the parties that have "approved" it will take the necessary measures to avoid a climate catastrophe, since we basically have zero years left to do so.*

Noam Chomsky: The IPCC report was sobering. Much, as you say, reinforces what we knew, but for me at least, shifts of emphasis were deeply disturbing. That's particularly true of the section on carbon removal. Instead of giving my own nonexpert reading, I'll quote the *MIT Technology Review*, under the heading "The UN climate report pins hopes on carbon removal technologies that barely exist."

The IPCC report

> offered a stark reminder that removing massive amounts of carbon dioxide from the atmosphere will be essential to prevent the gravest dangers of global warming. But it also un-

derscored that the necessary technologies barely exist—and will be tremendously difficult to deploy. . . . How much hotter it gets, however, will depend on how rapidly we cut emissions and how quickly we scale up ways of sucking carbon dioxide out of the air.

If that's correct, and I see no reason to doubt it, hopes for a tolerable world depend on technologies that "barely exist—and will be tremendously difficult to deploy." To confront this awesome challenge is a task for a coordinated international effort, well beyond the scale of John F. Kennedy's mission to the moon (whatever one thinks of that), and vastly more significant. To leave the task to private power is a likely recipe for disaster, for many reasons, including one brought up by the *New York Times* report on the idea: "There are risks: The very idea could offer industry an excuse to maintain dangerous habits . . . some experts warn that they could hide behind the uncertain promise of removing carbon later to avoid cutting emissions deeply today." The greenwashing is a constant ruse.

The significance of the IPCC report is beyond reasonable doubt. As to whether the necessary measures will be taken? That's up to us. We can have no faith in structures of power and what they will do unless pressed hard by an informed public that prefers survival to short-term gain for the "masters of the universe."

The immediate US government reaction to the IPCC report was hardly encouraging. President Joe Biden sent his national security adviser, Jake Sullivan, to censure the main oil-producing countries (OPEC) for not raising oil production high enough. The message was captured in a headline in the London *Financial Times*: "Biden to OPEC: Drill, Baby, Drill."

Biden was sharply criticized by the right wing here for calling on OPEC to destroy life on Earth. MAGA principles demand that US producers should have priority in this worthy endeavor.

Bob, what's your own take on the IPCC climate assessment report, and do you find anything in it that surprises you?

Robert Pollin: In total, the IPCC's Sixth Assessment Report on the physical basis of climate change is 3,949 pages long. So there's a whole lot to take in, and I can't claim to have done more than initially review the 42-page "Summary for Policymakers." Two things stand out from my initial review. These are, first, the IPCC's conclusion that the climate crisis is rapidly becoming more severe and, second, that their call for undertaking fundamental action has become increasingly urgent, even relative to their own 2018 report, "Global Warming of 1.50C." It is important to note that this hasn't always been the pattern with the IPCC. Thus, in its 2014 Fifth Assessment Report, the IPCC was significantly more sanguine about the state of play relative to its 2007 Fourth Assessment Report. In 2014, they were focused on a goal of stabilizing the global average temperature at 2.0 degrees Celsius above preindustrial levels, rather than the 1.5 degrees figure. As of 2014, the IPCC had not been convinced that the 1.5 degrees target was imperative for having any reasonable chance of limiting the most severe impacts of climate change in terms of heat extremes, floods, droughts, sea level rises, and biodiversity losses. The 2014 report concluded that reducing global CO_2 emissions by only 36 percent as of 2050 could possibly be sufficient to move onto a viable stabilization path. In this most recent report, there is no equivocation that hitting the 1.5 degrees target is imperative, and that to have any chance of achieving this goal, global CO_2 emissions must be at zero by 2050.

This new report does also make clear just how difficult it will be to hit the zero-emissions target, and thus to remain within the 1.5 degrees of warming threshold. But it also recognizes that a viable stabilization path is still possible, if just barely. There is no question as to what the first and most important single action has to be, which is to stop burning oil, coal, and natural gas to produce energy. Carbon-removal technologies will likely be needed as part of the overall stabilization program. But we should note here that there are already two carbon-removal technologies that operate quite effectively. These are: (1) to stop destroying forests, since trees absorb CO_2; and (2) to supplant corporate industrial practices with organic and regenerative agriculture. Corporate agricultural practices emit CO_2 and other greenhouses gases, especially through the heavy use of nitrogen fertilizer, while, through organic and regenerative agriculture, the soil absorbs CO_2. That said, if we don't stop burning fossil fuels to produce energy, then there is simply no chance of moving onto a stabilization path, no matter what else is accomplished in the area of carbon-removal technologies.

I would add here that the main technologies for building a zero-emissions economy—in the areas of energy efficiency and clean renewable energy sources—are already fully available to us. Investing in energy efficiency—through, for example, expanding the supply of electric cars and public transportation systems, and replacing old heating and cooling systems with electric heat pumps—will save money, by definition, for all energy consumers. Moreover, on average, the cost of producing electricity through both solar and wind energy is already, at present, about half that of burning coal combined with carbon capture technology. At this point, it is a matter of undertaking the investments at scale to build the clean energy infrastructure along with providing for a fair transition for the workers and communities who will be negatively impacted by the phaseout of fossil fuels.

The evidence is clear that human-caused emissions of carbon dioxide are behind global warming, and that warming, according to the IPCC report, is taking place faster than predicted. Most likely because of the latter, the Sixth Assessment report provides a detailed regional assessment of climate change, and (for the first time, I believe) includes a chapter on innovation and technology, with emphasis on carbon-removal technologies, which Noam, coincidentally, found "deeply disturbing." As one of the leading advocates of a Global Green New Deal, do you see a problem if regional climate and energy plans became the main frameworks, at least in the immediate future, for dealing with the climate emergency?

Pollin: In principle, I don't see anything wrong with regional climate and energy plans, as long as they are all seriously focused on achieving the zero-emissions goal and are advanced in coordination with other regions. The big question, therefore, is whether any given regional program is adequate to the requirements for climate stabilization. The answer, thus far, is "no." We can see this in terms of the climate programs in place for the US, the European Union, and China. These are the three most important regions in addressing climate change for the simple reason that these three areas are responsible for generating 54 percent of all global CO_2 emissions—with China at 30 percent, the US at 15 percent, and the EU at 9 percent.

In the US, the Biden administration is, of course, a vast improvement relative to the four disastrous years under Trump. Soon after taking office, Biden set out emission-reduction targets in line with the IPCC—that is, a 50 percent reduction by 2030 and net-zero emissions by 2050. Moreover, the American Jobs Plan that Biden introduced in March would have allocated about $130 billion per year in investments that would advance a clean energy infrastructure that would supplant our current fossil-fuel-dominant system.

This level of federal funding for climate stabilization would be unprecedented for the US. At the same time, it would provide maybe 25 percent of the total funding necessary for achieving the administration's own emission-reduction targets. Most of the other 75 percent would therefore have to come from private investors. Yet it is not realistic that private businesses will mount this level of investment in a clean energy economy—at about $400 billion per year—unless they are forced to by stringent government regulations. One such regulation could be a mandate for electric utilities to reduce CO_2 emissions by, say, 5 percent per year, or face criminal liability. The Biden administration has not proposed any such regulations to date. Moreover, with the debates in Congress over the Biden bill ongoing, the odds are long that the amount of federal government funding provided for climate stabilization will even come close to the $130 billion per year that Biden had initially proposed in March.

The story is similar in the EU. In terms of its stated commitments, the European Union is advancing the world's most ambitious climate stabilization program, what it has termed the European Green Deal. Under the European Green Deal, the region has pledged to reduce emissions by at least 55 percent as of 2030 relative to 1990 levels, a more ambitious target than the 45 percent reduction set by the IPCC. The European Green Deal then aligns with the IPCC's longer-term target of achieving a net-zero economy as of 2050.

Beginning in December 2019, the European Commission has been enacting measures and introducing further proposals to achieve the region's emission-reduction targets. The most recent measure to have been adopted, this past June, is the NextGenerationEU Recovery Plan, through which €600 billion will be allocated toward financing the European Green Deal. In July, the European Commission followed up on this spending commitment by outlining thirteen tax and regulatory measures to complement the spending program.

But here's the simple budgetary math: The €600 billion allocated over seven years through the NextGenerationEU Recovery Plan would amount to an average of about €85 billion per year. This is equal to less than 0.6 percent of EU GDP over this period, when a spending level in the range of 2 to 3 percent of GDP will be needed. As with the US, the EU cannot count on mobilizing the remaining 75 percent of funding necessary unless it also enacts stringent regulations on burning fossil fuels. If such regulations are to have teeth, they will mean a sharp increase in what consumers will pay for fossil fuel energy. To prevent all but the wealthy from then experiencing a significant increase in their cost of living, the fossil fuel price increases will have to be matched by rebates. The 2018 Yellow Vest Movement in France emerged precisely in opposition to President Emmanuel Macron's proposal to enact a carbon tax without including substantial rebates for nonaffluent people.

The Chinese situation is distinct from those in the US and EU. In particular, China has not committed to achieving the IPCC's emissions-reduction targets for 2030 or 2050. Rather, as of a September 2020 United Nations General Assembly address by President Xi Jinping, China committed to a less ambitious set of targets: emissions will continue to rise until they peak in 2030 and then begin declining. Xi also committed to achieving net-zero emissions by 2060, a decade later than the IPCC's 2050 target.

We do need to recognize that China has made major advances in support of climate stabilization. As one critical case in point, China's ambitious industrial policies are primarily responsible for driving down the costs of solar energy worldwide by 80 percent over the past decade. China has also been the leading supplier of credit to support clean energy investments in developing economies. Nevertheless, there is no getting around the fact that if China sticks to its stated emission-reduction plans, there is no chance whatsoever of achieving the IPCC's targets.

In short, for different reasons, China, the US, and the EU all need to mount significantly more ambitious regional climate stabilization programs. In particular, these economies need to commit higher levels of public investment to the global clean energy investment project.

The basic constraint with increasing public investment is that people don't want to pay higher taxes. Rich people can, of course, easily afford to pay higher taxes, after enjoying massive increases in their wealth and income under neoliberalism. That said, it is still also true that most of the funds needed to bring global clean energy investments to scale can be made available without raising taxes, by channeling resources from three sources: (1) transferring funds out of military budgets; (2) converting all fossil fuel subsidies into clean energy subsidies; and (3) mounting large-scale green bond purchasing programs by the US Federal Reserve, the European Central Bank, and the People's Bank of China. Such measures can be the foundation for tying together the US, EU, and Chinese regional programs that could, in combination, have a chance of meeting the urgent requirements for a viable global climate stabilization project.

Noam, I argued recently that we should face the global warming threat as the outbreak of a world war. Is this a fair analogy?

Chomsky: Not quite. A world war would leave survivors, scattered and miserable remnants. Over time, they could reconstruct some form of viable existence. Destruction of the environment is much more serious. There is no return.

Twenty years ago, I wrote a book that opened with biologist Ernst Mayr's rather plausible argument that we are unlikely to discover intelligence in the universe. To carry his argument further, if higher intelligence ever appears, it will probably find a way to self-destruct, as we seem to be bent on demonstrating.

The book closed with Bertrand Russell's thoughts on whether there will ever be peace on Earth: "After ages during which the earth produced harmless trilobites and butterflies, evolution progressed to the point at which it has generated Neros, Genghis Khans, and Hitlers. This, however, I believe is a passing nightmare; in time the earth will become again incapable of supporting life, and peace will return."

THE US-LED "WAR ON TERROR" HAS DEVASTATED MUCH OF THE WORLD

September 8, 2021

C. J. Polychroniou: *Nearly twenty years have passed since the September 11 terrorist attacks in 2001. With nearly three thousand dead, this was the deadliest attack on US soil in history and produced dramatic ramifications for global affairs, as well as startling impacts on domestic society. I want to start by asking you to reflect on the alleged revamping of US foreign policy under George W. Bush as part of his administration's reaction to the rise of Osama bin Laden and the jihadist phenomenon. First, was there anything new to the Bush Doctrine, or was it simply a codification of what we had already seen take place in the 1990s in Iraq, Panama, Bosnia, and Kosovo? Second, was the US-NATO-led invasion of Afghanistan legal under international law? And third, was the US ever committed to nation building in Afghanistan?*

Noam Chomsky: Washington's immediate reaction to 9/11/2001 was to invade Afghanistan. The withdrawal of US ground forces was timed to (virtually) coincide with the twentieth anniversary of the invasion. There has been a flood of commentary on the 9/11 anniversary and the termination of the ground war. It is highly illuminating, and consequential. It reveals how the course of events is perceived by the political class, and provides useful background for considering the substantive questions about the Bush Doctrine. It also yields some indication of what is likely to ensue.

Of utmost importance at this historic moment would be the

reflections of "the decider," as he called himself. And indeed, there was an interview with George W. Bush as the withdrawal reached its final stage, in the *Washington Post*.

In the Style section.

The article and interview introduce us to a lovable, goofy grandpa, enjoying banter with his children, admiring the portraits he had painted of Great Men that he had known in his days of glory. There was an incidental comment on his exploits in Afghanistan and the follow-up episode in Iraq:

> Bush may have started the Iraq War on false pretenses, but at least he hadn't inspired an insurrection that turned the U.S. Capitol into a combat zone. At least he had made efforts to distance himself from the racists and xenophobes in his party rather than cultivate their support. At least he hadn't gone so far as to call his *domestic* adversaries "evil."

"He looks like the Babe Ruth of presidents when you compare him to Trump," former Senate majority leader and one-time Bush nemesis Harry M. Reid (D-Nevada) said in an interview. "Now, I look back on Bush with a degree of nostalgia, with some affection, which I never thought I would do."

Way down on the list, meriting only incidental allusion, is the slaughter of hundreds of thousands; many millions of refugees; vast destruction; a regime of hideous torture; incitement of ethnic conflicts that have torn the whole region apart; and as a direct legacy, two of the most miserable countries on Earth.

First things first. He didn't bad-mouth fellow Americans.

The sole interview with Bush captures well the essence of the flood of commentary. What matters is us. There are many laments about the cost of these ventures: the cost to us, that is, which "have exceeded $8 trillion, according to new estimates by the Costs of War project at Brown University," along with American lives lost and disruption of our fragile society.

Next time we should assess the costs to us more carefully, and do better.

There are also well-justified laments about the fate of women under Taliban rule. The laments sometimes are no doubt sincere, though a natural question arises: Why weren't they voiced thirty years ago when US favorites, armed and enthusiastically supported by Washington, were terrorizing young women in Kabul who were wearing the "wrong" clothes, throwing acid in their faces and other abuses? Particularly vicious were the forces of the arch-terrorist, Gulbuddin Hekmatyar, recently on the US negotiating team.

The achievements in women's rights in Russian-controlled cities in the late '80s, and the threats they faced from the CIA-mobilized radical Islamist forces, were reported at the time by a highly credible source, Rasil Basu, a distinguished international feminist activist who was UN representative in Afghanistan in those years, with special concern for women's rights.

Basu reports:

> During the [Russian] occupation, in fact, women made enormous strides: illiteracy declined from 98% to 75%, and they were granted equal rights with men in civil law, and in the Constitution. This is not to say that there was complete gender equality. Unjust patriarchal relations still prevailed in the workplace and in the family with women occupying lower level sex-type jobs. But the strides they took in education and employment were very impressive.

Basu submitted articles on these matters to the major US journals, along with the feminist journal *Ms. Magazine*. No takers, wrong story. She was, however, able to publish her report in Asia: *Asian Age*, on December 3, 2001.

We can learn more about how Afghans in Kabul perceive the late years of the Russian occupation, and what followed, from another expert source, Rodric Braithwaite, British ambassador to Moscow from 1988 to 1992, and then chairman of the Joint Intelligence Committee, also author of the major scholarly work on the Soviets in Afghanistan.

Braithwaite visited Kabul in 2008, and reported his findings in the *London Financial Times*:

In Afghanistan today new myths are building up. They bode ill for current western policy. On a recent visit I spoke to Afghan journalists, former Mujahideen, professionals, people working for the "coalition"—natural supporters for its claims to bring peace and reconstruction. They were contemptuous of [US-imposed] President Hamid Karzai, whom they compared to Shah Shujah, the British puppet installed during the first Afghan war. Most preferred Mohammad Najibullah, the last communist president, who attempted to reconcile the nation within an Islamic state, and was butchered by the Taliban in 1996: DVDs of his speeches are being sold on the streets. Things were, they said, better under the Soviets. Kabul was secure, women were employed, the Soviets built factories, roads, schools and hospitals, Russian children played safely in the streets. The Russian soldiers fought bravely on the ground like real warriors, instead of killing women and children from the air. Even the Taliban were not so bad: they were good Muslims, kept order, and respected women in their own way. These myths may not reflect historical reality, but they do measure a deep disillusionment with the "coalition" and its policies.

The policies of the "coalition" were brought to the public in *New York Times* correspondent Tim Weiner's history of the CIA. The goal was to "kill Soviet Soldiers," the CIA station chief in Islamabad declared, making it clear that "the mission was not to liberate Afghanistan."

His understanding of the policies he was ordered to execute under President Ronald Reagan is fully in accord with the boasts of President Jimmy Carter's national security adviser Zbigniew Brzezinski about their decision to support radical Islamist jihadis in 1979 in order to draw the Russians into Afghanistan, and his pleasure in the outcome after hundreds of thousands of Afghans were killed and much of the country wrecked: "What is more important in world history? The Taliban or the collapse of the Soviet empire? Some agitated Moslems or the liberation of Central Europe and the end of the cold war?"

It was recognized early on by informed observers that the Russian invaders were eager to withdraw without delay. The study of Russian archives by historian David Gibbs resolves any doubts on the matter. But it was much more useful for Washington to issue rousing proclamations about Russia's terrifying expansionist goals, compelling the US, in defense, to greatly expand its own domination of the region, with violence when needed (the Carter Doctrine, a precursor of the Bush Doctrine).

The Russian withdrawal left a relatively popular government in place under Najibullah, with a functioning army that was able to hold its own for several years until the US-backed radical Islamists took over and instituted a reign of terror so extreme that the Taliban were widely welcomed when they invaded, instituting their own harsh regime. They kept on fairly good terms with Washington until 9/11.

Returning to the present, we should indeed be concerned with the fate of women, and others, as the Taliban return to power. For those sincerely concerned to design policies that might benefit them, a little historical memory doesn't hurt.

The same is true in other respects as well. The Taliban have promised not to harbor terrorists, but how can we believe them, commentators warn, when this promise is coupled with the outrageous claim by their spokesman Zabihullah Mujahid that there is "no proof" that Osama bin Laden was responsible for the 9/11 attack?

There is one problem with the general ridicule of this shocking statement. What Mujahid actually said was both accurate and very much worth hearing. In his words, "When Osama bin Laden became an issue for the Americans, he was in Afghanistan. Although there was no proof he was involved" in 9/11.

Let's check. In June 2002, eight months after 9/11, FBI director Robert Mueller made his most extensive presentation to the national press about the results of what was probably the most intensive investigation in history. In his words, "investigators believe the idea of the Sept. 11 attacks on the World Trade Center and Pentagon came from al Qaeda leaders in Afghanistan," though the plotting and financing apparently trace to Germany and the United Arab Emirates. "We think the masterminds of it were in Afghanistan, high in the al Qaeda leadership."

What was only surmised in June 2002 could not have been known eight months earlier when the US invaded. Mujahid's outrageous comment was accurate. The ridicule is another example of convenient amnesia.

Keeping Mujahid's accurate statement in mind, along with Mueller's confirmation of it, we can move toward understanding the Bush Doctrine.

While doing so, we might listen to Afghan voices. One of the most respected was Abdul Haq, the leading figure in the anti-Taliban Afghan resistance and a former leader of the US-backed Mujahideen resistance to the Russian invasion. A few weeks after the US invasion, he had an interview with Asia scholar Anatol Lieven.

Haq bitterly condemned the US invasion, which, he recognized, would kill many Afghans and undermine the efforts to overthrow the Taliban from within. He said that "the US is trying to show its muscle, score a victory and scare everyone in the world. They don't care about the suffering of the Afghans or how many people we will lose."

Haq was not alone in this view. A meeting of one thousand tribal elders in October 2001 unanimously demanded an end to the bombing, which, they declared, is targeting "innocent people." They urged that means other than slaughter and destruction be employed to overthrow the hated Taliban regime.

The leading Afghan women's rights organization, Revolutionary Association of the Women of Afghanistan (RAWA), issued a declaration on October 11, 2001, strongly opposing the "vast aggression on our country" by the US, which will shed the blood of innocent civilians. The declaration called for "eradication of the plague of the Taliban and al-Qaeda" by the "uprising of the Afghan nation," not by a murderous assault of foreign aggressors.

All public at the time, all ignored as irrelevant, all forgotten. The opinions of Afghans are not our concern when we invade and occupy their country.

The perception of the anti-Taliban Afghan resistance was not far from the stance of President Bush and his defense secretary, Donald Rumsfeld. Both dismissed Taliban initiatives to send bin Laden for trial abroad despite Washington's refusal to provide evidence (which it didn't have). Finally, they refused Taliban offers to surrender. As the president put it, "When I said no negotiations, I meant no negotiations." Rumsfeld added, "We don't negotiate surrenders." I.e., *we're going to show our muscle and scare everyone in the world.*

The imperial pronouncement at the time was that those who harbor terrorists are as guilty as the terrorists themselves. The shocking audacity of that proclamation passed almost unnoticed. It was not accompanied by a call to bomb Washington, as it obviously implied. Even putting aside the world-class terrorists in high places, the US harbors and abets retail terrorists who keep to such acts as blowing up Cuban commercial airliners, killing many people, part of the long US terrorist war against Cuba.

Quite apart from that scandal, it is worth stating the unspeakable: The US had no charge against the Taliban. No charge, before 9/11 or ever. Before 9/11, Washington was on fairly good terms with the Taliban. After 9/11, it demanded extradition (without even a pretense of providing required evidence), and when the Taliban agreed, Washington refused the offers: "We don't negotiate surrenders." The invasion was not only a violation of international law, as marginal a concern in Washington as the anti-Taliban Afghan resistance, but also had no credible pretext on any grounds.

Pure criminality.

Furthermore, ample evidence is now available showing that Afghanistan and al-Qaeda were not of much interest to the Bush-Cheney-Rumsfeld triumvirate. They had their eyes on much bigger game than Afghanistan. Iraq would be the first step, then the entire region. I won't review the record here. It's well documented in Scott Horton's book, *Fool's Errand.*

That's the Bush Doctrine. Rule the region, rule the world, show our muscle so that the world knows that "what we say goes," as Bush I put it.

It's hardly a new US doctrine. It's also easy to find precursors in imperial history. Simply consider our predecessor in world control, Britain, a grand master of war crimes, whose wealth and power derived from piracy, slavery, and the world's greatest narco-trafficking enterprise.

And in the last analysis, "Whatever happens, we have got the Maxim gun, and they have not." Hilaire Belloc's rendition of Western civilization. And pretty much Abdul Haq's insight into the imperial mindset.

Nothing reveals reigning values more clearly than the mode of withdrawal. The Afghan population was scarcely a consideration. The imperial "deciders" do not trouble to ask what people might want in the rural areas of this overwhelmingly rural society where the Taliban live and find their support, perhaps grudging support as the best of bad alternatives. Formerly a Pashtun movement, the "new Taliban" evidently have a much broader base. That was dramatically revealed by the quick collapse of their former enemies, the vicious warlord Abdul Rashid Dostum, along with Ismail Khan, bringing other ethnic groups within the Taliban network. There are also Afghan peace forces that should not be summarily dismissed. What would the Afghan population want if they had a choice? Could they, perhaps, reach local accommodations if given time before a precipitous withdrawal? Whatever the possibilities might have been, they do not seem to have been considered.

The depth of contempt for Afghans was, predictably, reached by Donald Trump. In his unilateral withdrawal agreement with the Taliban in February 2020, he did not even bother to consult with the official Afghan government. Worse still, Bush administration foreign policy specialist Kori Schake reports, Trump forced the Afghan government to release five thousand Taliban fighters and relax economic sanctions. He agreed that the Taliban could continue to commit violence against the government we were there to support, against innocent people and against those who'd assisted our efforts to keep Americans safe. All the Taliban had to do was say they would stop targeting US or coalition forces, not permit al-Qaeda and other terrorist organizations to use Afghan territory to threaten US security, and subsequently hold negotiations with the Afghan government.

As usual, what matters is us, this time amplified by Trump's signature cruelty. The fate of Afghans is of zero concern.

Trump timed the withdrawal for the onset of the summer fighting season, reducing the hope for some kind of preparation. President Joe Biden improved the terms of withdrawal a little, but not enough to prevent the anticipated debacle. Then came the predictable reaction of the increasingly shameless Republican leadership. They were barely able to remove their gushing tributes to Trump's "historic peace agreement" from their web page in time to denounce Biden and call for his impeachment for pursuing an improved version of Trump's ignominious betrayal.

Meanwhile, the Afghans are again hung out to dry.

Returning to the original question, the Bush Doctrine may have been formulated more crudely than the usual practice, but it is hardly new. The invasion violated international law (and Article VI of the US Constitution), but Bush's legal team had determined that such sentimentality was "quaint" and "obsolete," again breaking little new ground except for brazen defiance. As to "nation building," one way to measure the commitment to this goal is to ask what portion of the trillions of dollars expended went to the Afghan population, and what portion went to the US military system and its mercenaries ("contractors") along with the morass of corruption in Kabul and the warlords the US established in power.

At the outset, I referred to 9/11/2001, not just 9/11. There's a good reason. What we call 9/11 is the second 9/11. The first 9/11 was far more destructive and brutal by any reasonable measure: 9/11/73. To see why, consider per-capita equivalents, the right measure. Suppose that on 9/11/2001, thirty thousand people had been killed, five hundred thousand viciously tortured, the government overthrown, and a brutal dictatorship installed. That would have been worse than what we call 9/11.

It happened. It wasn't deplored by the US government, or by private capital, or by the international financial institutions that the US largely controls, or by the leading figures of "libertarianism." Rather, it was lauded and granted enormous support. The perpetrators, like Henry Kissinger, are highly honored. I suppose bin Laden is lauded among jihadis.

All should recognize that I am referring to Chile, 9/11/1973.

Another topic that might inspire reflection is the notion of "forever wars," finally put to rest with the withdrawal from Afghanistan. From the perspective of the victims, when did the forever wars begin? For the United States, they began in 1783. With the British yoke removed, the new nation was free to invade "Indian country," to attack Indigenous nations with campaigns of slaughter, terror, ethnic cleansing, violation of treaties—all on a massive scale, meanwhile picking up half of Mexico, then onto much of the world. A longer view traces our forever wars back to 1492, as historian Walter Hixson argues.

From the viewpoint of the victims, history looks different from the stance of those with the Maxim gun and their descendants.

In March 2003, the US initiated a war against Iraq as part of the neoconservative vision of remaking the Middle East and removing leaders that posed a threat to the interests and "integrity" of the United States. Knowing that the regime of Saddam Hussein had nothing to do with the 9/11 terrorist attacks, possessed no weapons of mass destruction, and subsequently posed no threat to the US, why did Bush invade Iraq, which left hundreds of thousands of Iraqis dead and may have cost more than $3 trillion?

September 11 provided the occasion for the invasion of Iraq, which, unlike Afghanistan, is a real prize: a major petrostate right at the heart of the world's prime oil-producing region. As the Twin Towers were still smoldering, Rumsfeld was telling his staff that it's time to "go massive—sweep it all up, things related and not," including Iraq. Goals quickly became far more expansive. Bush and associates made it quite clear that bin Laden was small potatoes, of little interest (see Horton for many details).

The Bush legal team determined that the UN Charter, which explicitly bars preemptive/preventive wars, actually authorizes them—formalizing what had long been operative doctrine. The official reason for war was the "single question": Hussein's weapons of mass destruction. When the question received the wrong answer, the reason for aggression instantly switched to "democracy promotion," a transparent fairy tale swallowed enthusiastically by the educated classes—though some demurred, including 99 percent of Iraqis, according to polls.

Some are now praised for having opposed the war from the start, notably Barack Obama, who criticized it as a strategic blunder. Perhaps my memory is faulty, but I don't recall praise for Nazi generals who regarded Hitler's Operation Barbarossa as a strategic blunder: they should have knocked out Britain first. A different judgment was rendered by the Nuremberg Tribunal. But the US doesn't commit crimes, by definition; only blunders.

The regime-change agenda that had defined US foreign policy under the Bush administration was apparently behind NATO's decision to remove Muammar Qaddafi from power in Libya in the wake of the "Arab Spring" revolutions in late 2010 and early 2011. But as in the case of Iraq, what were the real reasons for dealing with the leader of an alleged "rogue state" that had long ceased being one?

The Libya intervention was initiated by France, partly in reaction to humanitarian posturing of some French intellectuals, partly I suppose (we don't have much evidence) as part of France's effort to sustain its imperial role in francophone Africa. Britain joined in. Then Obama-Clinton joined, "leading from behind" as some White House official is supposed to have said. As Qaddafi's forces were converging on Benghazi, there were loud cries of impending genocide, leading to a UN Security Council resolution imposing a no-fly zone and calling for negotiations. That was reasonable in my opinion; there were legitimate concerns. The African Union proposed a ceasefire with negotiations with the Benghazi rebels about reforms. Qaddafi accepted it; the rebels refused.

At that point, the France-Britain-US coalition decided to violate the Security Council resolution they had introduced and to become, in effect, the air force of the rebels. That enabled the rebel forces to advance on ground, finally capturing and sadistically murdering Qaddafi. Hillary Clinton found that quite amusing, and joked with the press that "We came, we saw, he died."

The country then collapsed into total chaos, with sharp escalation in killings and other atrocities. It also led to a flow of jihadis and weapons to other parts of Africa, stirring up major disasters there. Intervention extended to Russia and Turkey, and the Arab dictatorships, supporting warring groups. The whole episode has been a catastrophe for Libya and much of West Africa. Clinton is not on record, as far as I know, as to whether this is also amusing.

Libya was a major oil producer. It's hard to doubt that that was a factor in the various interventions, but lacking internal records, little can be said with confidence.

The debacle in Afghanistan has shown beyond any doubt the failure of US strategy in the war on terror and of the regime-change operations. However, there is something more disturbing than these facts, which is that, after each intervention, the United States leaves behind "black holes" and even betrays those that fought on its side against terrorism. Two interrelated questions: First, do you think that the failed war on terror will produce any new lessons for future US foreign policymakers? And second, does this failure reveal anything about US supremacy in world affairs?

Failure is in the eyes of the beholder. Let's first recall that Bush II didn't declare the global war on terror. He re-declared it. It was Reagan and his secretary of state George Shultz who came into office declaring the global war on terror, a campaign to destroy the "evil scourge of terrorism," particularly state-backed international terrorism, a "plague spread by depraved opponents of civilization itself [in a] return to barbarism in the modern age."

The global war on terror quickly became a huge terrorist war directed or supported by Washington, concentrating on Central America but extending to the Middle East, Africa, and Asia. The global war on terror even led to a World Court judgment condemning the Reagan administration for "unlawful use of force"—a.k.a., international terrorism—and ordering the US to pay substantial reparations for its crimes.

The US of course dismissed all of this and stepped up the "unlawful use of force." That was quite proper, the editors of the *New York*

Times explained. The World Court was a "hostile forum," as proven by the fact that it condemned the blameless US. A few years earlier it had been a model of probity when it sided with the US in a case against Iran.

The US then vetoed a Security Council resolution calling on all states to observe international law, mentioning no one, although it was clear what was intended. I'm not sure whether it was even reported.

But we solemnly declare that states that harbor terrorists are as guilty as the terrorists themselves. So the invasion of Afghanistan was "right" and "just," though ill-conceived and too costly. *To us.*

Was it a failure? For US imperial goals? In some cases, yes. Reagan was the last supporter of the Apartheid regime in South Africa, but was unable to sustain it. In general, though, it extended Washington's imperial reach.

Bush's renewal of the global war on terror has not had similar success. When the US invaded Afghanistan, the base for radical Islamic fundamentalist terrorism was largely confined to a corner of Afghanistan. Now it is all over the world. The devastation of much of Central Asia and the Middle East has not enhanced US power.

I doubt that it has much impact on US global supremacy, which remains overwhelming. In the military dimension, the US stands alone. Its military spending eclipses rivals—in 2020, $778 billion as compared to China's $252 billion and Russia's $62 billion. The US military is also far more advanced technologically. US security is unrivaled. The alleged threats are at the borders of enemies, which are ringed with nuclear-armed missiles in some of the eight hundred US military bases around the world (China has one: Djibouti).

Power also has economic dimensions. At the peak of US power after World War II, the US had perhaps 40 percent of global wealth, a preponderance that inevitably declined. But as political economist Sean Starrs has observed, in the world of neoliberal globalization, national accounts are not the only measure of economic power. His research shows that US-based multinationals control a staggering 50 percent of global wealth and are first (sometimes second) in just about every sector.

Another dimension is "soft power." Here, America has seriously declined, well before Trump's harsh blows to the country's reputation. Even under Clinton, leading political scientists recognized that most of the world regarded America as the world's "prime rogue state" and "the single greatest external threat to their societies" (to quote Samuel Huntington and Robert Jervis, respectively). In the Obama years, international polls found that the US was considered the greatest threat to world peace, with no contender even close.

US leaders can continue to undermine the country, if they choose, but its enormous power and unrivaled advantages make that a hard task, even for the Trump wrecking ball.

A look back at the 9/11 attacks also reveals that the war on terror had numerous consequences on domestic society in the US. Can you comment on the impact of the war on terror on American democracy and human rights?

In this regard, the topic has been well enough covered so that not much comment is necessary. Another illustration just appeared in the *New York Times* Review of the Week, the eloquent testimony by a courageous FBI agent who was so disillusioned by his task of "destroying people" (Muslims) in the war on terror that he decided to leak documents exposing the crimes and to go to prison. That fate is reserved to those who expose state crimes, not the perpetrators, who are respected, like the goofy grandpa, George W. Bush.

There has of course been a serious assault on civil liberties and human rights, in some cases utterly unspeakable, like Guantánamo, where tortured prisoners still languish after many years without charges or because the torture was so hideous that judges refuse to allow them to be brought to trial. It's by now conceded that "the worst of the worst" (as they were called) were mostly innocent bystanders.

At home, the framework of a surveillance state with utterly illegitimate power has been established. The victims as usual are the most vulnerable, but others might want to reflect on Pastor Niemöller's famous plea under Nazi rule.

IT'S LIFE AND DEATH—INTELLECTUALS CAN'T KEEP SERVING THE STATUS QUO

October 7, 2021

C. J. Polychroniou: *Long ago, in your celebrated essay "The Responsibility of Intellectuals," you argued that intellectuals must insist on truth and expose lies, but must also analyze events in their historical perspective. Now, while you never implied that this is the only responsibility that intellectuals have, don't you think that the role of intellectuals has changed dramatically over the course of the last half century or so? I mean, true, critical/oppositional intellectuals were always few and far between in the modern Western era, but there were always giants in our midst whose voice and status were not only revered by a fair chunk of the citizenry, but, in some cases, produced fear and even awe among the members of the ruling class. Today, we have mainly functional/conformist "intellectuals" who focus on narrow, highly specialized, and technical areas, and do not dare to challenge the status quo or speak out against social evils out of fear of losing their job, being denied tenure and promotion, or not having access to grants. Indeed, whatever happened to public intellectuals like Bertrand Russell and Jean-Paul Sartre, and to iconic artists like Picasso with his fight against fascism?*

Noam Chomsky: Well, what did happen to Bertrand Russell?

Russell was jailed during World War I, along with the handful of others who dared to oppose that glorious enterprise: Rosa Luxemburg and Karl Liebknecht, Eugene Debs—who was even excluded from postwar amnesty by the vengeful Woodrow Wilson—to mention only the most famous. Some were treated more kindly, like Randolph Bourne, merely ostracized and barred from liberal intellectual circles and journals. Russell's later career had many ugly episodes, including his being declared by the courts to be too freethinking to be allowed to teach at City College, a flood of vilification from high places because of his opposition to the Vietnam War, scurrilous treatment even after his death.

Not all that unusual for those who break ranks, no matter how distinguished their contributions, as Russell's surely were.

The term "intellectual" itself is a strange one. It is not applied to a Nobel laureate who devotes his life to physics, or to the janitor in his building who may have little formal education but deep insight and perceptive understanding of human affairs, history, culture. The term is used, usually, to refer to a category of people with a degree of privilege who are somehow regarded to be the guardians of society's intellectual and moral values. They are supposed to uphold and articulate those values and call upon others to adhere to them.

Within this category there is a small minority who challenge power, authority, and received doctrine. It is sometimes held that their responsibility is "to speak truth to power." I've always found that troubling. The powerful typically know the truth quite well. They generally know what they are doing, and don't need our instructions. They also will not benefit from moral lessons, not because they are necessarily bad people, but because they play a certain institutional role, and if they abandon that role, somebody else will fill it as long as the institutions persist. There is no point instructing CEOs of the fossil fuel industry that their activities are damaging communities and destroying the environment and our climate. They've known that for a long time. They also know that if they depart from dedication to profit and concern themselves with the human impact of what they are doing, they'll be out on the streets and someone will replace them to carry out the institutionally required tasks.

There remains a range of options, but it is narrow.

It would make a lot more sense to speak truth not to power, but to its victims. If you speak truth to the powerless, it's possible that it could benefit somebody. It might help people confront the problems in their lives more realistically. It might even help them to act and organize in such ways as to compel the powerful to modify institutions and practices; and, even more significantly, to challenge illegitimate structures of authority and the institutions on which they are realized and thereby expand the scope of freedom and justice. It won't happen in any other way, and it's often happened in that way in the past.

But I don't think that's right either. The task of a responsible person—anyone who wants to uphold intellectual and moral values—is not to speak what they regard as truth *to* anybody—the powerful or the powerless—but rather to speak *with* the powerless and to try to learn the truth. That's always a collective endeavor and wisdom and understanding need not come from any particular turf.

But that's quite rare in the history of intellectuals.

Let's recall that the term "intellectual" came into use in its modern sense with the Dreyfus trial in France in the late nineteenth century. Today we admire and respect those who stood up for justice in their defense of Dreyfus, but if you look back at that time, they were a persecuted minority. The "immortals" of the French Academy bitterly condemned these preposterous writers and artists for daring to challenge the august leaders and institutions of the French State. The prominent figure of the Dreyfusards, Émile Zola, had to flee from France.

That's pretty typical. Take almost any society you like, and you will find that there is a fringe of critical dissidents and that they are usually subjected to one or another form of punishment. Those I mentioned are no exception. In recent history, in Russian-run Eastern Europe, they could be jailed; if it was in our own domains, in Central or South America, they could be tortured and murdered. In both cases, there was harsh repression of people who are critical of established power.

That goes back as far as you like, all the way back to classical Greece. Who was the person who drank the hemlock? It was the person who was "corrupting" the youth of Athens by asking searching questions that are better hidden away. Take a look at the biblical record, roughly about the same period. It's kind of oral history, but in what's reconstructed from it, there were people who by our standards might be called intellectuals—people who condemned the king and his crimes, called for mercy for widows and orphans, other subversive acts. How were they treated? They were imprisoned, driven into the desert, reviled. There were intellectuals who were respected, flatterers at the court. Centuries later, they were called false prophets, but not at the time. And if you think through history, that pattern is replicated quite consistently.

The basic operative principle was captured incisively by McGeorge Bundy, a leading liberal intellectual, noted scholar, former Harvard dean, national security adviser under presidents Kennedy and Johnson, then director of the Ford Foundation. In 1968, when protest against the Vietnam War was peaking, Bundy published an article in the main establishment journal *Foreign Affairs* in which he discussed protest against the war. Much of the protest was legitimate, he conceded: there had in retrospect been some mistakes in managing such a complex effort. But then there was a fringe of "wild men in the wings" who merit only contempt. The wild men actually descended so far as to look into motives. That is, they treated the US political leadership by the standards applied to others, and hence must be excluded from polite company.

Bundy's analysis was in fact the norm among liberal intellectuals. Their publications soberly distinguished the "technocratic and policy-oriented intellectuals" from the "value-oriented intellectuals." The former are the good guys, who orchestrate and inform policy, and are duly honored for their constructive work—the Henry Kissingers, the kind who loyally transmit orders from their half-drunk boss for a massive bombing campaign in Cambodia, "anything that flies against anything that moves." A call for genocide that's not easy to duplicate in the archival record. The latter are the wild men in the wings who prate about moral value, justice, international law, and other sentimentalities.

The US isn't El Salvador. The wild men don't have their brains blown out by elite battalions armed and trained in Washington, like the six leading Latin American intellectuals, Jesuit priests, who suffered this fate along with their housekeeper and her daughter on the eve of the fall of the Berlin Wall. Who even knows their names? Properly, one might argue, since there were many other religious martyrs among the hundreds of thousands slaughtered in Washington's crusade in Central America in the 1980s, managed with the assistance of technocratic and policy-oriented intellectuals.

It is, regrettably, all too easy to continue.

I believe it would be of great interest if you talked about the historical context of "The Responsibility of Intellectuals," but also if you elaborate on what you mean when you say intellectuals must see events from their historical perspective.

The essay was based on a talk given in 1966 to a student group at Harvard. It was published in the group's journal. They've probably expunged it since. It was the Harvard Hillel Society. The journal is *Mosaic*. This was a year before Israel's military victory in 1967, a great gift to the US, which led to a sharp reorientation in US-Israeli policies and major shifts in popular culture and attitudes in the US—an interesting and important story, but not for here.

The *New York Review of Books* published an edited version.

Since the talk was at Harvard, it was particularly important to focus on intellectual elites and their special links to government. The Harvard faculty was quite prominent in the Kennedy and Johnson administrations. Camelot mythology is in considerable part their creation. But as we've been discussing, it's just one phase in a long history of intellectual service to power. It's still unfolding without fundamental change, though the activism of the '60s and its aftermath has substantially changed much of the country, widening the wings in which "wild men" can pursue their value-oriented subversion.

This impact has also greatly broadened the historical perspective from which events of the world are perceived. No one today would write a major diplomatic history of the US recounting how after the British yoke was overthrown, the former colonists, in the words of

Thomas Bailey, "concentrated on the task of felling trees and Indians and of rounding out their natural boundaries"—in "self-defense," of course. Few in the '60s fully grasped the fact that our "forever wars" began in 1783. The horrendous four-hundred-year record of torture of African Americans was also scarcely acknowledged by mainstream academics; more, and worse, is constantly being unearthed. The same is true in other areas. Dedicated and conscientious activism can open many windows for valuable historical perspective to be gained.

The world has changed a great deal since the era of the Vietnam War, and I think you would agree with me that we are facing greater challenges today than ever before. Moreover, we live in a much smaller world, and some of the challenges facing us are truly global in nature and scope. In that context, what should be the role of intellectuals and of social movements in a globalized world and with a shared future for humanity?

You're quite right that we face far greater challenges today than during the Vietnam era. In 1968, when liberal intellectuals were excoriating the value-oriented "wild men," the leading issue was that "Viet-Nam as a cultural and historic entity [was] threatened with extinction [as] the countryside literally dies under the blows of the largest military machine ever unleashed on an area of this size," the judgment of the most respected Vietnam specialist, military historian Bernard Fall.

It is now organized human society worldwide that is "threatened with extinction" under the blows of environmental destruction, overwhelmingly by the rich, concentrated in the rich countries. That's apart from the no less ominous and growing threat of nuclear holocaust, being stoked as we speak.

We are living in an era of confluence of crises that has no counterpart in human history. For each of these, feasible solutions are known, though time is short. There is no need to waste words on responsibility.

Who is undertaking the historic task of addressing these crises? Who carried out the Global Climate Strike on September 24, a desperate attempt to wake up the dithering leaders of global society, and citizens who have been lulled into passivity by elite treachery?

We know the answer: the young, the inheritors of our folly. It should be deeply painful to witness the scene at Davos, the annual gathering where the rich and powerful posture in their self-righteousness, and applaud politely when Greta Thunberg instructs them quietly and expertly on the catastrophe they have been blithely creating.

Nice little girl. Now go back to school where you belong and leave the serious problems to us, the enlightened political leaders, the soulful corporations working day and night for the common good, the responsible intellectuals. We'll take care of it, ensuring that the betrayal will be apocalyptic—as it will be, if we grant them the power to run the world in accord with the principles they have established and implemented.

The principles are not obscure. Right now, governments of the world, the US foremost among them, are pressuring oil producers to increase production—having just been advised in the August IPCC report, by far the direst yet, that catastrophe is looming unless we begin right now to reduce fossil fuel use year by year, effectively phasing them out by mid-century. Petroleum industry journals are euphoric about the discovery of new fields to exploit as demand for oil increases. The business press debates whether the US fracking industry or OPEC is best placed to increase production.

Congress is debating a bill that might have slightly slowed the race to destruction. The denialist party is 100 percent opposed, so the fate of legislation is in the hands of the "moderate" Democrats, particularly Joe Manchin. He has made his position on climate explicit: "Spending on innovation, not elimination." Straight out of the playbook of PR departments of the fossil fuel companies, no surprise from Congress's leading recipient of fossil fuel compensation. Fossil fuel use must continue unimpeded, driving us to catastrophe in the interests of short-term profit for the very rich. Period.

On the rest of the Biden package, Manchin—the swing vote— has made it clear that he will accept only a trickle, also insisting on cumbersome and degrading means testing for what is standard practice in the civilized world. The posture is certainly not for the benefit of his constituents. As for other "moderates," it is much the same. Without far more intense public pressure, there was never much hope that this Congress would allow the country to begin to beat back the cruel assault of overwhelming business power.

There is no need to tarry on what this entails about responsibility.

And again, we dare not neglect the cloud that was cast over the world by human intelligence seventy-five years ago and has been darkening in recent years. The arms-control regime that had been laboriously constructed over many decades has been systematically dismantled by the last two Republican administrations, first Bush II and the Anti-Ballistic Missile Treaty, then Trump wielding his wrecking ball with abandon. He left office barely in time for Biden to salvage the New START Treaty, accepting Russia's pleas to extend it. Biden continues, however, to support the bloated military budget, to pursue the race to develop more dangerous weapons, and to carry out highly provocative acts where diplomacy and negotiations are surely possible.

A major point of contention right now is "freedom of navigation" in the South China Sea. More accurately, as Australian strategic analyst Clinton Fernandes points out, the conflict concerns military/ intelligence operations in China's Exclusive Economic Zone (EEZ) extending two hundred miles offshore. The US holds that such operations are permissible in all EEZs. China holds that they are not. India agrees with China's interpretation, and vigorously protested recent US military operations in its EEZ.

EEZs were established by the 1982 Law of the Sea (UNCLOS). The US is the only maritime power not to have ratified the law, but asserts that it will not violate it. The relevant wording about military operations in the law is not entirely precise. Surely this is a clear case where diplomacy is in order, not highly provocative actions in a region of considerable tension, with the threat of escalation, possibly without bounds.

All of this is part of the US effort to "contain China." Or, to put it differently, to establish "the fact that somehow, the rise of 20 per cent of humanity from abject poverty into something approaching a modern state, is illegitimate—but more than that, by its mere presence, an affront to the United States. It is not that China presents a threat to the United States—something China has never articulated or delivered—rather, its mere presence represents a challenge to United States pre-eminence."

This is the quite realistic assessment of former Australian prime minister Paul Keating, reacting to the recent AUKUS (Australia-UK-US) agreement to sell eight advanced nuclear submarines to Australia, to be incorporated in the US naval command in order to respond to the "threat of China."

The agreement abrogates a France-Australia agreement for sale of conventional subs. With typical imperial arrogance, Washington did not even notify France, instructing the European Union on its place in the US-run global order. In reaction, France recalled its ambassadors to the US and Australia, ignoring the UK, a mere vassal state.

Australian military correspondent Brian Toohey observes that Australia's submission to the US does not enhance its security—quite the contrary—and that AUKUS has no discernable strategic purpose. The subs will not be operational for over a decade, by which time China will surely have expanded its military forces to deal with this new military threat, just as it has done to deal with the fact that it is ringed by nuclear-armed missiles in some of the eight hundred military bases that the US has around the world (China has one, Djibouti).

Toohey outlines the naval military balance that is disrupted further by AUKUS. It's worth quoting directly to help understand how China threatens the US—not in the Caribbean or the California coast, but on China's borders:

> China's nuclear weapons are so inferior that it couldn't be confident of deterring a retaliatory strike from the US. Take the example of nuclear-powered, ballistic missile-armed submarines (SSBNs). China has four Jin-class SSBNs. Each can carry 12 missiles, each with a single warhead. The subs are easy to detect because they're noisy. According to the US Office of Naval Intelligence, each is noisier than a Soviet submarine first launched in 1976. Russian and US subs are now much quieter. China is expected to acquire another four SSBNs that are a little quieter by 2030. However, the missiles on the subs won't

have the range to reach the continental US from near their base on Hainan island in the South China Sea. To target the continental US, they would have to reach suitable locations in the Pacific Ocean. However, they are effectively bottled up inside the South China Sea. To escape, they have to pass through a series of chokepoints where they would be easily sunk by US hunter killer nuclear submarines of the type the [Australian] Morrison government wants to buy. In contrast, the US has 14 Ohio-class SSBNs. Each can launch 24 Trident missiles, each containing eight independently targetable warheads able to reach anywhere on the globe. This means a single US submarine can destroy 192 cities, or other targets, compared to 12 for the Chinese submarine. The Ohio class is now being replaced by the bigger Columbia class. These [are being] constructed at the same time as new US hunter killer submarines.

That's before eight new advanced nuclear subs are built for Australia. In nuclear forces generally and other relevant military capacity, China is of course far behind the US, as are all potential US adversaries combined.

AUKUS does serve a purpose, however: to establish more firmly that the US intends to rule the world, even if that requires escalating the threat of war, possibly terminal nuclear war, in a highly volatile region. And eschewing such "sissified" measures as diplomacy.

It is not the only example. One of these should have been on the front pages in the past few weeks as the US withdrew from Afghanistan, executing Trump's cynical sellout of Afghans in his February 2020 deal with the Taliban.

The obvious question is: Why did the Bush administration invade twenty years ago? The US had no interest in Afghanistan, as Bush's pronouncements at the time made explicit; the real prize was Iraq, then beyond. Bush also made it clear that the administration also had little interest in Osama bin Laden or al-Qaeda. That lack of concern was made fully explicit by Defense Secretary Donald Rumsfeld when the Taliban offered surrender. "We do not negotiate surrenders," Rumsfeld stormed.

The only plausible explanation for the invasion was given by the most highly respected leader of the anti-Taliban resistance, Abdul Haq. He was interviewed shortly after the invasion by Asia scholar Anatol Lieven.

Haq said that the invasion will kill many Afghans and undermine promising Afghan efforts to undermine the Taliban regime from within, but that's not Washington's concern: "The US is trying to show its muscle, score a victory and scare everyone in the world. They don't care about the suffering of the Afghans or how many people we will lose."

That also seems a fair description of current US strategy in "containing the China threat" by provocative escalation in place of diplomacy. It's no innovation in imperial history.

Returning to the responsibility of intellectuals and how it is being fulfilled, no elaboration should be necessary.

NOAM CHOMSKY, ROBERT POLLIN, AND COSTAS LAPAVITSAS

ARE WE WITNESSING THE DEMISE OF NEOLIBERALISM?

October 13, 2021

C. J. Polychroniou: *Noam, the neoliberal era of the last forty years has been defined to a large extent by growing inequalities, slow growth, and environmental degradation. Indeed, even the International Monetary Fund admitted some years ago that neoliberalism had failed. Yet, it took the outbreak of a pandemic for a consensus to emerge regarding the failures of neoliberalism. Why did neoliberalism triumph and endure in the first place, and is it actually dead?*

Noam Chomsky: My feeling is that a version of neoliberalism has triumphed because it has been highly successful—for the designers, whose power has been considerably enhanced by such predictable consequences as radical inequality, restricting democracy, destruction of unions, and atomization of the population so that there is limited defense against the version of neoliberalism that has been pursued with impressive dedication in this latest phase of class war. I say a "version" because the state-corporate managers of the system insist upon a very powerful state that can protect their interests internationally and provide them with massive bailouts and subsidies when their programs collapse, as they do regularly.

For similar reasons, I don't think that this version is dead, though it is being readjusted in response to growing popular anger and resentment, much fueled by the successes of the neoliberal assault on the population.

Bob, the pandemic has shown us that neoliberal capitalism is more than inadequate in addressing large-scale economic and public health crises. Are the resources mobilized by national states during the pandemic crisis a simple case of emergency Keynesianism, or do they represent a fundamental shift in the traditional role of government, which is to maximize society's welfare? Moreover, are the policies we have seen implemented so far at all levels of government sufficient to provide the basis for a progressive economic agenda in the post-pandemic era?

Robert Pollin: Neoliberalism is a variant of capitalism in which economic policies are weighted heavily in favor of supporting the privileges of big corporations, Wall Street, and the rich. Neoliberalism became dominant globally around 1980, beginning with the elections of Margaret Thatcher in the United Kingdom and Ronald Reagan in the US. The top priorities under neoliberalism, as practiced throughout the world, have included: cutting both taxes on the rich along with public spending on the non-rich; weakening protections for both working people and the environment and any semblance of a commitment to full and decent employment; and enabling financial speculation to run rampant while bailing out the speculators when the markets proceed, inevitably, into crises.

Neoliberalism represented a counterrevolution against social-democratic / New Deal / developmental state variants of capitalism, which emerged primarily as a result of successful political struggles by progressive political parties, labor unions, and allied social movements, out of the 1930s Depression and continuing through the early 1970s. Of course, social-democratic / New Deal / developmental state capitalism was still capitalism. Disparities of income, wealth, and opportunity remained intolerably high, along with the malignancies of racism, sexism, and imperialism. Nevertheless, the broadly social-democratic models produced dramatically more egalitarian versions of capitalism than the neoliberal regime that supplanted these models. The neoliberal model, in turn, has been highly successful in achieving its most basic aim, which is to shower ever-greater advantages on the already overprivileged. For example, under neoliberalism in the United States between 1978 and 2019, the average pay for big corporate CEOs has risen tenfold relative to the average nonsupervisory worker.

With the onset of the COVID pandemic in March 2020, government policies in the high-income countries did pursue measures to prevent a total, 1930s-level economic collapse. Depending on the country, these measures included direct cash support for lower- and middle-income people, significant increases in unemployment insurance, and large payroll subsidy programs to prevent layoffs. But by far, the most aggressive policy interventions were the bailouts provided for big corporations and Wall Street.

In the US, for example, nearly 50 percent of the entire labor force filed for unemployment benefits between March 2020 and February 2021. However, over this same period, Wall Street stock prices rose by 46 percent, one of the sharpest one-year increases on record. The same pattern prevailed globally. The International Labour Organization reported that "there were unprecedented global employment losses in 2020 of 114 million jobs relative to 2019." At the same time, global stock markets rose sharply—by 45 percent throughout Europe, 56 percent in China, 58 percent in the UK, and 80 percent in Japan, and with Standard & Poor's Global 1200 index rising by 67 percent.

So while there was a desperately needed expansion of social welfare programs helping people to survive under COVID, these measures were enacted within the framework of still larger efforts to prop up the still prevailing neoliberal order.

Of course, the severity of the climate crisis has continued to deepen during the pandemic. In February, UN secretary-general António Guterres said, "2021 is a make-or-break year to confront the global climate emergency. . . . Governments are nowhere close to the level of ambition needed to limit climate change to 1.5 degrees and meet the goals of the Paris Agreement. The major emitters must step up with much more ambitious emissions reductions targets for 2030 . . . well before the November UN Climate Conference in Glasgow."

We are now into October in the "make-or-break year," and yet, little has been accomplished since Guterres spoke in February. It is true that, throughout the high-income countries, social movements and climate activists are fighting to advance programs that combine climate stabilization and an egalitarian social agenda, under the rubric of a global Green New Deal. The extent to which they succeed will determine whether we will have established a basis for a progressive economic agenda and effective climate policies in the post-pandemic era. We do not yet know how successful these efforts will be. As we discussed at some length recently, the social infrastructure and climate proposal being debated right now in the US Congress is itself not ambitious enough to be truly transformative. But if it is enacted, it will still represent a significant break from neoliberal dominance that has prevailed since Thatcher and Reagan.

Costas, the COVID pandemic has exposed numerous structural flaws of capitalism, and the neoliberal order may be indeed on the verge of collapse. Still, can we speak of a "crisis of capitalism" given that we do not see large-scale opposition to the current system?

Costas Lapavitsas: There is no question that the pandemic shock represents a tremendous crisis of global capitalism, but I would urge strong caution regarding the collapse of neoliberalism. The period since the Great Crisis of 2007–2009 looks more like an interregnum (a term offered in the spirit of Antonio Gramsci) when the old is refusing to die and the new cannot be born. And like all such periods, it is prone to monsters, including fascism.

The Great Crisis of 2007–2009 was overcome by the state deploying its massive strength to defend financialized capitalism and globalization. But what followed was a decade of low growth, poor investment, weak productivity growth, sustained inequality, and partially revived profits. Economic performance was poor in core countries, providing further evidence of the failure of neoliberalism.

The Golden Era of financialization is well and truly over, despite the sustained rise of stock markets in the previous decade. Yet, economic performance was also mediocre in China, reflecting an underlying weakness of productive accumulation across the world.

When COVID-19 struck, it became crystal clear that contemporary capitalism is entirely dependent on massive state intervention. Core Western states were able to intervene on an unprecedented scale mostly because of monopoly command by central banks over fiat money. Unlike 2007–2009, however, the state also deployed fiat money to relax austerity, thus engaging in the unspoken nationalization of the wage bill and the income statements of thousands of enterprises.

It is a misunderstanding that neoliberalism necessarily means marginalizing the state and imposing austerity. Rather, it is about using the state selectively to defend the interests of a small elite, an oligarchy, associated with big business and the financial sector. Fundamentally, it stands for shifting the balance of power in favor of capital by removing controls on its activities. When the pandemic shock threatened the foundations of class rule, austerity and forbearing from direct economic intervention were abandoned in the blink of an eye. The neoliberal ideologists rapidly adapted to the new reality, though it is always possible that austerity will return. What has not taken place is an institutional shift in favor of workers' interests that would limit the freedom of capital. It is primarily in this sense that the old is refusing to die.

The pandemic also made it clear that there is great variety in the relationship between powerful states and domestic capitalist accumulation. Core Western states, in the grip of neoliberal ideology, derive their strength primarily from command over fiat money. In contrast, the Chinese state remains directly involved in both productive accumulation and finance as well as having possession over vast resources. Their respective responses to the pandemic differed greatly.

Inevitably there has been a tremendous escalation in the contest for global hegemony, including in the military field. For the first time since 1914, moreover, the hegemonic contest is also immediately economic. The Soviet Union was exclusively a political and military contestant to the US—the Lada could never compete with Chrysler.

But China can outcompete the US economically, making the struggle considerably deeper and removing any obvious point of equilibrium. The US ruling bloc realizes that it has made a strategic miscalculation, and this accounts for its current unrelenting aggressiveness. Conditions in the international arena are exceedingly dangerous.

Still, the global hegemonic struggle lacks entirely in ideological content. Western neoliberal democracies are exhausted, failed, and bereft of new ideas. The attempts of the US ruling bloc to present its aggressiveness as a defense of democracy are hollow and ludicrous. On the other hand, Chinese (and Russian) authoritarianism has considerable domestic support but no capacity to offer a globally appealing social and political perspective.

The characteristic feature of the interregnum since 2007–2009 is an ideological impasse. There is tremendous discontent with capitalism, particularly as the degradation of the environment and the warming of the planet have raised great concern among the young. But that concern has not translated into a broad-based mobilization behind fresh socialist ideas and politics. This is the challenge ahead, particularly as the far right is already taking advantage.

Postcapitalism (defined broadly as a social system in which the power of markets is restricted, productive activity is premised on automation, work is delinked from wages, and the state provides universal basic services and a basic income) is possible because of changes in information technology, according to some pundits. Should the left spend political capital by envisioning a postcapitalist future?

Lapavitsas: During the pandemic crisis, the domestic actions of nation-states displaced the precepts and prescriptions of neoliberal capitalism, foisted invasive measures on social and personal life centering on public health and hygiene, and imposed severe restrictions on civil liberties and economic activity. The state inflamed political tensions, heightened social polarization, and restricted freedoms.

Workers paid the greatest price through income loss, rising unemployment, and worsening public provision. But the middle strata were also left out in the cold, thus delivering a major blow to the class alliances that supported the neoliberal project. Giant oligopolies in new technology emerged as the main beneficiaries—Google, Amazon, Microsoft, and the rest. Their actions are steadily eclipsing the figure of the citizen as personal identities are increasingly organized around market links to the oligopolies. At the same time, the extreme right was strengthened, a trend that started before the pandemic and has accelerated through the agency of powerful oligarchies.

There has been no shortage of grassroots reactions to these developments. Heavy-handed state actions, official cultivation of fear, suspension of rights and liberties, the danger of permanent repression, and the crushing of workers and the middle strata during the lockdowns spurred various responses often in a libertarian direction.

Bear in mind that maintaining capitalist accumulation in the years to come will be exceedingly difficult across the world. The underlying weakness of accumulation is far from easy to confront. It is also clear that state intervention in the pandemic has created major difficulties with the disruption of supply chains, the rise of inflation eating into workers' incomes, and the tremendous escalation of public debt. And all that is without even mentioning the broader issues of environment and climate.

It is hardly possible that economic growth could be sustained without large-scale state intervention on the supply side through public investment that also involves profound distributional changes in income that benefit workers. It seems even less likely that this would happen without a major shift in property rights, redistributing wealth and productive resources in favor of workers and the poor.

Technology alone is never the answer for complex social problems. Indeed, one aspect of the technological revolution of the last four decades is its inability even to improve the economic conditions of accumulation since its effect on the average productivity of labor is modest. I see no reason at this stage to expect that artificial intelligence would prove dramatically different. Perhaps it will, but there are no guarantees.

Western neoliberal democracies are ideologically exhausted, and their capitalist economies are beset with problems. In this context, it is imperative for socialists and progressives to think of a postcapitalist future and ascertain its broad parameters. We need to think about the use of digital technologies, the greening of production, and the protection of the environment. But all that should take place in social conditions that favor working people and not capitalists, with a new sociality, collective action, and individual fulfillment through communal association. The rejuvenation of the socialist promise is the paramount need of the times.

Bob, during the neoliberal era, mainstream economics shaded easily into ideology. Indeed, it is rather easy to show that mainstream economic policy is full of misrepresentation of reality. The question is: How does an alleged science become ideology? And how likely is it that the coronavirus pandemic, in conjunction with the flaws of neoliberalism and the urgency of the climate crisis, will lead to an intellectual paradigm shift in "dismal science"?

Pollin: Let's recognize that all varieties of economists are heavily influenced by ideology, or what the great conservative economist Joseph Schumpeter more judiciously termed their "pre-analytic vision." Leftist economists, myself included, are as guilty as anyone else. Our ideology influences the questions that we decide are most important to ask. Ideology also provides us with some initial guesses as to what the answers to these questions are likely to be. Still, if we are also attempting to be the least bit scientific, or even minimally honest, as economic researchers, we will put our hunches and our preferred answers to the test of evidence and be open to challenges.

I think it is fair to say that, not all, but a high percentage of mainstream economists have not been committed to these minimally objective scientific standards. They rather have been so fully immersed in their ideological biases that they are unable to even think about how they might ask questions differently. Their biases have been reinforced by the fact that these prejudices provide succor to policy regimes that, as noted above, shower benefits on the already overprivileged.

Joan Robinson, the renowned Cambridge University economist of the Great Depression and post–World War II era, beautifully captured this allure of orthodox economics as follows: "One of the main effects (I will not say purposes) of orthodox traditional economics was . . . a plan for explaining to the privileged class that their position was morally right and was necessary for the welfare of society."

At the same time, there has been no shortage of progressive economists over the neoliberal era who have stood up to mainstream orthodoxy, as represented, for example, by the twenty-four people you interviewed in the new book, *Economics and the Left: Interviews with Progressive Economists*. In my view, how much influence economists such as these will have will depend primarily on how successful are the progressive movements in advancing the Green New Deal and related programs in the coming months and years.

There are hopeful signs. Just late last month, the Federal Reserve released a paper by Jeremy Rudd, a senior member of its own staff, which begins with the observation that "mainstream economics is replete with ideas that 'everyone knows' to be true, but that are actually arrant nonsense."

Rudd also notes on page 1 that he is leaving aside in this paper "the deeper concern that the primary role of mainstream economics in our society is to provide apologetics for a criminally oppressive, unsustainable, and unjust social order." There may well be more Jeremy Rudds out there, poised to spring from the shadows of the professional mainstream. This would be a most positive development. But I would also say that it's about time.

Noam, it's been said by far too many that it is easier to imagine the end of the world than the end of capitalism. Given that capitalism is actually destroying the earth, how, first would you respond to the above statement, and, secondly, how do you envision economy and society after capitalism?

Chomsky: I'd prefer to rephrase the question to refer to state capitalism. Those whom Adam Smith called "the masters of mankind," the dominant business classes, would never tolerate capitalism, which would expose them to the ravages of the market. That's for the victims. For the masters, a powerful state is required—insofar as they can control it and reduce the "underlying population" (Thorstein Veblen's ironic term) to subordination and passivity.

It does not seem to me too difficult to imagine at least a serious mitigation of the destructive and repressive elements of this system, and its eventual transformation to a far more fair and just society. In fact, we must not only imagine but proceed to implement such programs, or we'll all be finished—the masters, too.

It's even quite realistic to imagine—and implement—the overthrow of the basic state capitalist principle: renting oneself to a master (in a more anodyne formulation, having a job). After all, for millennia it's been recognized—in principle at least—that being subjected to the will of a master is an intolerable attack on human dignity and rights. The concept is not far back in our own history. In late nineteenth-century America, radical farmers and industrial workers were seeking to create a "cooperative commonwealth" in which they would be free of domination by illegitimate bosses robbing their labor and of northeast bankers and market managers. These powerful movements were so effectively crushed by state-corporate force that today even the highly popular ideas sound exotic. But they are not far below the surface and are even being revived in many important ways.

In short, there's reason to be hopeful that what must be done can be done.

NOAM CHOMSKY AND ROBERT POLLIN

COP26 PLEDGES WILL FAIL UNLESS PUSHED BY MASS ORGANIZING

October 28, 2021

C. J. Polychroniou: *Noam, COP26 is believed to be our "last best hope" for meaningful action to tackle the climate crisis. Why is COP26 so important? And wasn't pretty much the same thing said about COP21?*

Noam Chomsky: It was indeed, and correctly. The concept of "last best hope" keeps narrowing. What's the last best hope at one point is gone later, and the remaining last best hope becomes far more difficult to realize.

That's been true since the 1997 Kyoto Protocol, ratified by 192 nations, but not the US. The Senate would not accept it. George W. Bush pulled out completely; later Canada did as well. Kyoto was the last best hope in 1997. If the US had joined, the task of escaping devastating climate change would have been far easier.

By 2015 (the Paris Agreement, COP21), the "best hope" was much more remote and difficult to realize. Again, the US Senate blocked it. More precisely, the plan was for a verifiable treaty, but Republicans would not accept that, so it was reduced to toothless voluntary agreements. And shortly after, Trump pulled out completely. Biden has formally rejoined, but what that means remains to be seen.

121

Right now, the Republican commitment to destroying the planet in the interest of short-term profit for their prime constituency of extreme wealth seems unassailable. But it was not always so. As we've discussed before, in 2008, there were signs of a deviation toward minimal concern for the fate of humanity, but it didn't last long. A juggernaut by the huge Koch brothers energy conglomerate quickly returned the party to obedience, since unchanged.

In defense of the stand of what was once a genuine political party, we should take note of the fact that the US very rarely accepts international conventions, and when it does so, it is with reservations that render them inapplicable to the US. That's even true of the Genocide Convention.

One may plausibly argue, however, that these fine distinctions are all irrelevant. Even when the US fully accepts international treaties, it violates them at will, hence also violating the US Constitution, which declares them to be the supreme law of the land, binding on the political leadership. The clearest case is the UN Charter, the basis for modern international law. It bans "the threat or use of force" in international affairs, with reservations irrelevant to the constant violation of the treaty (and the Constitution) by US presidents.

So normal that it virtually never elicits a comment.

Discourse on international affairs has found a way around these inconvenient facts by devising the concept of a "rule-based international order," as contrasted with the old-fashioned "UN-based international order." The former is preferred, since the US can set the rules and determine how and when they can be enforced—an interesting topic, but not for now.

A treaty on climate change, if it can be reached, is in a different category. Survival is at stake. The basic facts are brutally clear, more so with each passing year. They are laid out clearly enough in the latest Intergovernmental Panel on Climate Change (IPCC) report, released on August 9. In brief, any hope of avoiding disaster requires taking significant steps right away to reduce fossil fuel use, continuing annually with the goal of effectively phasing out fossil fuel use by mid-century. We are approaching a precipice. A few steps more, and we fall over it, forever.

Falling off the precipice does not imply that everyone will die soon; there's a long way down. Rather, it means that irreversible tipping points will be reached, and barring some now-unforeseen technological miracle, the human species will be entering a new era: one of inexorable decline, with mounting horrors of the kind we can easily depict, extrapolating realistically from what already surrounds us—an optimistic estimate, since nonlinear processes may begin to take off and dangers lurk that are only dimly perceived.

It will be an era of *"sauve qui peut"*—run for your lives, everyone for themselves, material catastrophe heightened by social collapse and wholesale psychic trauma of a kind never before experienced. And on the side, an assault on nature of indescribable proportions.

All of this is understood at a very high level of confidence. Even a relic of rationality tells us that it is ridiculous to take a chance on its being mistaken, considering the stakes.

We might tarry for a moment on the date of the release of the IPCC report: August 9. Whether by accident or design, the choice is a momentous date in human affairs: the anniversary of the atomic bombing of Nagasaki. Putting aside the horrors and the dubious efforts at justification, the Hiroshima bombing a few days earlier demonstrated that human intelligence would soon reach the level of being able to destroy everything. Nagasaki demonstrated that the commitment to attain this goal was deeply entrenched in the reigning sociopolitical system and intellectual culture. What remained open was whether human moral capacities, and the institutions humans had created, had the capacity to overcome what human intellect was on the verge of achieving: total cataclysm. After seventy-five frightening years, the question still remains open even as prospects shrink for a hopeful answer.

The crisis of environmental destruction—which extends well beyond the crime of global heating—raises quite similar questions.

The evidence at hand is not encouraging. Let's go back to August 9, 2021, with its clear warning that we must begin now to reduce fossil fuel use.

Immediately on receipt of this grim warning, the president of the most powerful state in world history issued an appeal to the global oil cartel OPEC to increase production. Europe followed suit, joined by the rest of what is called "advanced society." The reason is an energy crunch. That's doubtless a problem. One way to deal with it is to race toward the precipice. Another is for the rich in the rich societies, the major culprits, to tighten their belts while we sharply accelerate transition to sustainable energy.

The choice is unfolding before our eyes.

Petroleum industry journals are euphoric, announcing promising new discoveries that they can exploit to enhance production and reveling in the prospects for growing demand for their poisons. A few examples fill in details.

Germany is reacting to the August warning by joining in the call for increasing fossil fuel use and making its own contribution, for example, by destroying villages to expand coal mining.

Turning to the US, a mere 60 percent of voters regard global warming as an urgent problem for government. It is only the most urgent problem that humans have ever faced.

The party breakdown is the usual one: Among Republicans, 45 percent of "liberal/moderate Republicans" see global warming as an urgent problem, along with 17 percent of "conservative Republicans." The persisting lethal denialism is not a great surprise in the light of pronouncements of the leadership and the media to which they are exposed.

Thanks to significant popular activism, Biden's major program, now being torn to shreds in Congress, did include some useful steps on climate change. Nothing seems likely to survive. Republicans are 100 percent opposed. Democrats need unanimity to pass anything. The Senate chair of the Committee on Energy and Natural Resources is a right-wing Democrat, also a coal baron and the leading recipient of fossil fuel funding in Congress: Joe Manchin. His position on climate concerns is simple: "spending on innovation, not elimination." Straight out of the fossil fuel industry playbook.

In South America, destruction of the Amazon is proceeding apace for the benefit of the domestic and international corporate sector, which has been hailing the policies of Chicago School economics minister Paulo Guedes: "privatize everything," and who cares about the consequences. Recent scientific studies have found that "the south-eastern Amazon was releasing more carbon [than] it was absorbing, even in rainy years when scientists had expected the forest to be in better health. It meant a part of the rainforest was no longer helping to slow climate change, but adding to the emissions driving it."

That is a disaster for Brazil and indeed for the world, given the role of the huge tropical forests in regulating the global climate.

A leaked report of governmental efforts to weaken the IPCC study shows that the usual scoundrels are at work.

Saudi Arabia calls for eliminating such phrases as "the need for urgent and accelerated mitigation actions at all scales" and "the focus of decarbonisation efforts in the energy systems sector needs to be on rapidly shifting to zero-carbon sources and actively phasing out fossil fuels." It is joined by OPEC, along with fossil fuel producers Argentina and Norway.

Saudi officials elaborated further. Giving no details, one Saudi prince explained that a transition to net-zero carbon emissions is welcome, but it must be reached through a "carbon circular economy"—a plan built around initiatives such as recycling and carbon removal.

Just innovation, no elimination.

Saudi officials and the chief executive of Saudi oil giant Aramco, the press reports, "expect demand for oil to continue and for it to be the dominant energy source for decades to come, and argue that reducing supply before demand drops risks a dangerous oil price spike, hurting economies such as Saudi Arabia's that are dependent on oil and gas."

Turning elsewhere, "A senior Australian government official rejects the conclusion that closing coal-fired power plants is necessary"—a stand that is perhaps related to Australia's position as the world's leading coal exporter.

Continuing with the submissions to the IPCC, "Brazil and Argentina, two of the biggest producers of beef products and animal feed crops in the world, argue strongly against evidence in the draft report that reducing meat consumption is necessary to cut greenhouse gas emissions. Both countries call on the authors to delete or change some passages in the text referring to 'plant-based diets' playing a role in tackling climate change, or which describe beef as a 'high carbon' food."

Again, not surprisingly, "A significant number of Switzerland's comments are directed at amending parts of the report that argue developing countries will need support, particularly financial support, from rich countries in order to meet emission-reduction targets."

In brief, as we fall off the precipice, the near-uniform reaction is that "I want to grasp my share of the loot as doomsday approaches."

Returning to the still-open question posed by the August 9 anniversary, do human moral capacities, and the institutions humans have created, have the capacity to overcome what human intellect and these institutions have shown themselves capable of achieving: total cataclysm?

The answer will soon be known.

And while reflecting on the unanswered question, we should never forget that human intellect has also forged feasible solutions to impending crises, easily at hand, though not for long.

Given our experience up to now with global climate talks, should we really have high expectations about the outcome of COP26? After all, in addition to everything you mentioned above, global oil demand is booming, China continues to build coal-fired power plants around the world, the US is bent on maintaining its hegemonic status in the world system, and we not only have a divided world but a world where now the majority of citizens say that their country's society is more divided than ever before. Indeed, what can we realistically expect from COP26?

Chomsky: The business press is generally fairly realistic. Its audience has a stake in knowing what's happening in the world. So, to answer the question, it is useful to open today's (October 24) business press and read the first paragraph of the major article on what we can realistically expect: "As the prospects for strong government action to curb climate change grow less certain, energy shares, and especially coal mining stocks, are generating astonishing returns." The article goes on to review the great opportunities for huge short-term profits for the super-rich while they destroy the diminishing hopes for a livable world for their children.

Economists soberly explain that this is a "market failure" caused by "externalities"—uncounted costs. Not false. The article quotes a recent International Monetary Fund (IMF) study that found that "market-based fossil fuel prices in 2020 failed to account for $5.9 trillion in global environmental costs, equivalent to 6.8 percent of global gross domestic product. The I.M.F. estimated that the gap will rise to 7.4 percent of world G.D.P. by 2025."

Not false, but misleading. Market failures occur all the time, with increasing intensity since the heralded "market revolution" that has assaulted the world since Ronald Reagan opened the doors to wholesale robbery forty years ago. But the anodyne phrase "market failure" does not begin to do justice to the monstrous crime that state-backed capitalist institutions are perpetrating.

The business press gives little reason to be optimistic about the outcome of COP26, but it's worth remembering that it does not consider what humans can accomplish, if they choose. With regard to human effort and action, the outcome of COP26 doesn't matter all that much. If governments make pledges, they won't implement them without extensive popular activism. If they don't make pledges, they won't be driven to adopt and implement them without extensive popular activism. The message is much the same whatever the outcome: more work, lots more, on many fronts, not excluding the long-term dedication to dismantle lethal institutions and the doctrines that chain people to them.

Bob, the economics of global warming and global climate stabilization are quite straightforward. Indeed, a broad consensus has emerged about the economic impacts of global warming, although there is disagreement among economists about the best solutions to achieve significant reductions in carbon emissions. Why is it so difficult to implement viable climate policies even at the national, let alone the global, level?

Robert Pollin: Let's start with the most obvious obstacle to advancing viable climate policies, which is the implacable opposition of the fossil fuel companies. Here I refer to both the private companies, such as ExxonMobil and Royal Dutch Shell, as well as public corporations such as

Saudi Aramco, Gazprom in Russia, and Petrobras in Brazil. Let's assume we are working with the target set out by the Intergovernmental Panel on Climate Change that we must stabilize the average global temperature at no more than 1.5 degrees Celsius above preindustrial levels. Within that framework, the most recent careful research by Tyler Hansen shows that the extent of total fossil fuel assets owned by these corporations that are "unburnable"—that is, cannot be burned to produce energy if the world has a chance of achieving the 1.5°C stabilization target—amounts to between $13–$15 trillion. Of this total, about 75 percent of these fossil fuel assets, between about $10–$11 trillion, are owned by the public corporations, with the remaining $3–$5 trillion owned by private corporations. We should not be surprised that the fossil fuel companies are fighting by all means available to them to continue profiting lavishly from selling this oil, coal, and natural gas still in the ground. They don't want to hear about dumping $15 trillion in assets.

It's true that the publicly owned national companies, controlling approximately 90 percent of the globe's total fossil fuel reserves, do not operate with precisely the same profit imperatives as big private energy corporations. But let's be clear that this does not mean that they are prepared to commit to fighting climate change simply because their stated mission is to serve the public as opposed to private shareholders, and because we, the public, face a global environmental emergency. Just as with the private companies, producing and selling fossil fuel energy generates huge revenue flows for these publicly owned companies. National development projects, lucrative careers, and political power all depend on continuing the flow of large fossil fuel revenues.

Overall, then, there is no getting around that the interests of these fossil fuel companies will simply have to be defeated. Obviously, that will not be easy to accomplish. We are seeing this right now in the US, with Senator Joe Manchin of West Virginia doing everything possible to kill even the minimally decent climate provisions of Biden's Build Back Better program. Manchin himself started his own coal brokerage company in the state and continues to receive large profits from it. We are also seeing it on a global scale, with Russian president

Vladimir Putin issuing dire warnings of upcoming energy shortages if investments to expand fossil fuel supply do not increase.

But it is also critical to recognize that the fossil fuel companies are not the only obstacle to advancing a viable global climate stabilization project. There is also the matter of pure inertia, which cannot be overlooked. We are faced with the challenge of building a new global energy infrastructure on the foundations of high efficiency and clean renewable energy, while also phasing out our existing fossil-fuel-dominant energy infrastructure. This has to be a hugely challenging project, even under the best of circumstances and even putting aside machinations of the fossil fuel companies. I have experienced this firsthand, for example, in our project at UMass–Amherst in which we built the first zero-emissions office building in western Massachusetts to house the Economics Department. There are lots of new ways of doing things that need to be learned, in terms of engineering, use of materials, and workers developing new skills. It also requires people cooperating effectively.

There is also the absolutely critical question of "just transition" for workers and communities whose livelihoods are, at present, dependent on the fossil fuel industry. In my view, just transition has to be at the center of any global Green New Deal project. There is no denying that these workers and communities throughout the world will lose out in the clean energy transition. In order for the global clean energy project to succeed, it must provide adequate transitional support for these workers and communities. It is a matter of simple justice, but it is also a matter of strategic politics. Without such adjustment assistance programs operating at a major scale, the workers and communities facing retrenchment from the clean energy investment project will, predictably and understandably, fight to defend their communities and livelihoods. This in turn will create unacceptable delays in proceeding with effective climate stabilization policies.

My coworkers and I have estimated the costs of a very generous just transition program for all workers in the United States now tied to the fossil fuel and ancillary industries, working with the assumption that all fossil fuel production will have been shut down by 2050. This program would include a reemployment guarantee with wages at least matching the workers' current pay, along with pension guarantees, and, as needed, retraining and relocation support. We estimated these total costs as averaging about $3 billion per year. This would be equal to roughly 1/100 of 1 percent (0.01 percent) of average US GDP between now and 2050. In other words, in terms of financing, it would be a trivial matter to establish this sort of just transition program throughout the US.

In fact, pathbreaking developments are occurring right now in California toward advancing a just transition program in the state. This movement is being led by visionary labor leaders in the state, including leaders of the state's oil refinery workers' union. One such leader, Norman Rogers, a vice president of United Steelworkers Local 675, recently wrote in the *Los Angeles Times* that

> though the energy transition is inevitable, a just version is not. Workers know what happens when whole industries go away: Companies maneuver behind our backs, squeeze every last drop of work out of a dying auto plant, steel mill or coal mine and shutter it overnight, devastating communities and stiffing workers out of jobs, pensions and healthcare. The fear is real of jobs lost with no plan for when operations begin to phase out.

Rogers emphasizes that "many speak of a 'just transition,' but we've never seen one. No worker or community member will ever believe that an equitable transition is possible until we see detailed, fully funded state safety net and job creation programs." But he, optimistically, is arguing that "with a fully funded equitable transition plan—meeting the immediate need for a safety net for workers and communities, and offering a bold vision to restructure our economy—we can jump-start recovery and move California's workers, communities, and the planet toward a more secure future."

The enactment of a robust just transition program in California, led by the state's labor unions, including its fossil fuel industry unions, will also provide a model for comparable measures to be adopted throughout the US and globally. Supporting such initiatives should therefore be understood as an absolute first-tier priority for the US and the global climate movement.

China has emerged as a global economic superpower in the last couple of decades and, in fact, since 2008 tops the annual list of being the largest emitter of greenhouse gas carbon dioxide, although we get a different picture if we look at carbon emissions per capita. Be that as it may, what sort of finance conditions need to be introduced in countries like China and in emerging economies for a successful transition to clean energy resources without sacrificing economic and social development?

Pollin: As of the most recent data, global carbon dioxide emissions were at about 34 billion tons. China is generating about 10 billion tons, 30 percent of this total, making it by far the country with the largest share of total emissions. The US is next at about 5 billion tons, 15 percent of the total. The countries of the European Union account for another 9 percent. Thus, China, the US, and the EU are responsible for 54 percent of all global emissions. They all need to drive their emissions down to zero no later than 2050 for there to be any chance of meeting the IPCC's global emissions reduction targets of a 45 percent decline by 2030 and a net-zero global economy by 2050.

It's true that in terms of emissions per person, China's figure, at 7.4 tons per person, is still less than half the 15.2 tons per person figure for the United States. But it remains the case that China must go from its current total emissions level of 10 billion tons down to zero by 2050, just as the US needs its emissions to fall absolutely, from 5 billion tons to zero.

It also follows that, even if China, the US, and the EU managed to push their carbon dioxide emissions down to zero tomorrow, we would still be only a bit more to halfway to achieving the global zero-emissions goal, since the rest of the world is today responsible for about 46 percent of all emissions. It is therefore obvious that the transition to a global clean energy system has to be a global project. The transition has to be advancing in India, Vietnam, Australia, Kenya, Puerto Rico, Chile, South Korea, South Africa, and Mexico just as much as in China, the US, and EU.

Building clean energy infrastructures in developing economies will not entail sacrificing economic and social development. Indeed,

the Green New Deal remains focused on expanding good job opportunities, raising mass living standards, and fighting poverty, along
with driving emissions to zero. All of these aims can be realistically
accomplished, since investments in clean energy will be a major
engine of job creation. Moreover, the costs of clean energy investments are already lower, on average, than those for fossil fuels. Building a clean energy infrastructure will also support the expansion of a
range of new public and private ownership forms. This includes small-
scale community ownership in rural low-income communities, such
as in sub-Saharan Africa. To date, roughly half of such communities
still do not have access to electricity of any kind, despite generations
of promises made by politicians of all stripes.

At the same time, we cannot expect low-income countries to
finance their clean energy and just transition programs on their own.
I have sketched out a global financing framework, in which there are
four main components. Other approaches could also be viable. These
four funding sources are: (1) a global carbon tax, in which 75 percent
of revenues are rebated back to the public, but 25 percent are chan-
neled into clean energy investment projects; (2) transferring funds
out of military budgets from all countries, but primarily the US; (3)
eliminating all existing fossil fuel subsidies and channeling 25 percent of the funds into clean energy investments; and (4) a Green Bond
lending program, initiated by the US Federal Reserve and European
Central Bank, with other major central banks in China, the UK, and
Japan also participating. Strong cases can be made for each of these
funding measures. But each proposal does also have vulnerabilities,
including around political feasibility. The most sensible approach is
therefore to combine the measures into a single package that mini-
mizes their respective weaknesses as standalone measures.

I work through some of the details of these proposals in our 2020
book, *Climate Crisis and the Global Green New Deal*. But let's briefly
consider the Green Bond financing proposal by way of illustration.
This program will not take money out of anyone's pocket. It rather
involves the world's major central banks effectively printing money
as needed. This would be just as they did during both the 2007–2009

global financial crisis and during the COVID recession, except on a far more modest scale than the largesse that the central banks showered on Wall Street and global financial elite to keep them afloat. To be clear, I am not suggesting that the US Fed or European Central Bank should rely on this policy—what is technically known as "debt monetization"—on a routine basis. But we need to be equally clear that this is a fully legitimate option that the major central banks have in their toolkit, and that this option should indeed be brought into action under crisis conditions. Note here that the funds will be generated by the major central banks but then distributed globally on an equitable basis, to underwrite the clean energy investment projects at scale in all regions of the globe. Public investment banks in all regions, but especially in low-income countries, will then serve as primary conduits in moving specific investment projects forward.

What would you consider as the optimal outcome of the talks at the COP26 summit?

Pollin: The optimal outcome would be for the summit to not produce another round of what Greta Thunberg has accurately described as the "blah, blah, blah" which has resulted from previous such gatherings. COP26 needs to establish truly binding commitments on all countries that would include the following:

1. Meeting at least the IPCC's emission-reduction targets, of a 45 percent global emissions cut by 2030 and to achieve zero emissions by 2050;

2. Mounting robust just transition programs in all countries and regions, to support workers and communities that will be negatively impacted by the emissions reduction project; and

3. Paying for these binding commitments through strongly egalitarian financing measures.

Noam, the impact of human activities on the environment is so real and profound that past, present, and future are interlinked in such a way that there can be no blurring between the empirical and the normative. The climate crisis has created a global storm and cooperation and solidarity are essential prerequisites to the survival of the planet. However, given the daunting task that lies ahead (shrinking and ultimately eliminating emissions while advancing at the same time a framework of development that embraces both developed and developing countries and guaranteeing a socially just transition), how do we encourage activists and concerned citizens alike to remain committed to a struggle where the outcome is uncertain without succumbing to defeatism?

Chomsky: Outcomes have always been uncertain. Defeatism is not an option; it translates as "species suicide, bringing down much of life on Earth with it."

There are steps forward. Crucially, there is widespread understanding of the measures that can be taken, quite realistically, to avert impending disaster and move on to a much better world. That includes the comprehensive and detailed studies by our friend and colleague economist Robert Pollin, by economist Jeffrey Sachs, and by the International Energy Agency, all coming to generally similar conclusions. These results have also reached Congress in a 2019 resolution recently reintroduced by its sponsors, Representative Alexandria Ocasio-Cortez and Senator Ed Markey. It's all there to be acted upon.

And while Senator Joe Manchin is working assiduously to block any congressional action that departs from the "no elimination" death warrant issued by the energy corporations, his constituents in West Virginia are showing more concern for survival. A recent report of the United Mine Workers recognizes that "change is coming, whether we seek it or not. Too many inside and outside the coalfields have looked the other way when it comes to recognizing and addressing specifically what that change must be, but we can look away no longer."

The union supports a transition to renewable energy, rightly insisting that workers receive good jobs—which should in fact be better jobs, as can be readily accomplished along lines that Bob Pollin has laid out in his studies and conveyed to the public in his grassroots work in West Virginia and other mining states, where unions are moving in the same direction.

There has also been considerable progress since COP21: sharp reduction in cost of sustainable energy, significant steps toward electrification and constant pressure to do more, mostly by the young, those who will have to endure the consequences of our folly and betrayal of their hopes. The recent global climate strike was a noteworthy example.

Another hopeful sign is the recovery of the labor movement from the state-corporate blows that were a salient feature of the neoliberal years from their outset, with deep roots in the origins of neoliberal doctrine in interwar Vienna. That's a long and important story, but there are many indications that it is underway, somewhat reminiscent of the early 1930s. The vibrant US labor movement had been almost crushed by state-corporate violence. But as the Depression hit, it began to revive, and spearheaded the New Deal moves toward social democracy that greatly improved the lives of (many, though not all) Americans. It wasn't until the late 1970s that the business counteroffensive became powerful enough to restore a system of radical inequality and suppression of the basic rights of the great majority. Today, that assault is being challenged and may be overcome. One sign of many is the massive refusal to return to the rotten, dangerous, precarious jobs offered to the workforce during the neoliberal class war. The catastrophic "market failure" of environmental destruction is a catalyzing factor.

If that happens, we can hope for—and try to nurture—a revival of core features of labor activism from the early days of the Industrial Revolution, among them solidarity and internationalism. We're all in this together, not each alone trying to collect as many crumbs as we can for ourselves. That consciousness is essential for survival, at home and abroad.

In particular, there must be an end to provocative confrontations with China and a serious rethinking of the alleged "China threat"—experiences we've been through before with dire consequences, now literally a matter of survival. The US and China will cooperate in approaching the urgent crises of today, or we're doomed.

The choices before us are stark. They cannot be evaded or ignored.

BUILD BACK BETTER FIASCO EXPOSES HOW BOTH PARTIES SERVE CORPORATE POWER

November 1, 2021

C. J. Polychroniou: *Noam, more than two decades after the "end [of] welfare as we know it," Democrats have the chance to reshape the country's safety net and close the gap with the US's liberal-democratic peers on social protection programs, as well as fight the climate crisis. However, in perhaps a rather unsurprising development, it looks like the obstructionist elements inside the Democratic Party will make sure that the US remains a noticeable outlier among developed countries by not having a major social welfare state. Indeed, Joe Manchin, one of the Democratic senators standing in the way of the passage of the reconciliation bill, said that the US should not turn into an "entitlement society." How do you assess all the drama in Congress around the $3.5 trillion in infrastructure, social programs, and combatting the climate crisis, and what does this whole experience reveal to us about the state of US politics in the post-Trump era?*

Noam Chomsky: It's not post-Trump, unfortunately. Former president Donald Trump's heavy hand has not been lifted. He owns the increasingly radicalized voting base of the Republican Party. The leadership slinks to his Mar-a-Lago palace to plead for his blessing, and the few who dare to raise their heads have them lopped off quickly.

The right-wing Democrats (mislabeled "moderate") follow along for their own reasons. These are not hard to discern in some cases: it's not a great surprise that a coal baron who is Congress's leading recipient of fossil fuel funding (Manchin) should proclaim the fossil fuel industry's "no elimination" slogan, or that a top recipient of donations from the pharmaceutical industry (Senator Kyrsten Sinema) should be holding back badly need drug pricing reforms. That's normal in a political system mired in corruption.

But the rot runs deeper.

It's often been observed that the US has a one-party political system—the business party—with two factions, Democrats and Republicans. In the past, the Republican faction has tended to be more dedicated to the concerns of extreme wealth and the corporate sector, but with the resurgence of the one-sided class war called "neoliberalism" under President Ronald Reagan, the leadership has been going off the rails. By now they barely resemble a political party in a functioning democracy.

Since the late president Jimmy Carter years, the Democrats have not lagged far behind, becoming a party of affluent professionals and Wall Street donors with the working class handed over to their bitter class enemy.

One of Trump's occasional true statements was that Republicans could never win a fair election on their actual programs. Recognizing this, since President Richard Nixon's Southern Strategy, the party has been mobilizing voters on "cultural issues"—white supremacy, abortion, guns, traditional patriarchal families, God (favoring the evangelical Christian variety) ... anything that doesn't lift the veil on their loyal service to their prime constituency. That way they can at least stay in the running, exploiting the deeply undemocratic features of the electoral system with its built-in advantages for their largely rural voting base.

All this and much more has been extensively discussed elsewhere. We need not elaborate here. It's playing out in the halls of Congress right now. The extent to which the US is an "outlier" glares at us wherever we look, sometimes in ways that verge on obscenity. Take paid maternity leave. In the US: none. In the next largest country in the hemisphere, Brazil: about four months. That's in addition to the universal health care, free higher education, and other public benefits that are found almost everywhere.

To be fair, the richest country in the world, with unparalleled advantages, is not alone in denying paid leave to new mothers. (Fathers? Forget about it.) The US is joined by the Marshall Islands, the Federated States of Micronesia, Nauru, Palau, Papua New Guinea, and Tonga.

Recently a lead columnist for the London *Financial Times* quipped that if Senator Bernie Sanders were in Germany, he could be running on the right-wing Christian Democrat ticket. Not just a witticism, and not a comment on Sanders. Rather, on the socioeconomic system that has been created in the one-party state, dramatically so in the era of vicious class war since Reagan.

It was not always thus. In the 1930s, while continental Europe succumbed to fascism, the US forged a path toward social democracy on a wave of militant labor activism, lively and diverse politics, and a sympathetic administration. Years earlier, the US had pioneered mass public education, a major contribution to democracy and social justice; Europe lagged far behind.

It's beyond irony that now Europe is upholding a tattered social democracy while the US declines to Trump-led protofascism, or that under Trump, the secretary of education sought to dismantle public education, carrying forward the neoliberal principles that underlie the sharp defunding of public education aimed at its elimination. All this is rooted in the "libertarian" doctrines of Milton Friedman, James Buchanan, and other leading figures of the movement, closely linked from its origins to the attack against government "overreach" by desegregating schools.

It's worth recalling that these doctrines had their origin in bitter class war in interwar Austria, as we've discussed before. They are well suited for its resumption in the neoliberal era.

The Biden effort to move the US somewhat toward the humane norms of other OECD countries is still not dead, but it has been virtually neutralized in Congress. The Republican organization is rock-solid opposed. Its red lines include preservation in full of their one legislative achievement under Trump, the "US Donor Relief Act of 2017," as Joseph Stiglitz termed the wholesale robbery, which punched a huge hole in the deficit (for a "good" cause, so OK). By charming coincidence this near-$2 trillion gift to the very rich and the corporate sector is about the same as the measly remnants of the Biden reconciliation bill (spread over ten years) that have barely survived the right-wing assault.

This time the "deficit threat" is definitely not OK, as is loudly proclaimed. Not a good cause this time. Wrong recipients: the poor, workers, mothers, and other "unpeople."

Should the progressives remain opposed to the infrastructure bill if Congress refuses to pass the social safety net bill in its original version?

It's a question of tactics, not principle. That's not to say that it's unimportant. Choice of tactics can have very far-reaching consequences. Rather, it means that it's not easy to answer. There are many imponderables, not least, how it will affect the coming elections. In earlier years, it was often not too important which faction of the business party took power. In recent years, it has been. Protofascism is on the march. Worse still, as we've discussed elsewhere, we're are advancing to a precipice from which there will be no return. Four more years of Trumpism might well tip the balance.

Which answer to the question you raise will reduce the likelihood of impending disasters? I don't see an easy answer. The question may by now be moot, with the vicious cuts in the reconciliation bill.

Won't there be grave political consequences if Democrats blow the chance to reshape federal priorities? After all, the majority of US people seem to be in support of Biden's Build Back Better Act.

The Republicans have been pursuing a careful and well-thought-out policy of maintaining power as a minority party dedicated to great wealth and corporate power. It has been openly announced by the most malicious and politically powerful of the gang: Senate Minority Leader Mitch McConnell, repeating what worked well for his reactionary cause during the President Barack Obama years (helped by Obama's quick betrayal of those who believed the pretty rhetoric about "hope and change").

So far, it's working. If it does work, with Trump and acolytes returning to power thanks to this malevolence, we will be well on our way to protofascism and to falling off the precipice. Failure of Biden's efforts to reshape federal priorities will have a terrible human cost. Beyond that, it will also provide a weapon for the McConnell strategy of harming the country as much as possible and blaming the outcome on the Democrats.

Brutal, but not stupid.

Is there a way to fend off these grave political consequences? Not within the confines of the deeply corrupt and undemocratic political system. The only way that has ever worked, and can work now, is mass popular pressure—what the powerful call "the peasants coming with their pitchforks."

Trump has been out of office for several months, yet his influence among Republican voters remains unwavering. What continues to drive the pro-Trump crowd?

We've often discussed it before, and there has been extensive investigation by social scientists—most convincingly, in my opinion, by Tony DiMaggio.

It's not just Trump, though he has shown real genius in tapping poisons that run deep in US history and contemporary culture, and in portraying himself as "your savior"—even "the chosen one"—while stabbing you in the back. That's no small accomplishment for a person with few talents other than chicanery, fraud, and wielding the wrecking ball to destroy everything he can't claim as his own.

But it's not just Trump. We can also ask why Nixon's racist Southern Strategy succeeded, or Reagan's quite overt racism—in his case, apparently sincerely held. We can ask why the abortion and gun frauds took hold, or why in the face of overwhelming evidence, segments of the left join the far right in anti-vax campaigns, at enormous human costs, or why "more than half of President Trump's supporters [in 2020] embraced the QAnon conspiracy theory of a global satanic pedophile ring that was plotting against the 45th president of the United States," who was valiantly trying to save the children from such "prominent pedophiles" as Biden, Hillary Clinton, and other "Deep State" suspects.

The signs of collapse of the social order are too numerous and familiar to review once again. To a large extent, it can be attributed to the impact of the one-sided and vicious class war of the past forty-plus years. There are deeper cultural and historical roots. It's not just the US. European racism and xenophobia are even more malevolent in some respects. One sign is the corpses in the Mediterranean, victims of the frenzy of Europe's dedication to torture the survivors of its centuries of destruction of Africa.

The effort to reveal the roots of such pathologies is no mere academic enterprise, and not just these. We can add the pathologies of the rich and powerful, including the deplorables who hurl the epithet at others. These have been far more consequential. Efforts to understand are of value primarily as a guide to self-reflection and to action to find remedies.

And quickly. Our strange species doesn't have a lot of time to spare.

NOAM CHOMSKY AND ROBERT POLLIN

PROTESTS OUTSIDE OF COP26 OFFERED MORE HOPE THAN THE SUMMIT

November 22, 2021

C. J. Polychroniou: *COP26, touted as our "last best hope" to avert a climatic catastrophe, has produced an outcome that was a "compromise," according to United Nations secretary-general António Guterres, while activists conducted a funeral ceremony at the Glasgow Necropolis to symbolize the failure of the summit. Noam, can you give us your analysis of the COP26 climate agreement?*

Noam Chomsky: There were two events at Glasgow: within the stately halls, and in the streets. They may have not been quite at war, but the conflict was sharp. Within, the dominant voice mostly echoed the concerns of the largest contingent, corporate lobbyists; rather like the US Congress, where the impact of lobbyists, always significant, has exploded since the 1970s as the corporate-run neoliberal assault against the general population gained force. The voice within had some nice words but little substance. In the streets, tens of thousands of protesters, mostly young, were desperately calling for real steps to save the world from looming catastrophe.

The outcome of this conflict will determine the course of history—or more precisely, will determine whether future human history will be "nasty, brutish, and short" (to lift philosopher Thomas Hobbes's words) or full of promise and opportunity.

The conflict is nicely encapsulated in a report of Brazil's National Institute of Space Research. It is dated October 27, just a few days before COP26 opened, offering space for fine words and eloquent promises about saving the Amazon forests, a precious resource for Brazil's future, and the world's.

The institute reported that "the area deforested in Brazil's Amazon reached a 15-year high after a 22% jump from the prior year, [an outcome that] flies in the face of [the Jair] Bolsonaro government's recent attempts to shore up its environmental credibility," to put it politely.

It was put less politely by spokespersons for Brazilian and international environmental organizations. One said, "We are seeing the Amazon rainforest being destroyed by a government which made environmental destruction its public policy." Another said: "This is the real Brazil that the Bolsonaro government tries to hide with fantastical speeches and actions of greenwashing abroad. The reality shows that the Bolsonaro government accelerated the path of Amazon destruction."

Within the halls there were many "fantastical speeches," while the outside world revealed much that "flies in their face." Within, there was great enthusiasm about the $130 trillion that will be provided by financial institutions to rescue us. US chief negotiator John Kerry was exultant that the market is now on our side.

He might be right, if we understand the phrase "the market" to refer not to the "fantastical" concept that is conjured up in public discourse but to the real-world market: What Robert Pollin and Gerald Epstein call the neoliberal "bailout economy."

How the holy market works in this case is outlined by political economist Adam Tooze. Lending by the holders of the rescue package of $130 trillion "will not be concessional," he writes.

The trillions, Kerry insisted to his Glasgow audience, will earn a proper rate of return. But how then will they flow to low-income countries? After all, if there was a decent chance of making profit by wiring west Africa for solar power, the trillions would already be at work. For that, Larry Fink of BlackRock, the world's largest fund manager, has a ready answer. He can direct trillions towards the energy transition in low-income countries, if the International Monetary Fund and the World Bank are there to "derisk" the lending, by absorbing the first loss on projects in Africa, Latin America and Asia. Even more money will flow if there is a carbon price that gives clean energy a competitive advantage.

"It is a neat solution," Tooze adds: "The same neat neoliberal solution that has been proffered repeatedly since the 1990s. The same solution that has not been delivered." And won't be delivered unless the friendly taxpayers (excluding the rich, who are granted ways to exempt themselves) perform their neoliberal duty in the "bailout economy."

Others added their own interpretation of the lofty rhetoric within the halls. Not least Washington. "We must seize this moment," President Joe Biden declared in Glasgow. On returning home, he "opened the largest oil and gas lease sale in U.S. history," carrying out a program set in motion by former president Donald Trump.

In defense, the administration held that it was obligated to proceed because of "a preliminary injunction issued by a federal judge in June, saying that its proposed pause on new leases would be illegal." Environmental groups point out a variety of options, but the main conclusions stare us in the face: The reigning institutions, whether federal or judicial, are unwilling to take the steps needed to save us from catastrophe.

Threats will mount when, as seems likely, the denialist party storms back into power, having successfully blocked government programs that would help the population but bolster their political opposition, along with a flood of lies about saving innocent little children from the "critical race theory" villains who are teaching them that they are by nature brutal oppressors, and whatever other hysteria they can whip up.

As Trump took over sole possession of the Republican Party, the percentage of Republicans who regarded global warming as a "serious

problem" declined from 49 percent to 39 percent while, "the propor-
tion of Democrats who see climate change as an existential threat rose
by 11 points to 95 percent over seven years." It's not hard to imagine
how the wrecker and his minions will gleefully exploit the renewed
opportunity to race as quickly as possible toward irreversible tipping
points, while enriching their corporate masters.

The "last, best hope" in Glasgow was not the conference of 120 world
leaders, but the competing event that was taking place in the streets outside. They are the ones who can compel the powerful in government and
corporate headquarters to act expeditiously to use the options available
to avert the race to destruction and to create a better world.

*Can we draw hope from the promise made by the countries meeting in
Glasgow to "revisit and strengthen" new plans by the end of 2022, or
should we interpret this pledge as another way on the part of world leaders
to just keep kicking the can down the road?*

Chomsky: There were a few positive developments within the halls in
Glasgow, though far short of what is urgently needed. The question of
how to interpret the pledge brings to mind Karl Marx's eleventh thesis
on Ludwig Feuerbach: The task of those committed to decent survival
is not to interpret the pledge but to act to ensure that it is more than
pious verbiage.

*Bob, first what's your own assessment of the key outcomes from COP26,
and what do you make of the position of those countries which were fiercely
opposed to calls for the inclusion of fossil fuels in any final agreement and
phasing out coal and fossil fuel subsidies?*

Robert Pollin: The first thing to say about the COP26 conference is
that it demonstrated, yet again, the breathtaking capacity of high-level
diplomats to discuss issues of human survival almost entirely discon-
nected from reality. For example, it was considered an achievement
of the conference that, for the first time, the burning of fossil fuels to
produce energy was officially recognized as a cause of climate change.

The only way that we can consider this progress is in relationship to the flat-out absurdity that the previous twenty-five COP agreements had all failed to acknowledge the long-established reality that burning fossil fuels is responsible for producing about 75 to 80 percent of the greenhouse gases causing climate change.

Beyond this measure of "progress," the COP26 diplomats still wrangled over whether they objected, *full stop*, to governments providing fossil fuel subsidies or rather, whether they objected only to fossil fuel subsidies that are "inefficient," whatever that means. Not surprisingly, the final document ended up only opposing "inefficient" subsidies. Similarly, at the very end of the meetings, China and India managed to substitute a reference to "phasing *down*" coal rather than the original text that referred to "phasing *out*" coal.

Amid such word-parsing exercises, the underlying reality is that, even with all the pledges made at the last major COP conference, COP21 in Paris in 2015, almost nothing has been accomplished in terms of reducing CO_2 emissions. Thus, in its 2021 "World Energy Outlook," the International Energy Agency (IEA) projects that, according to its "stated policies" scenario—that is, a scenario that takes account of all government pledges made at Paris along with what they have actually accomplished relative to these pledges— global CO_2 emissions will not fall at all as of 2030 and will fall by less than 6 percent as of 2050, from 36 billion tons of emissions today to 33.9 billion tons as of 2050. This, again, is within the context of the Paris Agreement, in which all 196 countries committed to stabilizing the global average temperature at 1.5 degrees Celsius above preindustrial levels. To succeed in stabilizing the global average temperature at 1.5°C above preindustrial levels, the Intergovernmental Panel on Climate Change has established that global CO_2 emissions must fall by 45 percent by 2030 and reach zero emissions by 2050.

All of this tells us that we will never move on to a viable climate stabilization by relying on the words or pledges agreed to in any such diplomatic documents. The only way to move seriously onto a viable climate stabilization path is through grassroots political organizing that forces governments to take actions that they will otherwise never take. If there was any good news out of COP26, it is that political organizers were in the streets in Glasgow in full force and could not be ignored.

Their presence did force some concessions into the final document: About half of the nearly two hundred country delegations agreed to cut methane emissions by 30 percent as of 2030. The full body pledged to end deforestation by 2030. The full body also acknowledged "with deep regret" that the rich countries that are responsible for the climate crisis have not fulfilled their financial pledges to support green transition programs in low-income countries. It remains an open question as to whether this "deep regret" will lead to serious financing commitments that will actually be met.

Why is the transition to clean energy so slow? Is it a question of lack of investments and technological know-how, or something else?

Pollin: By some metrics, the transition to clean energy is proceeding fairly quickly. For example, as of 1985, solar energy provided less than 0.01 percent of the world's electricity supply. By 2020, that figure is up to 3.3 percent. This is an increase of nearly 3,000 percent in thirty-five years. Of course, we are starting in 1985 with a miniscule base of solar production. More importantly, the level of solar supply can't remain stuck in the range of 3 percent of electricity in order to meet the climate goals. It rather needs to be in the range of 60 to 70 percent as of 2050.

A major factor that had prevented the expansion of clean renewable energy from expanding more rapidly had been cost. As recently as 2010, the average cost globally of producing a kilowatt of electricity through solar energy was thirty-eight cents. As of 2020, the average cost had fallen to less than seven cents. Meanwhile, the comparative average cost for fossil-fuel-generated electricity has remained stable over this decade at between five and fifteen cents per kilowatt hour. In other words, solar is now fully cost competitive with fossil fuels, which had not been true previously. Both onshore and offshore wind are also now fully cost competitive with fossil fuels. As such, when we include energy efficiency investments along with those for renewable energy, the overall result is that this clean energy infrastructure can deliver both a zero-emissions economy and lower energy costs.

Even with renewable energy costs dropping sharply, several critical issues still remain outstanding. One is the intermittency of solar and wind power supply—that is, the sun doesn't shine at night and wind doesn't blow all day everywhere. So, transmission and storage questions do need to be addressed—for example, how to deliver wind-powered electricity reliably and at low cost from a farm in western Pennsylvania to the center of Philadelphia? A lot of progress is being made toward resolving these issues. But also keep in mind that we don't need to solve them completely right now, before we can proceed with the clean energy transition. We aren't going to eliminate the use of fossil fuels next week, no matter what. We have roughly two decades to develop the transmission and storage technologies that we will need to operate the global economy on 100 percent renewable energy supply.

Another challenge with building the renewable energy infrastructure is land use. This is a serious question that has emerged in many places. Where do we site the wind turbines and arrays of solar panels without wrecking neighborhoods or natural environments? Part of the solution is to make as much use as possible of artificial surfaces—such as putting solar panels on rooftops or building solar canopies in parking lots. Such measures are becoming increasingly viable, with the costs of even residential solar installations now also reaching cost parity with both fossil fuels as well as utility-scale solar farms. A similar pattern is also occurring with offshore wind platforms.

Broadly speaking then, the technology, intermittency, and land use issues are being addressed effectively despite inadequate levels of government support. Still, we need to find the funds to build this global clean energy infrastructure. That is going to require something like 2.5 to 3 percent of global GDP per year—that is, about $2.5 trillion next year, then averaging about $4.5 trillion per year between now and 2050, according to figures in our book, *Climate Crisis and the Global Green New Deal*.

What was clear from COP26 is that government funding at sufficient levels will never be forthcoming without political struggles. This is despite the fact that the 2.5 percent of GDP that is required can be provided readily through some financing combinations that we have discussed previously. For example, converting all existing fossil fuel subsidies into clean energy subsidies, transferring only 5 to 10 percent of military spending into clean energy investments, or having the major central banks purchasing global green investment bonds. Such bond purchases could be in the range of 2 percent of the bailout injections that the Federal Reserve injected into Wall Street to prevent a financial collapse brought on by the COVID recession.

Democratic Representative Alexandria Ocasio-Cortez said that people shouldn't expect international climate summits like COP26 or governments to solve the climate crisis, but at the same time defended the Green New Deal plan. How do we realize the goals of the Green New Deal from below? This is a question addressed to both of you.

Chomsky: How was the New Deal realized, or any other step forward in human history? Virtually without exception by dedicated persistent activism. This time will not be different.

Elements are there. Thanks in no small part to Bob Pollin's active engagement, backed by sound analytic work, unions are taking up the cause. That includes the United Mine Workers, proceeding well ahead of coal baron Senator Joe Manchin, a congressional champion-in-receiving-funding-from-fossil-fuel-industries who is cooperating with rock-solid Republican opposition to steps to reverse the race to destruction.

There's ample precedent for organized labor taking the lead, as it did in bringing the New Deal to fruition. One of the earliest environmental activists was Tony Mazzocchi of the Chemical and Atomic Workers International Union, workers who are the most immediate victims of poisoning the atmosphere. His efforts to form a Labor Party failed, and it's not easy in the rigidly monopolized US political system, but there are ways to progress even in this domain. There are encouraging signs that labor is reviving from the bitter forty-year neoliberal assault. The mass refusal to return to rotten and dangerous jobs is only one sign. The malaise that is leading to an unprecedented wave of "deaths of despair" in the white working class can, and must, be overcome and directed to the kind of militant labor action that ninety years ago created a base for social democracy in the US while Europe was descending into fascist horror.

A third of Americans, overwhelmingly Republicans, don't even regard global warming (let alone the much broader crisis of environmental destruction) as a "serious problem." All must come to recognize, soon, that it is not only a serious problem but an urgent one, and that how we deal with it, right now, will determine the fate of human life as well as that of the countless species we are casually destroying. To achieve that essential goal requires major educational and organizational efforts, omitting no sector of the society, including those in thrall of Trump-style malevolence.

In Congress, Representative Alexandria Ocasio-Cortez and Senator Ed Markey have reintroduced a 2019 resolution calling for a comprehensive Green New Deal along the lines of the detailed work of Robert Pollin and his colleagues and, with somewhat different models from economist Jeffrey Sachs, now also backed by the IEA. Local and state-level initiatives are underway. There are major international actions, mostly by the young.

That's the barest sample. There's lots of work to do. This is not the time for musing on the sidelines.

Pollin: We need to be organizing at all levels of society to advance the global Green New Deal project. This means fighting to stop any and all communities and institutions from relying on burning fossil fuels to provide energy and to build a zero-emissions energy infrastructure through investments in both energy efficiency and clean renewables. Note that this is distinct from demanding that institutions divest their ownership shares of fossil fuel stock and bonds. The divestment movement has played a critical role in raising consciousness about the climate crisis. But its effectiveness is limited by the reality that if, say, a university sells its stocks in ExxonMobil, those stocks are getting purchased by hedge funds that are happy to buy the stocks at reduced prices. The hedge fund will then continue to earn dividends from their fossil fuel stocks as long as people continue to consume oil, coal, and natural gas to meet their energy needs. So, the Green New Deal program must start with the project of ending reliance on fossil fuels. And we certainly can't wait for the next COP conference to settle the matter.

We then need to be clear that the case for the Green New Deal is overwhelming, at many levels: it is the way through which we can realistically get to zero emissions by 2050. The investments to build the clean energy infrastructure will be a major engine of new job opportunities, in all regions of the world. My coworkers and I have estimated that clean energy investments at about 2.5 percent of GDP per year would generate, for example, about four to five million jobs per year in the US and about twenty million jobs in India. Creating these new jobs will also open opportunities to increase union organizing and raise the pay and benefits associated with these jobs. Building the clean energy infrastructure will also create new possibilities for small-scale public, private, and cooperative ownership of renewable energy assets. It will eliminate the largest sources of outdoor air pollution, thus significantly raising public health standards. The Green New Deal must, critically, also be committed to just transition for the workers and communities that are currently dependent on the fossil fuel industry that will need to be phased out.

In combination, these various features of the global Green New Deal provide a powerful platform for committed and effective organizing. The diplomats that argued last week over what may constitute "inefficient" fossil fuel subsidies will then be forced into finally seeing the reality before their eyes.

US-CHINA COOPERATION IS ESSENTIAL TO AVERT A NEW COLD WAR

December 22, 2021

C. J. Polychroniou: *Noam, the US-China relationship has gone through ups and downs over the course of the last thirty or so years. Clearly, the sort of relationship that exists today between the two countries is far more antagonistic than it was even ten years ago. In your own view, what forces or processes are responsible for the increasing tensions we are witnessing today in US-China relations?*

Noam Chomsky: After the fall of the USSR, there was much euphoria about the end of history with "liberal democracy" (a code word for the US) having achieved total victory. A corollary was that China could now be brought within the "rule-based international order."

The latter is a now-conventional phrase, one worth pondering. It refers to an international order in which the US sets the rules, displacing the international order established by the United Nations, which the US deems antiquated and irrelevant. The UN Charter is the supreme law of the land under the US Constitution, constantly violated, a matter of no concern to those who pledge reverence for the holy text. Its provisions have been considered inappropriate for the modern world ever since the US lost control of the UN with decolonization, and occasional backsliding among the privileged as well. UN members no longer know "how to play," to borrow Thomas Friedman's ridicule of France when it failed to support the benign US invasion of Iraq, accompanied by his call for the miscreant to be deprived of its permanent membership in the Security Council. The self-described "world's greatest deliberative body" contented itself with renaming French fries as "Freedom fries" in the Senate cafeteria.

Right-thinking people understand that the outdated UN-based international order is to be replaced by the rule-based order, including such constructions as the highly protectionist "free-trade agreements," right now yielding such pleasures as barring a "People's Vaccine" that would alleviate the COVID disaster. The Clintonites were particularly enthusiastic about incorporating a well-disciplined China within this forward-looking, rule-based order.

It didn't work as planned. China refuses to play when it doesn't want to. Worse still, it can't be intimidated. It goes its own way. That way is often ugly, but that's of no relevance to the rule-based order, which easily tolerates vicious crimes by the righteous—notably the Master—with equanimity and often approval.

China is not Europe. The countries of Europe may fume when the US decides to destroy the joint agreement with Iran (the JCPOA) and to impose harsh sanctions to punish Iran for Washington's demolition of the agreement. They may even proclaim that they will develop ways to avoid the murderous US sanctions. But in the end, they go along, not willing to incur the wrath of the Godfather, or his punitive measures, such as expulsion from the international financial system, controlled by Washington. Same in many other cases.

China is different. It insists on the UN-based system (which it violates when it chooses to). As former Australian prime minister Paul Keating explained, the much-heralded "China threat" reduces to the fact that China exists and is successfully defying the rules.

It is not the first to do so. The charge of "successful defiance" comes from the annals of the US State Department in the 1960s. It was directed against the "Cuban threat," namely, Cuba's "successful defiance" of US policies dating back to the Monroe Doctrine of 1823, which declared Washington's intention to dominate the hemisphere once the British nuisance had been removed. That was anticipated by the great grand strategist John Quincy Adams, intellectual author of Manifest Destiny. He instructed his cabinet colleagues that US power would increase while Britain's declined, so that Cuba (indeed the hemisphere) would fall into US hands by the laws of "political gravitation" as an apple falls from a tree. That happened in 1898 when the US intervened to prevent Cuba's liberation from Spanish rule, turning Cuba into a virtual colony, events recorded in properly sanitized history as Washington's "liberation" of Cuba.

Cuba has been punished viciously for this successful defiance, including John F. Kennedy's terrorist war, which almost brought about terminal nuclear war, and a crushing blockade. US punishment of Cuba is opposed by the whole world: 184–2 in the latest UN vote, with Israel alone voting with its US protector. But Europe obeys, however reluctantly.

Sometimes China's practices sink to almost indescribable depths of evil. Once Washington realized that China is successfully defying the rules, it turned to the project of impeding China's technological development—harming itself in the process, but overcoming the "China threat" is of transcendent importance. One aspect of the campaign to impede Chinese development is to keep others from using Chinese technology. But the devious Chinese are defying the rule-based international order by "setting up a network of vocational colleges around the world [to] train students in dozens of countries in technical areas . . . on Chinese technology with Chinese standards as part of a full court press to globalize Chinese tech. It is a component of a bigger effort to tighten the economic linkages between China and the Global South, which Beijing sees as key to competition with the United States," according to foreign policy scholars Niva Yau and Dirk van der Kley. Worse still, they note, "the Chinese government has been willing to listen to host countries," and is training local instructors who will upgrade the skills of the local trainees and be able to develop their own societies, within the Chinese orbit and using Chinese technology.

These projects fall within the broader Chinese global policy framework now being realized most extensively throughout Eurasia, probably soon reaching to Turkey and on to Eastern and Central Europe. If Afghanistan can survive US sanctions, it too will probably be brought within the orbit of the China-based Shanghai Cooperation Organization, joining Russia, India, Pakistan, Iran, and the Central Asian states. China might manage to shift Afghanistan's economy from opium export, the staple when it was under US control, to exploiting its considerable mineral resources, to China's benefit. Chinese economic initiatives also extend to Southeast Asia, Africa, the Middle East (including Israel), and even to Washington's backyard in Latin America, despite strenuous US efforts to block such intrusion.

Critics of these initiatives "accuse China of pursuing a policy of 'debt-trap diplomacy': luring poor, developing countries into agreeing [to] unsustainable loans to pursue infrastructure projects so that, when they experience financial difficulty, Beijing can seize the asset, thereby extending its strategic or military reach." Perhaps, but the charges are contested by reputable Western sources, including a Chatham House study that "demonstrates that the evidence for such views is limited," and studies by US researchers assert that these charges, including those leveled by Donald Trump and Mike Pompeo, are baseless and that "Chinese banks are willing to restructure the terms of existing loans and have never actually seized an asset from any country," in particular, the prize example in the charges, a port in Sri Lanka.

Nonetheless, debt traps are a concern, one that the US understands well. Right now, for example, Washington is deeply concerned about a debt trap afflicting Cambodia, which is under pressure to repay a loan as it easily can, the lender claims, also arguing that it "would set a bad precedent for other states" if the debt were canceled.

The lender is, of course, Washington. The debt was incurred by the government the US was supporting (or more realistically, had imposed), in the early 1970s, when official US policy, in Henry Kissinger's immortal words, was a "massive bombing campaign in Cambodia. . . . Anything that flies on anything that moves," a call for genocide that would be hard to match in the archival record. The consequences were, predictably, horrendous. The perpetrator is greatly honored. The victims must repay their debts. We wouldn't want to set a bad precedent.

Occasionally, depravity reaches such a level that words fail.

The report on Cambodia's debt trap adds that "if Washington were to wipe out a large chunk of the debt, it would only do so if it believed this gesture was met by good-faith reciprocity from Phnom Penh. Frankly, there's zero reason for such a belief now. A case in point occurred last month, when, after [US deputy secretary of state Wendy] Sherman's visit to Phnom Penh, the Cambodian government allowed the defense attaché at the US Embassy, Marcus M. Ferrara, to tour the Ream Naval Base.... Yet he turned up to find that he was only allowed to visit parts of the site. Phnom Penh was in its rights to limit Ferrara's visit, yet it did nothing to absolve US fears that Cambodia is hiding something."

It might be hiding a deal with China, which never ceases its malevolence.

As we have discussed earlier, much of the frenzied rhetoric about the China threat concerns alleged threats off the coast of China, where the US military advantage is overwhelming (and a small fraction of the US military advantage worldwide). That was so even before the recent US-UK decision to provide Australia with a fleet of nuclear-powered submarines to confront China's four old noisy diesel submarines bottled up by US power in the South China Sea.

The US claims to be defending freedom of navigation with its military maneuvers in China's Exclusive Economic Zone—pure fraud, as we have already discussed. There are actually serious issues concerning Chinese abuses of the Law of the Sea, which has been ratified by all maritime powers except one: the usual outlier, the US. These should be addressed by diplomacy led by the regional powers, not by highly provocative acts that increase the threat of escalation to full-scale war.

Taiwan has returned as one of the thorniest issues in US-Chinese relations. The Chinese military has stepped up its activities in the Taiwan Strait and, according to some military experts, is even acquiring the equipment necessary for an invasion. In fact, Taipei has warned that China is getting ready to invade the island by 2025, although one would have to assume that such a scenario is most unlikely because of the impact that it would have on China's relations with the rest of the world. Still, would it be likely, as President Biden stated in late October during a CNN "town hall," that the US would defend Taiwan if China invaded? And is there really a "Taiwan agreement" between the US and China, as Biden also seems to have suggested earlier in that month?

The critical agreement is the "one-China" doctrine that has been held for over forty years. It is kept ambiguous. The rational policy now is for both the US and China to refrain from provocative acts, and for Taiwan to adhere to the ambiguous agreement, the best outcome that can be hoped for at this point.

As China is bent on expanding its nuclear arsenal, the US appears willing now to push for arms-control talks. What are the lessons from the Cold War era to help us feel confident that a US-China arms race can be prevented?

The main lesson from the Cold War era is that it's a virtual miracle that we have survived. There should be no need here to run through the record once again, but it is worth remembering how many opportunities to reduce the dangers radically were lost.

The most instructive case I think was sixty years ago. Nikita Khrushchev understood well that Russia could not carry out the economic development he hoped for if it was trapped in an arms race with a far richer and more powerful adversary. He therefore proposed sharp mutual reductions in offensive weapons. The incoming Kennedy administration considered the offer and rejected it, instead turning to rapid military expansion, even though it was already far in the lead. The prominent international relations scholar Kenneth Waltz described what happened at the time: the Kennedy administration "undertook the largest strategic and conventional peace-time military build-up the world has yet seen . . . even as Khrushchev was trying at once to carry through a major reduction in the conventional forces and to follow a strategy of minimum deterrence, and we did so even though the balance of strategic weapons greatly favored the United States."

As often has been the case, the policy harmed national security while enhancing state power, what really matters to Washington.

By now it's widely recognized—including a joint statement by Henry Kissinger; Reagan's secretary of state George Shultz; the Senate's leading specialist on armaments, Sam Nunn; and former secretary of defense William Perry—that we should move expeditiously to eliminate nuclear weapons, a process that the signers of the nonproliferation treaty are obligated to undertake. The UN Treaty on the Prohibition of Nuclear Weapons entered into force this year. Though not yet implemented because of US interference, nuclear-weapons-free zones have been established in much of the world.

In brief, there are ways to greatly enhance security.

China so far has held back in nuclear weapons development. It would be wise to continue this policy. The US can facilitate it by ending its highly provocative actions and moving toward an arms-control agreement with China. There are feasible means, outlined by arms-control specialists. While the Republican administrations since 2000 have been dismantling the arms-control regime that has been laboriously constructed over the past sixty years, even Trump's wrecking ball didn't manage to demolish all of them; Biden was able to rescue the New START Treaty just before its expiration. The system can be resurrected and carried forward to the point where this scourge is removed from the earth.

The essential conclusion is simple: either the US and China will work together on the critical issues that we all face, or they will expire together, bringing the rest of the world down with them.

OUTDATED US COLD WAR POLICY WORSENS ONGOING RUSSIA-UKRAINE CONFLICT

December 23, 2021

C. J. Polychroniou: *Following the undoing of the USSR between 1980 and 1991, people in Ukraine voted overwhelmingly in 1991 to declare independence from the crumbling communist empire. Since then, Ukraine has sought to align closely with the European Union and NATO, but Moscow has objected to such plans, as it has always considered Ukraine to be part of Russia, and, accordingly, continued to meddle in the country's internal affairs. In fact, Ukraine became a battleground in 2014 when Putin decided to annex Crimea, which he called the "spiritual source" of the Russian state, and, since then, tensions between the two countries have been very hard to defuse. In your own view, what's really behind the conflict between Russia and Ukraine?*

Noam Chomsky: There's more to add, of course. What happened in 2014, whatever one thinks of it, amounted to a coup with US support that replaced the Russia-oriented government by a Western-oriented one. That led Russia to annex Crimea, mainly to protect its sole warm water port and naval base, and apparently with the agreement of a considerable majority of the Crimean population. There's extensive scholarship on the complexities, particularly Richard Sakwa's *Frontline Ukraine* and more recent work.

There's an excellent discussion of the current situation in a recent article in the *Nation* by Anatol Lieven. Lieven argues realistically that Ukraine is "the most dangerous [immediate] problem in the world," and "also in principle the most easily solved." The solution has already been proposed and accepted—in principle: the Minsk II agreement, adopted by France, Germany, Russia, and Ukraine in 2015, and endorsed unanimously by the UN Security Council. The agreement tacitly presupposes withdrawal of George W. Bush's invitation to Ukraine to join NATO, reaffirmed by Barack Obama, vetoed by France and Germany, an outcome that no Russian leader is likely to accept. It calls for disarmament of the separatist Russia-oriented region (Donbas) and withdrawal of Russian forces ("volunteers"), and spells out the key elements of settlement, with "three essential and mutually dependent parts: demilitarization; a restoration of Ukrainian sovereignty, including control of the border with Russia; and full autonomy for the Donbas in the context of the decentralization of power in Ukraine as a whole." Such an outcome, Lieven observes, would not be unlike other federations, including the US.

Minsk II has not been implemented because of disagreements about timing of its various measures. The issue has been "buried" in US political circles and media, Lieven writes, "because of the refusal of Ukrainian governments to implement the solution and the refusal of the United States to put pressure on them to do so." The US, he concludes, has been keeping to "a zombie policy—a dead strategy that is wandering around pretending to be alive and getting in everyone's way, because US policymakers have not been able to bring themselves to bury it."

The imminent dangers make it imperative to bury the policy and adopt a sound one.

To overcome the impasse will not be easy, but as Lieven observes, the only alternatives are too horrendous to consider. The essentials are understood: Austrian-style neutrality for Ukraine, which means no military alliances or foreign military bases, and an internal resolution in the general terms of Minsk II.

"The most dangerous problem in the world" can therefore be solved with a modicum of rationality.

The broader context reaches back to the collapse of the Soviet Union thirty years ago. There were three contrasting visions of the global order that should be established in the wake of its collapse. All accepted that

Germany would be unified and would join NATO—a remarkable concession by Russia, considering that Germany alone, not part of a hostile military alliance, had virtually destroyed Russia twice in the past century, a third time joining with the West (including the US), in the "intervention" immediately after the Bolsheviks took power.

One proposal was Mikhail Gorbachev's: a Eurasian security system from the Atlantic to Vladivostok, with no military blocs. The US never considered that as an option. A second proposal was offered by George H. W. Bush and his secretary of state James Baker, endorsed by West Germany: NATO would not move "one inch to the East," meaning East Berlin; nothing beyond was contemplated, at least publicly. The third was Bill Clinton's: NATO would move all the way to the Russian border, carry out military maneuvers in the states adjoining Russia, and place weapons on the Russian border that the US would certainly regard as offensive weapons in the (inconceivable) event that it would even tolerate anything remotely comparable anywhere in its vicinity. It was the Clinton Doctrine that was implemented.

The asymmetry is far more deeply rooted. It is a core component of the "rule-based international order" that the US advocates (while by coincidence, setting the rules), replacing the supposedly archaic UN-based international order that bans "the threat or use of force" in international affairs. The latter condition is unacceptable to rogue states that demand the right to employ the threat of force constantly, and to resort to force at will. An important topic that we have discussed before.

One crucial illustration of the rule-based asymmetry that should be familiar is President Kennedy's response to Nikita Khrushchev's sending of nuclear missiles to Cuba—in reaction to the threat of invasion as the culmination of JFK's terrorist war against Cuba, and to his huge arms buildup in response to Khrushchev's offer for mutual reduction of offensive weapons even though the US was far in the lead. The critical issue that almost led to devastating war was the status of US nuclear-armed missiles aimed at Russia in Turkey. As the crisis moved ominously close to war, the key issue was whether the missiles should be publicly withdrawn (as Khrushchev requested) or only secretly (as Kennedy demanded). In fact, the US had already ordered them withdrawn to be replaced by far more menacing Polaris submarines, so there was no withdrawal at all, only escalation.

The crucial asymmetry is presupposed, an inviolable principle of world order, established more extensively as the Clinton's NATO Doctrine was imposed.

It should be recalled that this was only one component of a more expansive Clinton Doctrine, which accords the US the right to use military force "unilaterally when necessary" to defend vital interests such as "ensuring uninhibited access to key markets, energy supplies and strategic resources." No one else can claim such a right.

There is extensive scholarly debate about the status of the Bush-Baker proposal. The agreement was only verbal, as argued in justification when Washington instantly violated it, moving troops to East Berlin. But the basic facts are not seriously in doubt.

NATO was founded in response to the alleged threat posed to Western democracies by the Soviet Union. Yet, NATO not only did not disappear after the end of the Cold War, but continued its expansion eastward and, as a matter of fact, regards Ukraine today as a potential member. What is the relevance of NATO today, and to what extent is it responsible for escalating tensions on Russia's borders and for potentially ushering in a new Cold War?

The expansion to the East, including regular military maneuvers and threatening weapons systems, is clearly a factor in escalating tensions, the offer to Ukraine to join NATO even more so, as just discussed.

In thinking about the acutely dangerous current situation, it's useful to bear in mind the founding of NATO and the "alleged threat." There's a good deal to say about that topic, specifically about how the Russian threat was actually perceived by planners. Inquiry shows that it was quite different from the fevered rhetoric employed "to scare the hell out of the country" in a manner "clearer than truth" (Senator Arthur Vandenberg and Dean Acheson, respectively).

It is well known that the influential planner George Kennan considered the Russian threat to be political and ideological, not military. He was, in fact, sent out to pasture early on for failure to join in the largely manufactured panic. Still, it's always instructive to see how the world is perceived at the dovish extreme.

As head of the State Department planning staff, Kennan was so concerned about the threat from postwar Russia in 1946 that he felt that partition of Germany might be necessary in violation of wartime agreements. The reason was the need to "rescue Western zones of Germany by walling them off against Eastern penetration," not, of course, by military force, but by "political penetration," where the Russians had the advantage. In 1948, Kennan advised that "the problem of Indonesia [is] the most crucial issue of the moment in our struggle with the Kremlin," even though the Kremlin was nowhere in sight. The reason was that if Indonesia falls under "Communism" it could be an "infection [that] would sweep westward" through all of South Asia, even endangering US control of the Middle East.

The internal record is littered with similar illustrations of oblique, sometimes quite explicit, recognition of reality. In general, "The Kremlin" became a metaphor for anything that might fall out of US control—until 1949, when the "Sino-Soviet conspiracy" could sometimes fill the bill.

Russia was indeed a threat, within its Eastern European domains, just as many around the world can attest to threats of the US and its Western allies. There should be no need to sample that awful history. NATO had little role in it.

With the collapse of the USSR, the official justification for NATO was gone, and something new had to be devised. More generally, some new pretext had to be devised for violence and subversion. One device, quickly seized upon, was "humanitarian intervention." This was soon framed within the doctrine of "Responsibility to Protect" (R2P). Two versions were formulated. The official version was adopted by the UN in 2005. It keeps to the strictures of the UN Charter banning the threat or use of force in international affairs apart from conditions irrelevant to R2P, proceeding beyond only in calling on states to observe humanitarian law.

That's the official version of R2P. A second version was formulated by the *Report of the International Commission on Intervention and*

State Sovereignty on Responsibility to Protect (2001), produced under the initiative of former Australian foreign minister Gareth Evans. It departs from the official version in one crucial respect: a situation in which "the Security Council rejects a proposal or fails to deal with it in a reasonable time." In that case, the report authorizes "action within area of jurisdiction by regional or sub-regional organizations under Chapter VIII of the Charter, subject to their seeking subsequent authorization from the Security Council."

In practice, the right to intervene is reserved to the powerful—in today's world, to the NATO powers, which are also unilaterally able to determine their own "area of jurisdiction." They did in fact do so. NATO unilaterally determined that its "area of jurisdiction" includes the Balkans, then Afghanistan, and well beyond. NATO secretary-general Jaap de Hoop Scheffer instructed a NATO meeting in June 2007 that "NATO troops have to guard pipelines that transport oil and gas that is directed for the West," and more generally have to protect sea routes used by tankers and other "crucial infrastructure" of the energy system. NATO's area of jurisdiction is therefore worldwide.

To be sure, some do not agree; in particular, the traditional victims of the kind tutelage of Europe and its offshoots. Their opinion, as always dismissed, was made explicit in the first meeting of the South Summit of 133 states (April 2000). Its declaration, surely with the recent bombing of Serbia in mind, rejected "the so-called 'right' of humanitarian intervention, which has no legal basis in the United Nations Charter or in the general principles of international law." The wording of the declaration reaffirms earlier UN declarations to the same effect, and is mirrored in the official version of R2P.

Standard practice since has been to refer to the official UN version as justification for whatever is done but to keep to the Evans Commission version for determination of choice of action.

There are indications that Russia is building capacity to attack Ukraine, with some military analysts claiming that this could happen in the first couple months of the new year. While it is not likely that NATO would intervene militarily in a conflict between Russia and Ukraine, a Russian invasion of Ukraine would surely bring about a dramatic transformation of the international landscape. What would be the most realistic solution to the Ukraine conflict?

The indications are real, and ominous. Most serious analysts doubt that Putin would launch an invasion. He would have a great deal to lose— maybe everything if the US reacted with force, as we all might. At best from his perspective, Russia would be engaged in a bitter "endless war" and subjected to very severe sanctions and other harsh measures. I presume that Putin's intention is to warn the West not to disregard what he takes to be Russian interests, with some justice.

There is a realistic solution: the one that Anatol Lieven outlined. As he discusses, it is not easy to imagine another one. And none has been proposed.

Fortunately, this solution is within reach. It is of great importance to keep popular opinion from being inflamed by all-too-familiar devices that have led to catastrophe in the past.

GOP'S SOFT COUP IS STILL UNDERWAY ONE YEAR AFTER CAPITOL ASSAULT

January 6, 2022

C. J. Polychroniou: *A year ago, on January 6, 2021, a mob of Donald Trump's supporters broke into the US Capitol in an attempt to block certification of the electoral votes—a routine procedure following a presidential election—that would have formalized Joe Biden's victory. The Capitol building had been breached on a few occasions in the past, but this was the first time in the history of the country that an assault on democracy was actually incited by an outgoing president. In fact, months later, former president Trump would go so far as to condemn the criminal prosecution of those who took part in the Capitol attack that day, even though he had denounced the insurrection after he had been impeached over it. From your perspective, Noam, how should we understand what happened on January 6, 2021?*

Noam Chomsky: Participants in the assault on the Capitol doubtless had varying perceptions and motives, but were united in the effort to overthrow an elected government; in short, an attempted coup, by definition. It was furthermore an attempt that could have succeeded if a few prominent Republican figures had changed their stance and gone along with the coup attempt, and if the military command had made different decisions. Trump was making every effort to facilitate the coup, which would surely have been applauded by a large majority of Republican voters and by the Republican political leadership, which, with a few exceptions, grovels at his feet in a shameful display of cowardice.

Implications for the future are all too clear. The Republican organization—it's hard to regard them any longer as an authentic political party—is now carefully laying the groundwork for success next time, whatever the electoral outcome may be. It's all completely in the open, not only not concealed but in fact heralded with pride by its leaders. And regularly reported, so that no one who is interested enough to pay attention to the American political scene can miss it. To mention just the most recent discussion I've seen, the Associated Press describes how the GOP is carrying out a "slow-motion insurrection" and has become "an anti-democratic force," something that has not happened before in American politics. A few weeks earlier, Barton Gellman outlined the plans in detail in the *Atlantic*.

There is no need to review the many well-known flaws of the formal democratic system: the radically undemocratic Senate, the enormous role of concentrated wealth and private power in determining electoral outcomes and legislation, the structural advantages provided to a traditionalist rural minority, and much else. But there are also broader issues.

What was progressive in the eighteenth century is by now so antiquated that if the US were to apply for membership in the European Union, it would probably be rejected as not satisfying democratic norms. That raises questions that merit more attention than they receive.

With all due respect for the founders, one question—raised by Thomas Jefferson in his own terms—is why we should revere the sentiments of a group of wealthy, white male eighteenth-century slaveowners, particularly now that the amendment system has succumbed to the deep flaws of the formal political system. No less curious are the legal doctrines of originalism/textualism that call on us to decipher their pronouncements with little regard to social and economic conditions as a decisive guide to judicial action. Looking at our political culture from a distance, there is a lot that would seem passing strange.

But even the tattered system that still survives is intolerable to GOP wreckers. Nothing is overlooked in their systematic assault on the fragile structure. Methods extend from "taking hold of the once-overlooked machinery of elections" at the ground level, to passing laws to bar the "wrong people" from voting, to devising a legal framework to establish the principle that Republican legislatures can "legally" determine choice of electors, whatever the irrelevant public may choose.

In the not-too-distant background are calls to "save our country," by force if necessary, where "our country" is a white supremacist, Christian nationalist, patriarchal society in which non-white folk can take part as long as they "know their place"; not at the table.

[White people's] fear of "losing our country" is [in part a response to] demographic tendencies that are eroding white majorities, resisting even the radical gerrymandering that is imposed to amplify the structural advantages of the scattered conservative rural vote. Another threat to "our country" is that white supremacy is increasingly rejected, particularly by younger people, as is devotion to religious authority, even church membership.

So, while the charges of right-wing propagandists are largely fantasy and delusion, they have enough of a basis in reality to enflame those who see their familiar world of dominance disappearing before their eyes. And with the social order crumbling under the neoliberal assault, these fears can easily be manipulated by demagogues and opportunists—while their masters in the executive suites and mansions relish the opportunity to carry forward the highway robbery that they have engaged in for forty years if future challenges can be beaten down, by state and private violence if necessary.

That's a world that may not be remote, though it won't last long with the supreme climate denialists in charge. When Hungary, the current darling of the right, descends toward fascism, it's bad enough. If the US does, long-term survival of human society is a dim prospect.

What does the January 6 Capitol attack tell us about the state of US democracy in the twenty-first century? And do you agree with the view that Trump was the product of bad political institutions?

It tells us that the limited political democracy that still exists is hanging by a delicate thread.

If political institutions—more generally, intertwined socioeconomic-political institutions—can yield a President Trump, they are infected with profound malignancies. A moment's reflection shows that the malignancies are so profound that they are driving organized human society to suicide, and not in the distant future, with Trump and his acolytes and apologists enthusiastically in the lead. By now it takes real literary talent to exaggerate.

What are these institutions? That's much too far-reaching an inquiry to undertake here, but there are some instructive highlights.

The so-called founders outlined clearly enough the kind of society they envisioned: "Those who own the country ought to govern it" and ensure that "the minority of the opulent are protected from the majority" (John Jay, James Madison, respectively). Their model was England, where the reigning institutions had been described accurately a few years earlier by Adam Smith in words that bear repetition: The "masters of mankind," the merchants and manufacturers of England, are the "principal architects" of government policy and ensure that their own interests are "most peculiarly attended to" no matter how "grievous" the impact on others, including the people of England but also, much more severely, the victims of "the savage injustice of the Europeans," notably the people of India, then the richest country in the world, which England was robbing and despoiling for the benefit of the masters. Under the protection of the state they control, the masters can pursue their "vile maxim": "All for ourselves and nothing for other people," the maxim of the feudal lords adopted by the masters of mankind who had been replacing them since the "glorious revolution" of the preceding century.

The masters of mankind have always understood that free-market capitalism would destroy them and the societies they owned. Accordingly, they have always called for a powerful state to protect them from the ravages of the market, leaving the less fortunate exposed. That has been dramatically plain in the course of the "bailout economy" of the past forty years of class war, masked under "free market" rhetoric.

These core features of the reigning state capitalist institutions have been exacerbated by the rot spreading from interwar Vienna, adopting the term "neoliberalism" in the international Walter Lippmann symposium in Paris in 1938, then in the Mont Pelerin Society. The ideas were implemented under almost perfect experimental conditions during Augusto Pinochet's murderous dictatorship in Chile, crashing the economy in half a dozen years, but no matter. By then, they had bigger game in sight: the global economy in the era of vigorous class war launched by Ronald Reagan and Margaret Thatcher and carried forward by Bill Clinton and other successors, establishing more firmly the vile maxim and dismantling such troublesome impediments as a limited welfare system and labor unions.

That's the kind of terrain in which a Trump can appear, though there are of course multiple factors of varied nature that interact.

It seems that political violence has become an accepted norm among many Americans today. First, what do you think are Trump's motives for continuing to spin the "Big Lie"? Second, do you share the view that neofascism is gaining ground and that election subversion remains a real threat?

Trump's motives are clear enough. We don't need a degree in advanced psychiatry to know that a sociopathic megalomaniac must always win; nothing else can be contemplated. Furthermore, he's a canny politician who understands that his worshippers will easily accept the "Big Lie."

Many have wondered at the willingness of two-thirds of Republicans to believe the ludicrous pretense that the election was stolen. Should we really be surprised? Have a look at the views of Republicans on other matters. For example, on whether humans were created as they are today: about half of Republicans. Or on whether Muslims are seeking to impose sharia law on the US: 60 percent of Republicans who trust Fox News. Or on a host of other premodern beliefs in which the US (mostly Republicans) stands virtually alone among comparable societies.

So why not a stolen election?

Election subversion is not merely a threat. It's happening in the "soft coup" that is underway right now. As is the drift toward a form of fascism. There is evidence that general attitudes of Trump voters on a range of issues are similar to those of European voters for far-right parties with fascist origins. And these sectors are now a driving force in the GOP.

There's also substantial evidence that this drift to the far right may be driven in part by blind loyalty to Trump. That seems to be the case on the most critical issue that humans have ever faced: environmental destruction. During Trump's years in office, Republican recognition of climate change as a "serious issue," already shockingly low, declined by 20 percent, even as nature has been issuing dramatic warnings, loud and clear, that we are racing toward disaster.

The phenomenon is deeply disturbing, and not without grim precedent. A century ago, Germany was at the peak of Western civilization, producing great contributions to the sciences and the arts. The Weimar Republic was regarded by political scientists as a model democracy. A few years later, Germans were worshipping *Der Führer* and accepting the vilest lies, and acting on them. That included some of the most respected figures, like Martin Heidegger; I recall very well my shock when I started to read his 1935 *Introduction to Metaphysics* when it appeared in English 60 years ago. And I'm old enough to remember hearing similar atrocious thoughts as a child in the '30s, close to home. Sinclair Lewis's 1935 classic on how fascism might be implanted in America by Christian nationalists (*It Can't Happen Here*) was not mere fantasy when it appeared, and it's no surprise that it has been returning to the best-seller lists in the Trump era.

State-level contests have moved to the very center of US politics, but the Democrats are failing to catch up with this new reality. What's going on? Why do state politics matter more these days, and why do the Democrats seem to have embarked on a suicide mission as far as political strategy is concerned?

The neglect of state politics by Democrats seems to have taken off under Barack Obama. That critical area of American politics was handed over to Republicans who, by that time, were already moving toward their current stance of rejecting democratic politics as an impediment to their task of "saving the country" (the version for the voting base) and maintaining power so as to serve the rich and the corporate sector (the understanding of the leadership).

So far, there have been, surprisingly enough, no breakthroughs in the House committee investigation of the January 6 attack. Do you think that the congressional select committee involved in this task will establish accountability for what happened on that infamous day? And if it does, what could be the political implications of such an outcome?

The Republican leadership has already neutralized the select committee by refusal to participate on acceptable terms, then by rejecting subpoenas—a sensible strategy to delay the proceedings by court proceedings until they can simply disband the committee, or even better, reshape it to pursuing their political enemies. That's the kind of tactic that Trump has used successfully throughout his career as a failed businessman, and it is second nature to corrupt politicians.

That aside, the events of January 6 have been investigated so fully, and even visually presented so vividly, that nothing much of substance is likely to be revealed. Republican elites who want to portray the insurrection as an innocent picnic in the park, with some staged violence by antifa to make decent law-abiding citizens look bad, will persist no matter what is revealed. And though there is more to learn about the background, it is not likely to have much effect on what seems now a reasonably plausible picture.

Suppose that the select committee were to come up with new and truly damning evidence about Trump's role or other high-level connivance in the coup attempt. The Rupert Murdoch–controlled mainstream media would have little difficulty in reshaping that as further proof that the "Deep State," along with the "Commie rats" and "sadistic pedophiles" who supposedly run the Democratic Party, have conspired to vilify the "Great Man." His adoring worshippers would probably be emboldened by this additional proof of the iniquity of the evil forces conniving at the "Great Replacement." Or whatever fabrication is contrived by those capable of converting critical race theory into an instrument for destroying the "embattled white race," among other propaganda triumphs.

My guess is that the committee's work will end up being a gift to the protofascist forces that are chipping away at what remains of formal democracy, much as the impeachment proceedings turned out to be.

It's worth proceeding for the sake of history—assuming that there will be any history that will even care if the plan to establish lasting Republican rule succeeds.

No exaggeration.

US APPROACH TO UKRAINE AND RUSSIA HAS "LEFT THE DOMAIN OF RATIONAL DISCOURSE"

February 4, 2022

C. J. Polychroniou: *Tensions continue to escalate between Russia and Ukraine, and there is little room for optimism since the US offer for de-escalation fails to meet any of Russia's security demands. As such, wouldn't it be more accurate to say that the Russia-Ukraine border crisis stems in reality from the US's intransigent position over Ukrainian membership in NATO? In the same context, is it hard to imagine what might have been Washington's response to the hypothetical event that Mexico wanted to join a Moscow-driven military alliance?*

Noam Chomsky: We hardly need to linger on the latter question. No country would dare to make such a move in what former president Franklin Delano Roosevelt's secretary of war Henry Stimson called "our little region over here," when he was condemning all spheres of influence (except for our own—which in reality, is hardly limited to the Western Hemisphere). Secretary of State Antony Blinken is no less adamant today in condemning Russia's claim to a "sphere of influence," a concept we firmly reject (with the same reservation).

There was, of course, one famous case when a country in our little region came close to a military alliance with Russia, the 1962 missile crisis. The circumstances, however, were quite unlike Ukraine. President John F. Kennedy was escalating his terrorist war against

Cuba to a threat of invasion; Ukraine, in sharp contrast, faces threats as a result of its potentially joining a hostile military alliance. Soviet leader Nikita Khrushchev's reckless decision to provide Cuba with missiles was also an effort to slightly rectify the enormous US preponderance of military force after JFK had responded to Khrushchev's offer of mutual reduction of offensive weapons with the largest military buildup in peacetime history, though the US was already far ahead. We know what that led to.

The tensions over Ukraine are extremely severe, with Russia's concentration of military forces at Ukraine's borders. The Russian position has been quite explicit for some time. It was stated clearly by Foreign Minister Sergey Lavrov at his press conference at the United Nations: "The main issue is our clear position on the inadmissibility of further expansion of NATO to the East and the deployment of strike weapons that could threaten the territory of the Russian Federation." Much the same was reiterated shortly after by Putin, as he had often said before.

There is a simple way to deal with deployment of weapons: don't deploy them. There is no justification for doing so. The US may claim that they are defensive, but Russia surely doesn't see it that way, and with reason.

The question of further expansion is more complex. The issue goes back over thirty years, to when the Union of Soviet Socialist Republics was collapsing. There were extensive negotiations among Russia, the US, and Germany. (The core issue was German unification.) Two visions were presented. Soviet leader Mikhail Gorbachev proposed a Eurasian security system from Lisbon to Vladivostok with no military blocs. The US rejected it: NATO stays, Russia's Warsaw Pact disappears.

For obvious reasons, German reunification within a hostile military alliance is no small matter for Russia. Nevertheless, Gorbachev agreed to it, with a quid pro quo: No expansion to the East. President George H. W. Bush and Secretary of State James Baker agreed. In their words to Gorbachev: "Not only for the Soviet Union but for other European countries as well, it is important to have guarantees that if the United States keeps its presence in Germany within the framework of NATO, not an inch of NATO's present military jurisdiction will spread in an eastern direction."

"East" meant East Germany. No one had a thought about anything beyond, at least in public. That's agreed on all sides. German leaders were even more explicit about it. They were overjoyed just to have Russian agreement to unification, and the last thing they wanted was new problems.

There is extensive scholarship on the matter—Mary Sarotte, Joshua Shifrinson, and others—debating exactly who said what, what they meant, what's its status, and so on. It is interesting and illuminating work, but what it comes down to, when the dust settles, is what I quoted from the declassified record.

President H. W. Bush pretty much lived up to these commitments. So did President Bill Clinton at first, until 1999, the fiftieth anniversary of NATO; with an eye on the Polish vote in the upcoming election, some have speculated. He admitted Poland, Hungary, and the Czech Republic to NATO. President George W. Bush—the lovable, goofy grandpa who was celebrated in the press on the twentieth anniversary of his invasion of Afghanistan—let down all the bars. He brought in the Baltic states and others. In 2008, he invited Ukraine to join NATO, poking the bear in the eye. Ukraine is Russia's geostrategic heartland, apart from intimate historic relations and a large Russia-oriented population. Germany and France vetoed Bush's reckless invitation, but it's still on the table. No Russian leader would accept that, surely not Gorbachev, as he made clear.

As in the case of deployment of offensive weapons on the Russian border, there is a straightforward answer. Ukraine can have the same status as Austria and two Nordic countries throughout the whole Cold War: neutral, but tightly linked to the West and quite secure, part of the European Union to the extent they chose to be.

The US adamantly rejects this outcome, loftily proclaiming its passionate dedication to the sovereignty of nations, which cannot be infringed: Ukraine's right to join NATO must be honored. This principled stand may be lauded in the US, but it surely is eliciting loud guffaws in much of the world, including the Kremlin. The world is hardly unaware of our inspiring dedication to sovereignty, notably in the three cases that particularly enraged Russia: Iraq, Libya, and Kosovo-Serbia.

Iraq need not be discussed: US aggression enraged almost everyone. The NATO assaults on Libya and Serbia, both a slap in Russia's face during its sharp decline in the '90s, is clothed in righteous humanitarian terms in US propaganda. It all quickly dissolves under scrutiny, as amply documented elsewhere. And the richer record of US reverence for the sovereignty of nations needs no review.

It is sometimes claimed that NATO membership increases security for Poland and others. A much stronger case can be made that NATO membership threatens their security by heightening tensions. Historian Richard Sakwa, a specialist on East Europe, observed that "NATO's existence became justified by the need to manage threats provoked by its enlargement"—a plausible judgment.

There is much more to say about Ukraine and how to deal with the very dangerous and mounting crisis there, but perhaps this is enough to suggest that there is no need to inflame the situation and to move on to what might well turn out to be a catastrophic war.

There is, in fact, a surreal quality to the US rejection of Austrian-style neutrality for Ukraine. US policymakers know perfectly well that admission of Ukraine to NATO is not an option for the foreseeable future. We can, of course, put aside the ridiculous posturing about the sanctity of sovereignty. So, for the sake of a principle in which they do not believe for a moment, and in pursuit of an objective that they know is out of reach, the US is risking what may turn into a shocking catastrophe. On the surface, it seems incomprehensible, but there are plausible imperial calculations.

We might ask why Putin has taken such a belligerent stance on the ground. There is a cottage industry seeking to solve this mystery: Is he a madman? Is he planning to force Europe to become a Russian satellite? What is he up to?

One way to find out is to listen to what he says: for years, Putin has tried to induce the US to pay some attention to the requests that he and Foreign Minister Lavrov repeated, in vain. One possibility is that the show of force is a way to achieve this objective. That has been suggested by well-informed analysts. If so, it seems to have succeeded, at least in a limited way.

Germany and France have already vetoed earlier US efforts to offer membership to Ukraine. So why is the US so keen on NATO expansion eastward to the point of treating a Russian invasion of Ukraine as imminent, even when Ukrainian leaders themselves don't seem to think so? And since when did Ukraine come to represent a beacon of democracy?

It is indeed curious to watch what is unfolding. The US is vigorously fanning the flames while Ukraine is asking it to tone down the rhetoric. While there is much turmoil about why the demon Putin is acting as he is, US motives are rarely subject to scrutiny. The reason is familiar: by definition, US motives are noble, even if its efforts to implement them are perhaps misguided.

Nevertheless, the question might merit some thought, at least by "the wild men in the wings," to borrow former national security adviser McGeorge Bundy's phrase, referring to those incorrigible figures who dare to subject Washington to the standards applied elsewhere.

A possible answer is suggested by a famous slogan about the purpose of NATO: to keep Russia out, to keep Germany down, and to keep the US in. Russia is out, far out. Germany is down. What remains is the question of whether the US will be in Europe—more accurately, should be in charge. Not all have quietly accepted this principle of world affairs, among them: Charles de Gaulle, who advanced his concept of Europe from the Atlantic to the Urals; former German chancellor Willy Brandt's Ostpolitik; and French president Emmanuel Macron, with his current diplomatic initiatives that are causing much displeasure in Washington.

If the Ukraine crisis is resolved peacefully, it will be a European affair, breaking from the post–World War II "Atlanticist" conception that places the US firmly in the driver's seat. It might even be a precedent for further moves toward European independence, maybe even moving toward Gorbachev's vision. With China's Belt and Road Initiative encroaching from the East, much larger issues of global order arise.

As virtually always in the past when it comes to foreign affairs, we see a bipartisan frenzy over Ukraine. However, while Republicans in Congress are urging President Joe Biden to adopt a more aggressive stance toward Russia, the protofascist base is questioning the party line. Why, and what does the split among Republicans over Ukraine tell us about what is happening to the Republicans?

One cannot easily speak of today's Republican Party as if it were a genuine political party participating in a functioning democracy. More apt is the description of the organization as "a radical insurgency—ideologically extreme, scornful of facts and compromise, and dismissive of the legitimacy of its political opposition." This characterization by political analysts Thomas Mann and Norman Ornstein of the American Enterprise is from a decade ago, pre–Donald Trump. By now it's far out of date. In the acronym "GOP," what remains is "O."

I don't know whether the popular base that Trump has whipped up into a worshipful cult is questioning the aggressive stance of Republican leaders, or if they even care. Evidence is skimpy. Leading right-wing figures closely associated with the GOP are moving well to the right of European opinion, and of the stance of those who hope to retain some semblance of democracy in the US. They are going even beyond Trump in their enthusiastic support for Hungarian president Viktor Orbán's "illiberal democracy," extolling it for saving Western civilization, no less.

This effusive welcome for Orbán's dismantling of democracy might bring to mind the praise for Italian fascist leader Benito Mussolini for having "saved European civilization [so that] the merit that Fascism has thereby won for itself will live on eternally in history"; the thoughts of the revered founder of the neoliberal movement that has reigned for the past forty years, Ludwig von Mises, in his 1927 classic *Liberalism*.

Fox News commentator Tucker Carlson has been the most outspoken of the enthusiasts. Many Republican senators either go along with him or claim ignorance of what Orbán is doing, a remarkable confession of illiteracy at the peak of global power. The highly regarded senior senator Charles Grassley reports that he knows about Hungary only from Carlson's TV expositions, and approves. Such performances tell us a good deal about the radical insurgency. On Ukraine, breaking with the GOP leadership, Carlson asks why we should take any position on a quarrel between "foreign countries that don't care anything about the United States."

Whatever one's views on international affairs, it's clear that we've left the domain of rational discourse far behind and are moving into territory with an unattractive history, to put it mildly.

US PUSH TO "REIGN SUPREME" STOKES THE UKRAINE CONFLICT

February 16, 2022

C. J. Polychroniou: *The political culture in the United States seems to have a propensity toward alarmism when it comes to political developments that are not in tune with the economic interests, ideological mindset, and strategic interests of the powers-that-be. Indeed, from the anti-Spanish panic of the late 1890s to today's rage about Russia's security concerns over Ukraine, and China's growing role in world affairs and everything in between, the political establishment and the media of this country tend to respond with full-blown alarm to developments that are not in alignment with US interests, values, and goals. Can you comment about this peculiar state of affairs, with particular emphasis on what's happening today in connection with Ukraine and China?*

Noam Chomsky: Quite true. Sometimes it's hard to believe. One of the most significant and revealing examples is the rhetorical framework of the major internal planning document of the early Cold War years, NSC-68 of 1950, shortly after "the loss of China," which set off a frenzy in the US. The document set the stage for a huge expansion of the military budget. It's worth recalling today when strains of this madness are reverberating—not for the first time; it's perennial.

The policy recommendations of NSC-68 have been widely discussed in scholarship, though avoiding the hysterical rhetoric. It reads like a fairy tale: ultimate evil confronted by absolute purity and noble idealism. On one side is the "slave state" with its "fundamental design" and inherent "compulsion" to gain "absolute authority over the rest of the world," destroying all governments and the "structure of society" everywhere. Its ultimate evil contrasts with our sheer perfection. The "fundamental purpose" of the United States is to assure "the dignity and worth of the individual" everywhere. Its leaders are animated by "generous and constructive impulses, and the absence of covetousness in our international relations," which is particularly evident in the traditional domains of US influence, the Western Hemisphere, long the beneficiary of Washington's tender solicitude as its inhabitants can testify.

Anyone familiar with history and the actual balance of global power at the time would have reacted to this performance with utter bewilderment. Its State Department authors couldn't have believed what they were writing. Some later gave an indication of what they were up to. Secretary of State Dean Acheson explained in his memoirs that in order to ram through the huge planned military expansion, it was necessary to "bludgeon the mass mind of 'top government'" in ways that were "clearer than truth." The highly influential senator Arthur Vandenberg surely understood this as well when advising [in 1947] that the government must "scare the hell out of the American people" to rouse them from their pacifist backwardness.

There are many precedents, and the drums are beating right now with warnings about American complacency and naivete about the intentions of the "mad dog" Putin to destroy democracy everywhere and subdue the world to his will, now in alliance with the other "Great Satan," Xi Jinping.

The February 4 Putin-Xi summit, timed with the opening of the Olympic games, was recognized to be a major event in world affairs. Its review in a major article in the *New York Times* is headlined "A New Axis," the allusion unconcealed. The review reported the intentions of the reincarnation of the Axis powers: "The message that China and Russia have sent to other countries is clear," David Leonhardt writes. "They will not pressure other governments to respect human rights or hold elections." And to Washington's dismay, the Axis is attracting two countries from "the American camp," Egypt and Saudi Arabia, stellar examples of how the US respects human rights and elections in its camp—by providing a massive flow of weapons to these brutal dictatorships and directly participating in their crimes. The New Axis also maintains that "a powerful country should be able to impose its will within its declared sphere of influence. The country should even be able to topple a weaker nearby government without the world interfering"—an idea that the US has always abhorred, as the historical record reveals.

Twenty-five hundred years ago, the Delphi Oracle issued a maxim: "Know Thyself." Worth remembering, perhaps.

As in the case of NSC-68, there is method in the madness. China and Russia do pose real threats. The global hegemon does not take them lightly. There are some striking common features in how US opinion and policy are reacting to the threats. They merit some thought.

The Atlantic Council describes the formation of the New Axis as a "tectonic shift in global relations" with plans that are truly "head spinning": "The sides agreed to more closely link their economies through cooperation between China's Belt and Road Initiative and Putin's Eurasian Economic Union. They will work together to develop the Arctic. They'll deepen coordination in multilateral institutions and to battle climate change."

We should not underestimate the grand significance of the Ukraine crisis, adds Damon Wilson, president of the National Endowment for Democracy. "The stakes of today's crisis are not about Ukraine alone, but about the future of freedom," no less.

Strong measures have to be taken right away, says Senate Minority Leader Mitch McConnell: "President Biden should use every tool in his tool box and impose tough sanctions ahead of any invasion and not after it happens." There is no time to dilly-dally with Macron-style appeals to the raging bear to temper his violence.

Received doctrine is that we must confront the formidable threat of China and stand firm on Ukraine, while Europe wavers and Ukraine asks us to tone down the rhetoric and pursue diplomatic measures.

Luckily for the world, Washington is unflinching in its dedication to what is right and just, even if it is almost alone, as when it righteously invades Iraq and strangles Cuba in defiance of virtually uniform international protest, to take just two from a plethora of examples.

To be fair, adherence to the doctrine is not uniform. There's deviation, most forcefully on the far right: Tucker Carlson, probably the most influential TV voice. He's said we shouldn't be involved in defending Ukraine against Russia—because we should be devoting all our resources to confronting the far more awesome China threat. Have to get our priorities straight in combating the Axis.

Warnings about Russia's mobilization to invade Ukraine have been an annual media event since the crises of 2014, with regular reports of tens or hundreds of thousands of Russian troops preparing to attack. Today, however, the warnings are far more shrill, with a mixture of fear and ridicule for so-called Mad Vlad, whom the *New York Times*'s Thomas Friedman describes as a "one-man psycho-drama, with a giant inferiority complex toward America that leaves him always stalking the world with a chip on his shoulder so big it's amazing he can fit through any door," or from another perspective, the Russian leader seeking in vain for some response to his repeated requests for some attention to Russia's expressed concerns. An analysis by *MintPress* found that 90 percent of the opinion pieces in the three major national newspapers have adopted a hawkish militant stance, with a bare scattering of questioning—a familiar phenomenon, as in the days before the Iraq invasion and, in fact, routinely when the state has delivered the word.

As in the case of the Sino-Soviet conspiracy to gain "absolute authority over the rest of the world" in 1950, the word now is that the US must act decisively to counter the threat of the New Axis to the "rule-based global order" that is hailed by US commentators, an interesting concept to which I'll return briefly.

The "tectonic shift" is not a myth, and it does pose a threat to the US. It threatens US primacy in shaping world order. That's true of both of the crisis areas, on the borders of Russia and of China. In both cases, negotiated settlements are within reach: regional settlements.

If they are achieved, the US will only have an ancillary role, which it may not be willing to accept even at the cost of inflaming extremely hazardous confrontations.

In Ukraine, the basic outlines of a settlement are well known on all sides; we've discussed them before. To repeat, the optimal outcome for the security of Ukraine (and the world) is the kind of Austrian/Nordic neutrality that prevailed through the Cold War years, offering the opportunity to be part of Western Europe to whatever extent they chose, in every respect apart from providing the US with military bases, which would have been a threat to them as well as to Russia. For internal Ukrainian conflicts, Minsk II provides a general framework.

As many analysts observe, Ukraine is not going to join the North Atlantic Treaty Organization (NATO) in the foreseeable future. George W. Bush rashly issued an invitation to join, but it was immediately vetoed by France and Germany. Though it remains on the table under US pressure, it is not an option. All sides recognize this. The astute and knowledgeable Central Asia scholar Anatol Lieven comments that "the whole issue of Ukraine's NATO membership is in fact purely theoretical, so that, in some respects, this whole argument is an argument about nothing—on both sides, it must be said, Russian as well as the West."

His comment brings to mind [Argentinian writer Jorge Luis] Borges's description of the Falklands/Malvinas War: two bald men fighting over a comb.

Russia pleads security concerns. For the US, it is a matter of high principle: We cannot infringe on the sacred right of sovereignty of nations, hence the right to join NATO, which Washington knows is not going to happen.

On the Russian side, a formal pledge of nonalignment hardly increases Russian security, any more than Russian security was enhanced when Washington guaranteed to Gorbachev that "not an inch of NATO's present military jurisdiction will spread in an eastern direction," soon abrogated by Clinton, then more radically by W. Bush. Nothing would have changed if the promise had risen from a gentlemen's agreement to a signed document.

The US plea hardly rises to the level of comedy. The US has utter disdain for the principle it proudly proclaims, as recent history once again dramatically confirms.

For Washington, there is a deeper issue: a regional settlement would be a serious threat to the US global role. That concern has been simmering right through the Cold War years. Will Europe assume an independent role in world affairs, as it surely can, perhaps along Gaullist lines: Europe from the Atlantic to the Urals, revived in Gorbachev's 1989 advocacy of a "common European home," a "vast economic space from the Atlantic to the Urals"? Even more unthinkable would be Gorbachev's broader vision of a Eurasian security system from Lisbon to Vladivostok with no military blocs, shot down without discussion in the negotiations thirty years ago over a post–Cold War settlement.

The commitment to maintain the Atlanticist order in Europe, in which the US reigns supreme, has had policy implications that reach beyond Europe itself. One crucial example was Chile in 1973, when the US was working hard to overthrow the parliamentary government, finally succeeding with the installation of the murderous Pinochet dictatorship. A prime reason for destroying democracy in Chile was explained by its prime architect, Henry Kissinger. He warned that parliamentary social reforms in Chile might provide a model for similar efforts in Italy and Spain that might lead Europe on an independent path, away from subordination to US control and the US model of harsher capitalism. The domino theory, often derided, never abandoned, because it is an important instrument of statecraft. The issue arises again with regard to a regional settlement of the Ukraine conflict.

Much the same is true in the confrontation with China. As we've discussed earlier, there are serious issues concerning China's violation of international law in the neighboring seas—though as the one maritime country that refuses even to ratify the UN Law of the Sea, the US is hardly in a strong position to object. Nor does the US alleviate these problems by sending a naval armada through these waters or providing Australia with a fleet of nuclear submarines to enhance the already overwhelming military superiority of the US off the coasts of China. The issues can and should be addressed by the regional powers.

As in the case of Ukraine, however, there is a downside: The US will not be in charge.

Also as in the case of Ukraine, the US professes its commitment to high principle in taking the lead to confront the threat of China: its horror at China's human rights abuses, which are doubtless severe. Again, it is easy enough to assess the sincerity of this stand. One revealing index is US military aid. At the top, in a category by themselves, are Israel and Egypt. On the Israeli record on human rights, we can now refer to the detailed reports of Amnesty International and Human Rights Watch, reviewing the crimes of what they describe as the world's second apartheid state. Egypt is suffering under the harshest dictatorship of its tortured history. More generally, for many years, there has been a striking correlation between US military aid and torture, massacre, and other severe human rights abuses.

There is no more need to tarry on Washington's concern for human rights than on its dedication to the sacred principle of sovereignty. The fact that these absurdities can even be discussed illustrates how deeply the rhetorical flights of NSC-68 permeate the intellectual culture.

Hebrew University lecturer Guy Laron usefully reminds us of another facet of the Ukraine crisis: the long struggle between the US and Russia over control of Europe's energy, again in the headlines today. Even before Russia was a player, the US sought to shift Europe (and Japan) to an oil-based economy, where the US would have the hand on the spigot. Much of Marshall Plan aid was directed to this end. From George Kennan to Zbigniew Brzezinski commenting on the invasion of Iraq (which he opposed, but felt might confer advantages to the US with the anticipated control over major oil resources), planners have recognized that control over energy resources could provide "critical leverage" over allies. Later years saw many struggles in the Cold War framework Laron describes, now very prominent. Ukraine has had a large part in these confrontations.

Throughout, the shape of world order has of course been a driving concern of policymakers. For post–World War II Washington, there is only one acceptable form: under its leadership. And it must be a particular form of world order: the "rule-based international order," which has displaced an earlier commitment to the "UN-based international order" established under US lead after World War II. It's not hard to discern the reasons for the transition in policy and accompanying commentary. In the rule-based order, the US sets the rules.

The same was true in the UN-based order in the early years after World War II. US global dominance was so overwhelming that the UN served virtually as a tool of US foreign policy and a weapon against its enemies. Not surprisingly, the UN was highly regarded in US popular and intellectual culture, along with the UN-based international order, guided by Washington.

That turned out to be a passing phase. The UN began to fall out of favor in US elite opinion as it lurched out of control with the recovery of other industrial societies but particularly with decolonization, which brought discordant voices into the UN and also in independent structures such as the Non-Aligned Movement and many others—all very vocal and active, though effectively barred from the international information order dominated by the traditional imperial societies.

Within the UN there were calls for a "New International Economic Order" that would offer the Global South something better than a continuation of the large-scale robbery, violent intervention, and subversion that the colonized world had enjoyed during the long reign of Western imperialism. There were other threats, such as a call for a New International Information Order that would provide some opportunity for voices of the former colonies to enter the international information system, a near monopoly of the imperial powers.

The masters of the world undertook vigorous campaigns to beat back these efforts, a major, though largely ignored, chapter of modern history—though not completely; there is some fine work of exposure and analysis.

One effect of the Global South's disruptive efforts was to turn US practice and elite opinion against the UN, no longer a reliable agency of US power as it had been in the early Cold War years. Furthermore, the foundations of modern international law in the few UN treaties that the US ratified became completely unacceptable as the years passed, particularly the banning of "the threat or use of force" in international affairs, a practice in which the US is far in the lead. It is conventional to say that the US and Russia engaged in proxy wars during the Cold War years—omitting the fact that with rare exceptions, these were conflicts in which Russia provided some support to victims of US attack. All topics that should have far more prominence.

In this context, the "rule-based international order" became the favored pillar of world order, and there is much annoyance when China calls instead for the UN-based international order as it did at the rancorous March 2021 China-US summit in Alaska (putting aside the sincerity of these pronouncements).

It's intriguing to see how the conflict with China plays out in US policy and discourse in other domains. A front-page story in the *New York Times* is headlined, "House Passes Bill Adding Billions to Research to Compete with China; The vote sets up a fight with the Senate, which has different recommendations for how the United States should bolster its technology industry to take on China." The official name of the bill is "The America COMPETES Act of 2022"— meaning "compete" with China.

The passage of the bill was hailed in the left-liberal press: "The House gave President Joe Biden another reason to celebrate on Friday with the passage of a bill aimed at boosting competitiveness with China."

Could Congress support research and development because it would help American society, as this bill surely would? Apparently not; only because it would "take on China." Republicans reflexively opposed the bill as usual, in this case because it "concedes too much to China." Republicans also opposed what they called "far left" initiatives such as addressing climate change. The bill was derided by House Republican leader Kevin McCarthy as the "coral reefs bill." How does saving humanity from self-destruction help to compete with China?

A side comment: An amendment to the bill was introduced by Pramila Jayapal, chair of the Progressive Caucus, a call to release the near $10 billion the Afghan government held in New York banks, so as to help relieve the horrendous humanitarian crisis facing the population. It was voted down. Forty-four Democrats joined Republican brutality. It appears that the China-based Shanghai Cooperation Organization might be planning aid, more of the China threat.

There is no denying that China is a rising superpower confronting the US. Reporting a study of Harvard's Belfer Center for Science and International Affairs, Graham Allison argued further that the so-called Thucydides Trap is likely to lead to a US-China war.

That cannot happen. US-China war means simply: game over. There are critical global issues on which the US and China must cooperate. They will either work together, or collapse together, bringing the world down with them.

One of the most striking developments in the international arena today is that while the US is pulling back from the Mideast, and elsewhere, China is moving in but with a different strategic approach and overall agenda. Instead of bombs, missiles, and coercive diplomacy, China is expanding its influence with the use of "soft power." Indeed, US overseas expansion was always overwhelmingly dependent on the use of hard power, and, as a result, it would only leave black holes behind after its withdrawal. To what extent, as some might argue, is this the result of a young nation ignorant of history and with lack of experience in global affairs (although it would be hard to find any examples of benign imperialism)?

I don't think the US has forged new paths in Western imperial brutality. Simply consider its immediate predecessors in world control. British wealth and global power derived from piracy (such heroic figures as Sir Francis Drake), despoiling India by guile and violence, hideous slavery, the world's greatest narco-trafficking enterprise, and other such gracious acts. France was no different. Belgium broke records in hideous crimes. Today's China is hardly benign within its much more limited reach. Exceptions would be hard to find.

The two cases you mention have highly instructive features, brought out clearly, if unintentionally, by how they are depicted. Take an article in the *New York Times* about the growing China threat. The headline reads, "As the US Pulls Back from the Mideast, China Leans In; . . . expanding its ties to Middle Eastern states with vast infrastructure investments and cooperation on technology and security."

That's accurate; it's one example of what's happening all over the world. The US is withdrawing military forces that have battered the Mideast region for decades in traditional imperial style. The evil Chinese are exploiting the retreat by expanding China's influence with investment, loans, technology, development programs. What's called "soft power."

Not just in the Mideast. The most extensive Chinese project is the huge Belt and Road Initiative (BRI) that is taking shape within the framework of the Shanghai Cooperation Organization, which incorporates the Central Asia states, India, Pakistan, Russia, now Iran, reaching to Turkey, and with its eye on Central Europe. It may well include Afghanistan if it can survive its current catastrophe. Chinese aid and development might manage to shift the Afghan economy from heroin production for Europe, the core of the economy during the US occupation, to exploitation of its rich mineral resources.

The BRI has offshoots in the Middle East, including Israel. There are accompanying programs in Africa, and now even Latin America, over strenuous US objections. Recently, China announced that it's taking over the manufacturing facilities in São Paulo that Ford abandoned, and will initiate large-scale electric vehicles production, an area in which China is far ahead.

The US has no way to counter these efforts. Bombs, missiles, special forces raids in rural communities just don't work.

It's an old dilemma. Sixty years ago in Vietnam, US counterinsurgency efforts were stymied by a problem that was despairingly recognized by US intelligence and by province advisers: the Vietnamese resistance—the Viet Cong (VC), in US discourse—were fighting a political war, a domain in which the US was weak. The US was responding with a military war, the arena in which it is strong.

But that couldn't overcome the appeal of VC programs to the peasant population.

The only way the Kennedy administration could react to the VC political war was by US Air Force bombing of rural areas, authorizing napalm, large-scale crop and livestock destruction, and other programs to drive the peasants to virtual concentration camps where they could be "protected" from the guerrillas whom the US knew they were supporting. The consequences we know.

Earlier, the dilemma had been explained by Secretary of State John Foster Dulles, addressing the National Security Council about US problems with Brazil, where elites, he said, are "like children, with no capacity for self-government." Worse still, in his words, the US is "hopelessly far behind the Soviets in developing controls over the minds and emotions of unsophisticated peoples" of the Global South, even educated elites. Dulles lamented to the president about the Communist "ability to get control of mass movements, . . . something we have no capacity to duplicate. The poor people are the ones they appeal to and they have always wanted to plunder the rich."

Dulles left unsaid the obvious: the poor people somehow don't respond well to our appeal of the rich to plunder the poor, so with great reluctance we have to turn to the arena of violence, where we dominate.

That's not unlike the dilemma posed when China "leans in" to the Global South by "expanding its ties with vast infrastructure investments and cooperation on technology and security." That is one central element of the China threat that is eliciting such fears and anguish.

The US is reacting to this growing China threat in the arena where it is strong. The US of course has overwhelming military dominance worldwide, even right off the coast of China. But it's being enhanced. Last December, military analyst Michael Klare reports, President Biden signed the National Defense Authorization Act. It calls for "an unbroken chain of US-armed sentinel states—stretching from Japan and South Korea in the northern Pacific to Australia, the Philippines, Thailand, and Singapore in the south and India on China's eastern flank"—meant to encircle China.

Klare adds that "ominously enough Taiwan too is included in the chain of armed sentinel states." The word "ominously" is well chosen. China, of course, regards Taiwan as part of China. So does the US, formally. The official US one-China policy recognizes Taiwan as part of China, with a tacit agreement that no steps will be taken to force-fully change its status. Donald Trump and Secretary of State Mike Pompeo chipped away at this formula. It's now being driven to the brink. China has the choice of either succumbing or resisting. It is not going to succumb.

This is only one component of the program to defend the US from the China threat. A complementary element is to undermine China's economy by means too well known to review. In particular (in the US's eyes), China must be prevented from advancing in the technol-ogy of the future—actually extending its lead in some areas, such as electrification and renewable energy, the technologies that might save us from our race to destroy the environment that sustains life.

One aspect of these efforts to undermine China's progress is to pressure other countries to reject superior Chinese technology. China has found a way to get around these efforts. They are planning to establish technical schools in countries of the Global South to teach advanced technology—Chinese technology, which graduates will then use. Again, the kind of aggression that is hard to confront.

US influence is clearly declining across the international system, but one would not easily reach this conclusion by looking at the current US National Security Strategy, which is still designed around the principle of the "two-war" doctrine even without expressly saying so. In this context, could it be argued that the US empire is weakening in the twenty-first cen-tury, and that the end of the US empire might not be a peaceful event?

It has been widely predicted in foreign policy circles for many years that China is poised to surpass the US and to dominate world affairs, a du-bious prospect, in my opinion, unless the US continues on its current course of self-destruction, probably to be accelerated with the predict-ed congressional victory of the denialist party in November.

As we have discussed before, for some years the former Republican Party has been more accurately described as a "radical insurgency" that has abandoned normal parliamentary politics, to borrow the terms of political analysts Thomas Mann and Norman Ornstein of the American Enterprise Institute a decade ago—when Trump's takeover of the insurgency was not yet a nightmare.

The Trump administration established a two-war doctrine in all but name. A war between two nuclear powers can quickly get out of control, meaning the end.

A step toward utter irrationality was taken last December 27, perhaps in celebration of Christmas, when President Biden signed the National Defense Authorization Act, discussed earlier, enhancing the policy of "encirclement" of China, "containment" being out of date. That includes formation of the Quad: US-India-Japan-Australia, supplementing the AUKUS alliance (Australia, UK, US) and the Anglosphere's Five Eyes, all of them strategic military alliances confronting China. China has only a troubled hinterland. As discussed earlier, the radical military imbalance in favor of the US is being enhanced by other provocative acts, carrying great risk. Apparently, we cannot let down our guard with the Axis powers on the march once again.

It's all too easy to sketch a likely trajectory that is far from a pleasant prospect. But we should never forget the usual proviso. We do not have to be passive spectators, thereby contributing to potential disaster.

US MILITARY ESCALATION AGAINST RUSSIA WOULD HAVE NO VICTORS

March 1, 2022

C. J. Polychroniou: *Noam, Russia's invasion of Ukraine has taken most people by surprise, sending shockwaves throughout the world, although there were plenty of indications that Putin had become quite agitated by NATO's expansion eastward and Washington's refusal to take seriously his "red line" security demands regarding Ukraine. Why do you think he decided to launch an invasion at this point in time?*

Noam Chomsky: Before turning to the question, we should settle a few facts that are uncontestable. The most crucial one is that the Russian invasion of Ukraine is a major war crime, ranking alongside the US invasion of Iraq and the Hitler-Stalin invasion of Poland in September 1939, to take only two salient examples. It always makes sense to seek explanations, but there is no justification, no extenuation.

Turning now to the question, there are plenty of supremely confident outpourings about Putin's mind. The usual story is that he is caught up in paranoid fantasies, acting alone, surrounded by groveling courtiers of the kind familiar here in what's left of the Republican Party traipsing to Mar-a-Lago for the Leader's blessing.

The flood of invective might be accurate, but perhaps other possibilities might be considered. Perhaps Putin meant what he and his associates have been saying loud and clear for years. It might be, for example, that "since Putin's major demand is an assurance that NATO will take no further members, and specifically not Ukraine or Georgia, obviously there would have been no basis for the present crisis if there had been no expansion of the alliance following the end of the Cold War, or if the expansion had occurred in harmony with building a security structure in Europe that included Russia." The author of these words is former US ambassador to Russia Jack Matlock, one of the few serious Russia specialists in the US diplomatic corps, writing shortly before the invasion. He goes on to conclude that the crisis "can be easily resolved by the application of common sense. . . . By any common-sense standard it is in the interest of the United States to promote peace, not conflict. To try to detach Ukraine from Russian influence—the avowed aim of those who agitated for the 'color revolutions'—was a fool's errand, and a dangerous one. Have we so soon forgotten the lesson of the Cuban Missile Crisis?"

Matlock is hardly alone. Much the same conclusions about the underlying issues are reached in the memoirs of CIA head William Burns, another of the few authentic Russia specialists. [Diplomat] George Kennan's even stronger stand has belatedly been widely quoted, backed as well by former defense secretary William Perry, and outside the diplomatic ranks by the noted international relations scholar John Mearsheimer and numerous other figures who could hardly be more mainstream.

None of this is obscure. US internal documents, released by WikiLeaks, reveal that Bush II's reckless offer to Ukraine to join NATO at once elicited sharp warnings from Russia that the expanding military threat could not be tolerated. Understandably.

We might incidentally take note of the strange concept of "the left" that appears regularly in excoriation of "the left" for insufficient skepticism about the "Kremlin's line."

The fact is, to be honest, that we do not know why the decision was made, even whether it was made by Putin alone or by the Russian Security Council in which he plays the leading role. There are, however, some things we do know with fair confidence, including the record reviewed in some detail by those just cited, who have been in high places on the inside of the planning system. In brief, the crisis has been brewing for twenty-five years as the US contemptuously rejected Russian security concerns, in particular their clear red lines: Georgia and especially Ukraine.

There is good reason to believe that this tragedy could have been avoided, until the last minute. We've discussed it before, repeatedly. As to why Putin launched the criminal aggression right now, we can speculate as we like. But the immediate background is not obscure—evaded but not contested.

It's easy to understand why those suffering from the crime may regard it as an unacceptable indulgence to inquire into why it happened and whether it could have been avoided. Understandable, but mistaken. If we want to respond to the tragedy in ways that will help the victims, and avert still worse catastrophes that loom ahead, it is wise, and necessary, to learn as much as we can about what went wrong and how the course could have been corrected. Heroic gestures may be satisfying. They are not helpful.

As often before, I'm reminded of a lesson I learned long ago. In the late 1960s, I took part in a meeting in Europe with a few representatives of the National Liberation Front of South Vietnam ("Viet Cong," in US parlance). It was during the brief period of intense opposition to the horrendous US crimes in Indochina. Some young people were so infuriated that they felt that only a violent reaction would be an appropriate response to the unfolding monstrosities: breaking windows on Main Street, bombing an ROTC center. Anything less amounted to complicity in terrible crimes. The Vietnamese saw things very differently. They strongly opposed all such measures. They presented their model of an effective protest: a few women standing in silent prayer at the graves of US soldiers killed in Vietnam. They were not interested in what made American opponents of the war feel righteous and honorable. They wanted to survive.

It's a lesson I've often heard in one or another form from victims of hideous suffering in the Global South, the prime target of imperial violence. One we should take to heart, adapted to circumstances. Today that means an effort to understand why this tragedy occurred and what could have been done to avert it, and to apply these lessons to what comes next.

The question cuts deep. There is no time to review this critically important matter here, but repeatedly the reaction to real or imagined crisis has been to reach for the six-gun rather than the olive branch. It's almost a reflex, and the consequences have generally been awful—for the traditional victims. It's always worthwhile to try to understand, to think a step or two ahead about the likely consequences of action or inaction. Truisms of course, but worth reiterating, because they are so easily dismissed in times of justified passion.

The options that remain after the invasion are grim. The least bad is support for the diplomatic options that still exist, in the hope of reaching an outcome not too far from what was very likely achievable a few days ago: Austrian-style neutralization of Ukraine, some version of Minsk II federalism within. Much harder to reach now. And—necessarily—with an escape hatch for Putin, or outcomes will be still more dire for Ukraine and everyone else, perhaps almost unimaginably so.

Very remote from justice. But when has justice prevailed in international affairs? Is it necessary to review the appalling record once again?

Like it or not, the choices are now reduced to an ugly outcome that rewards rather than punishes Putin for the act of aggression—or the strong possibility of terminal war. It may feel satisfying to drive the bear into a corner from which it will lash out in desperation—as it can. Hardly wise.

Meanwhile, we should do anything we can to provide meaningful support for those valiantly defending their homeland against cruel aggressors, for those escaping the horrors, and for the thousands of courageous Russians publicly opposing the crime of their state at great personal risk, a lesson to all of us.

And we should also try to find ways to help a much broader class of victims: all life on Earth. This catastrophe took place at a moment where all of the great powers, indeed all of us, must be working together to control the great scourge of environmental destruction that is already exacting a grim toll, with much worse soon to come unless major efforts are undertaken quickly. To drive home the obvious, the IPCC just released the latest and by far most ominous of its regular assessments of how we are careening to catastrophe.

Meanwhile, the necessary actions are stalled, even driven into reverse, as badly needed resources are devoted to destruction and the world is now on a course to expand the use of fossil fuels, including the most dangerous and conveniently abundant of them, coal.

A more grotesque conjuncture could hardly be devised by a malevolent demon. It can't be ignored. Every moment counts.

The Russian invasion is in clear violation of Article 2(4) of the UN Charter, which prohibits the threat or use of force against the territorial integrity of another state. Yet Putin sought to offer legal justifications for the invasion during his speech on February 24, and Russia cites Kosovo, Iraq, Libya, and Syria as evidence that the United States and its allies violate international law repeatedly. Can you comment on Putin's legal justifications for the invasion of Ukraine and on the status of international law in the post–Cold War era?

There is nothing to say about Putin's attempt to offer legal justification for his aggression. Its merit is zero.

Of course, it is true that the US and its allies violate international law without a blink of an eye, but that provides no extenuation for Putin's crimes. Kosovo, Iraq, and Libya did, however, have direct implications for the conflict over Ukraine.

The Iraq invasion was a textbook example of the crimes for which Nazis were hanged at Nuremberg, pure unprovoked aggression. And a punch in Russia's face.

In the case of Kosovo, NATO aggression (meaning US aggression) was claimed to be "illegal but justified" (for example, by the International Commission on Kosovo chaired by Richard Goldstone) on grounds that the bombing was undertaken to terminate ongoing atrocities. That judgment required reversal of the chronology. The evidence is overwhelming that the flood of atrocities was the consequence of the invasion: predictable, predicted, anticipated.

Furthermore, diplomatic options were available, [but] as usual, ignored in favor of violence.

High US officials confirm that it was primarily the bombing of Russian ally Serbia—without even informing them in advance—that reversed Russian efforts to work together with the US somehow to construct a post–Cold War European security order, a reversal accelerated with the invasion of Iraq and the bombing of Libya after Russia agreed not to veto a UN Security Council Resolution that NATO at once violated.

Events have consequences; however, the facts may be concealed within the doctrinal system.

The status of international law did not change in the post–Cold War period, even in words, let alone actions. President Clinton made it clear that the US had no intention of abiding by it. The Clinton Doctrine declared that the US reserves the right to act "unilaterally when necessary," including "unilateral use of military power" to defend such vital interests as "ensuring uninhibited access to key markets, energy supplies and strategic resources." His successors as well, and anyone else who can violate the law with impunity.

That's not to say that international law is of no value. It has a range of applicability, and it is a useful standard in some respects.

The aim of the Russian invasion seems to be to take down the Zelenskyy government and install in its place a pro-Russian one. However, no matter what happens, Ukraine is facing a daunting future for its decision to become a pawn in Washington's geostrategic games. In that context, how likely is it that economic sanctions will cause Russia to change its stance toward Ukraine—or do the economic sanctions aim at something bigger, such as undermining Putin's control inside Russia and ties with countries such as Cuba, Venezuela, and possibly even China itself?

Ukraine may not have made the most judicious choices, but it had nothing like the options available to the imperial states. I suspect that the sanctions will drive Russia to even greater dependency on China. Barring a serious change, of course, Russia is a kleptocratic petrostate relying on a resource that must decline sharply or we are all finished. It's not clear whether its financial system can weather a sharp attack, through sanctions or other means. All the more reason to offer an escape hatch with a grimace.

Western governments, mainstream opposition parties, including the Labour Party in the UK, and corporate media alike have embarked on a chauvinistic anti-Russian campaign. The targets include not only Russia's oligarchs but musicians, conductors, and singers, and even football owners such as Roman Abramovich of Chelsea FC. Russia has even been banned from Eurovision in 2022 following the invasion. This is the same reaction that the corporate media and the international community in general exhibited toward the US following its invasion and subsequent destruction of Iraq, wasn't it?

Your wry comment is quite appropriate. And we can go on in ways that are all too familiar.

Do you think the invasion will initiate a new era of sustained contestation between Russia (and possibly in alliance with China) and the West?

It's hard to tell where the ashes will fall—and that might turn out not to be a metaphor. So far, China is playing it cool, and is likely to try to carry forward its extensive program of economic integration of much of the world within its expanding global system, a few weeks ago incorporating Argentina within the Belt and Road Initiative, while watching rivals destroy themselves.

As we've discussed before, contestation is a death warrant for the species, with no victors. We are at a crucial point in human history. It cannot be denied. It cannot be ignored.

A NO-FLY ZONE OVER UKRAINE COULD UNLEASH UNTOLD VIOLENCE

March 8, 2022

C. J. Polychroniou: *Noam, nearly two weeks into the Russian invasion of Ukraine, Russian forces continue to pummel cities and towns while more than 140 countries voted in favor of a UN nonbinding resolution condemning the invasion and calling for a withdrawal of Russian troops. In light of Russia's failure to comply with rules of international law, isn't there something to be said at the present juncture about the institutions and norms of the postwar international order? It's quite obvious that the Westphalian state-centric world order cannot regulate the geopolitical behavior of state actors with respect to issues of war/peace and even sustainability. Isn't it therefore a matter of survival that we develop a new global normative architecture?*

Noam Chomsky: If it really is literally a matter of survival, then we are lost, because it cannot be achieved in any relevant time frame. The most we can hope for now is strengthening what exists, which is very weak. And that will be hard enough.

The great powers constantly violate international law, as do smaller ones when they can get away with it, commonly under the umbrella of a great power protector, as when Israel illegally annexes the Syrian Golan Heights and Greater Jerusalem—tolerated by Washington, authorized by Donald Trump, who also authorized Morocco's illegal annexation of Western Sahara.

Under international law, it is the responsibility of the UN Security Council to keep the peace and, if deemed necessary, to authorize force. Superpower aggression doesn't reach the Security Council: US wars in Indochina, the US-UK invasion of Iraq, or Putin's invasion of Ukraine, to take three textbook examples of the "supreme international crime" for which Nazis were hanged at Nuremberg. More precisely, the US is untouchable. Russian crimes at least receive some attention.

The Security Council may consider other atrocities, such as the French-British-Israeli invasion of Egypt and the Russian invasion of Hungary in 1956. But the veto blocks further action. The former was reversed by orders of a superpower (the US), which opposed the timing and manner of the aggression. The latter crime, by a superpower, could only be protested.

Superpower contempt for the international legal framework is so common as to pass almost unnoticed. In 1986, the International Court of Justice condemned Washington for its terrorist war (in legalistic jargon, "unlawful use of force") against Nicaragua, ordering it to desist and pay substantial reparations. The US dismissed the judgment with contempt (with the support of the liberal press) and escalated the attack. The UN Security Council did try to react with a resolution calling on all nations to observe international law, mentioning no one, but everyone understood the intention. The US vetoed it, proclaiming loud and clear that it is immune to international law. It has disappeared from history.

It is rarely recognized that contempt for international law also entails contempt for the US Constitution, which we are supposed to treat with the reverence accorded to the Bible. Article VI of the Constitution establishes the UN Charter as "the supreme law of the land," binding on elected officials, including, for example, every president who resorts to the threat of force ("all options are open")—banned by the charter. There are learned articles in the legal literature arguing that the words don't mean what they say. They do.

It's all too easy to continue. One outcome, which we have discussed, is that in US discourse, including scholarship, it is now de rigueur to reject the UN-based international order in favor of a "rule-based international order," with the tacit understanding that the US effectively sets the rules.

Even if international law (and the US Constitution) were to be obeyed, its reach would be limited. It would not reach as far as Russia's horrendous Chechnya wars, leveling the capital city of Grozny, perhaps a hideous forecast for Kyiv unless a peace settlement is reached; or in the same years, Turkey's war against Kurds, killing tens of thousands, destroying thousands of towns and villages, driving hundreds of thousands to miserable slums in Istanbul, all strongly supported by the Clinton administration, which escalated its huge flow of arms as the crimes increased. International law does not bar the US specialty of murderous sanctions to punish "successful defiance," or stealing the funds of Afghans while they face mass starvation. Nor does it bar torturing a million children in Gaza or a million Uighurs sent to "reeducation camps." And all too much more.

How can this be changed? Not much is likely to be achieved by establishing a new "parchment barrier," to borrow James Madison's phrase, referring to mere words on paper. A more adequate framework of international order may be useful for educational and organizing purposes—as indeed international law is. But it is not enough to protect the victims. That can only be achieved by compelling the powerful to cease their crimes—or in the longer run, undermining their power altogether. That's what many thousands of courageous Russians are doing right now in their remarkable efforts to impede Putin's war machine. It is what Americans have done in protesting the many crimes of their state, facing much less serious repression, with good effect even if insufficient.

Steps can be taken to construct a less dangerous and more humane world order. For all its flaws, the European Union is a step forward beyond what existed before. The same is true of the African Union, however limited it remains. And in the Western hemisphere, the same is true for such initiatives as UNASUR [the Union of South American Nations] and CELAC [the Community of Latin American and Caribbean States], the latter seeking Latin American–Caribbean integration separate from the US-dominated Organization of American States.

The questions arise constantly in one or another form. Up to virtually the day of the Russian invasion of Ukraine, the crime very possibly could have been averted by pursuing options that were well understood: Austrian-style neutrality for Ukraine, some version of Minsk II federalism reflecting the actual commitments of Ukrainians on the ground. There was little pressure to induce Washington to pursue peace. Nor did Americans join in the worldwide ridicule of the odes to sovereignty on the part of the superpower that is in a class by itself in its brutal disdain for the notion.

The options still remain, though narrowed after the criminal invasion.

Putin demonstrated the same reflexive resort to violence although peaceful options were available. It's true that the US continued to dismiss what even high US officials and top-ranking diplomats have long understood to be legitimate Russian security concerns, but options other than criminal violence remained open. Organization for Security and Co-operation in Europe observers had been reporting sharply increased violence in the Donbas region, which many—not just Russia—charge was largely at Ukrainian initiative. Putin could have sought to establish that charge, if it is correct, and to bring it to international attention. That would have strengthened his position.

More significantly, Putin could have pursued the opportunities, which were real, to appeal to Germany and France to carry forward the prospects for a "common European home" along the lines proposed by de Gaulle and Gorbachev, a European system with no military alliances from the Atlantic to the Urals, even beyond, replacing the Atlanticist NATO-based system of subordination to Washington. That has been the core background issue for a long time, heightened during the current crisis. A "common European home" offers many advantages to Europe. Intelligent diplomacy might have advanced the prospects.

Instead of pursuing diplomatic options, Putin reached for the revolver, an all-too-common reflex of power. The result is devastating for Ukraine, with the worst probably still to come. The outcome is also a very welcome gift to Washington, as Putin has succeeded in establishing the Atlanticist system even more solidly than before. The gift is so welcome that some sober and well-informed analysts have speculated that it was Washington's goal all along.

We should be thinking hard about these matters. One useful exercise is to compare the rare appearance of "jaw-jaw" with the deluge on "war-war," to borrow Churchill's rhetoric.

Perhaps peacemakers are indeed the blessed. If so, the good Lord doesn't have to put in overtime hours.

Speaking of the need for a new global architecture and diplomatic practice to adopt to the present-day global dynamic, Putin repeated, in a recent telephone conversation he had with French president Emmanuel Macron, the list of Russia's grievances against the West, and hinted at a way out of the crisis. Yet, there was, again, rejection of Putin's demands and, even more inexplicably, complete suppression of this ray of light offered by Putin. Do you wish to comment on this matter?

Regrettably, it is not inexplicable. Rather, it is entirely normal and predictable.

Buried in the press report of the Putin-Macron conversation, with the routine inflammatory headline about the goals of Putin, was a brief report of what Putin actually said: "In its own readout of the call, the Kremlin said that Mr. Putin had told his French counterpart that his main goal was 'the demilitarization and neutral status of Ukraine.' Those goals, the Kremlin said, 'will be achieved no matter what.'"

In a sane world, this comment would be headlined, and commentators would be calling on Washington to seize what may be an opportunity to end the invasion before a major catastrophe that will devastate Ukraine and may even lead to terminal war if Putin is not offered an escape hatch from the disaster he has created. Instead, we're hearing the usual "war-war" pronouncements, pretty much across the board, beginning with the renowned foreign policy analyst Thomas Friedman. Today the *New York Times* tough guy counsels, "Vladimir, you haven't felt the half of it yet."

Friedman's essay is a celebration of the "cancellation of Mother Russia." It may be usefully compared to his reaction to comparable or worse atrocities for which he shares responsibility. He is not alone.

That's how things are in a very free but deeply conformist intellectual culture.

A rational response to Putin's reiteration of his "main goal" would be to take him up on it and to offer what has long been understood to be the basic framework for peaceful resolution: to repeat, "Austrian-style neutrality for Ukraine, some version of Minsk II federalism reflecting the actual commitments of Ukrainians on the ground." Rationality would also entail doing this without the pathetic posturing about sovereign rights for which we have utter contempt—and which are not infringed any more than Mexico's sovereignty is infringed by the fact that it cannot join a Chinese-based military alliance and host joint Mexico-China military maneuvers and Chinese offensive weapons aimed at the US.

All of this is feasible, but it assumes something remote, a rational world, and furthermore, a world in which Washington is not gloating about the marvelous gift that Putin has just presented to it: a fully subordinate Europe, with no nonsense about escaping the control of the Master.

The message for us is the same as always, and as always simple and crystal clear. We must bend every effort to create a survivable world.

Ukrainian president Volodymyr Zelenskyy condemned NATO's decision not to close the sky over Ukraine. An understandable reaction given the catastrophe inflicted on his homeland by Russian armed forces, but wouldn't a declaration of a no-fly zone be a step closer to World War III?

As you say, Zelenskyy's plea is understandable. Responding to it would very likely lead to the obliteration of Ukraine and well beyond. The fact that it is even discussed in the US is astonishing. The idea is madness. A no-fly zone means that the US Air Force would not only be attacking Russian planes but would also be bombing Russian ground installations that provide antiaircraft support for Russian forces, with whatever "collateral damage" ensues. Is it really difficult to comprehend what follows?

As things stand, China may be the only great power out there with the ability to stop the war in Ukraine. In fact, Washington itself seems to be eager to get the Chinese involved, as Xi Jinping could be the only leader to force Putin to reconsider his actions in Ukraine. Do you see China playing the role of a peace mediator between Russia and Ukraine, and perhaps even emerge soon as a global peace mediator?

China could try to assume this role, but it doesn't seem likely. Chinese analysts can see as easily as we can that there had always been a way to avert catastrophe, along lines that we've discussed repeatedly in earlier interviews, briefly reiterated here. They can also see that while the options are diminished, it would still be possible to satisfy Putin's "main goal" in ways that would be beneficial to all, infringing on no basic rights. And they can see that the US government is not interested, nor the commentariat. They may see little inducement to plunge in.

It's not clear that they would even want to. They're doing well enough by keeping out of the conflict. They are continuing to integrate much of the world within the China-based investment and development system, with Turkey—a NATO member—very possibly next in line.

China also knows that the Global South has little taste for "canceling Mother Russia" but would prefer to maintain relations. The South may well share the horror at the cruelty of the invasion, but their experiences are not those of Europe and the US. They are, after all, the traditional targets of European-US brutality, alongside of which the suffering of Ukraine hardly stands out. The experiences and memories are shared by China from its "century of humiliation" and far more.

While the West may choose not to perceive this, China can certainly understand. I presume that they'll keep their distance and proceed on their current path.

Assuming that all diplomatic undertakings fail, is Russia really in a position to occupy an entire country the size of Ukraine? Couldn't Ukraine become Putin's Afghanistan? Indeed, back in December 2021, the head of the Russian Academy of Science's Center for Ukrainian Research, Viktor Mironenko, warned that Ukraine could become another Afghanistan. What are your thoughts on this matter? Hasn't Putin learned any lessons from Afghanistan?

If Russia does occupy Ukraine, its miserable experience in Afghanistan will resemble a picnic in the park.

We should bear in mind that the cases are quite different. The documentary record reveals that Russia invaded Afghanistan very reluctantly, several months after President Carter authorized the CIA to "provide . . . support to the Afghan insurgents" who were opposing a Russian-backed government—with the strong support if not initiative of National Security Adviser Zbigniew Brzezinski, as he later proudly declared. There was never any basis for the frenzied pronouncements about Russian plans to take over the Middle East and beyond. Again, George Kennan's quite isolated rejection of these claims was astute and accurate.

The US provided strong support for the Mujahideen who were resisting the Russian invasion, not in order to help liberate Afghanistan but rather to "kill Soviet Soldiers," as explained by the CIA station chief in Islamabad who was running the operation.

For Russia, the cost was terrible, though of course, hardly a fraction of what Afghanistan suffered—continuing when the US-backed Islamic fundamentalists ravaged the country after the Russians withdrew.

One hesitates even to imagine what occupying Ukraine would bring to its people, if not to the world.

It can be averted. That is the crucial point.

PEACE TALKS IN UKRAINE "WILL GET NOWHERE" IF US KEEPS REFUSING TO JOIN

March 14, 2022

C. J. Polychroniou: *Noam, while a fourth round of negotiations was scheduled to take place today between Russian and Ukrainian representatives, it is now postponed until tomorrow, and it still seems unlikely that peace will be reached in Ukraine anytime soon. Ukrainians don't appear likely to surrender, and Putin seems determined to continue his invasion. In that context, what do you think of Ukrainian president Volodymyr Zelenskyy's response to Vladimir Putin's four core demands, which were (a) cease military action; (b) acknowledge Crimea as Russian territory; (c) amend the Ukrainian constitution to enshrine neutrality; and (d) recognize the separatist republics in eastern Ukraine?*

Noam Chomsky: Before responding, I would like to stress the crucial issue that must be in the forefront of all discussions of this terrible tragedy: We must find a way to bring this war to an end before it escalates, possibly to utter devastation of Ukraine and unimaginable catastrophe beyond. The only way is a negotiated settlement. Like it or not, this must provide some kind of escape hatch for Putin, or the worst will happen. Not victory, but an escape hatch. These concerns must be uppermost in our minds.

I don't think that Zelenskyy should have simply accepted Putin's demands. I think his public response on March 7 was judicious and appropriate.

In these remarks, Zelenskyy recognized that joining NATO is not an option for Ukraine. He also insisted, rightly, that the opinions of people in the Donbas region, now occupied by Russia, should be a critical factor in determining some form of settlement. He is, in short, reiterating what would very likely have been a path for preventing this tragedy—though we cannot know, because the US refused to try.

As has been understood for a long time, decades in fact, for Ukraine to join NATO would be rather like Mexico joining a China-run military alliance, hosting joint maneuvers with the Chinese army and maintaining weapons aimed at Washington. To insist on Mexico's sovereign right to do so would surpass idiocy (and, fortunately, no one brings this up). Washington's insistence on Ukraine's sovereign right to join NATO is even worse, since it sets up an insurmountable barrier to a peaceful resolution of a crisis that is already a shocking crime and will soon become much worse unless resolved—by the negotiations that Washington refuses to join.

That's quite apart from the comical spectacle of the posturing about sovereignty by the world's leader in brazen contempt for the doctrine, ridiculed all over the Global South though the US and the West in general maintain their impressive discipline and take the posturing seriously, or at least pretend to do so.

Zelenskyy's proposals considerably narrow the gap with Putin's demands and provide an opportunity to carry forward the diplomatic initiatives that have been undertaken by France and Germany, with limited Chinese support. Negotiations might succeed or might fail. The only way to find out is to try. Of course, negotiations will get nowhere if the US persists in its adamant refusal to join, backed by the virtually united commissariat, and if the press continues to insist that the public remain in the dark by refusing even to report Zelenskyy's proposals.

In fairness, I should add that on March 13, the *New York Times* did publish a call for diplomacy that would carry forward the "virtual summit" of France-Germany-China, while offering Putin an "offramp," distasteful as that is. The article was written by Wang Hui-yao, president of a Beijing nongovernmental think tank.

It also seems to me that, in some quarters, peace in Ukraine is hardly on top of the agenda. For example, there are plenty of voices both in the US and in UK urging Ukraine to keep on fighting (although Western governments have ruled out sending troops to defend Ukraine), probably in the hopes that the continuation of the war, in conjunction with the economic sanctions, may lead to regime change in Moscow. Yet, isn't it the case that even if Putin actually falls from power, it would still be necessary to negotiate a peace treaty with whatever Russia government comes next, and that compromises would have to be made for the withdrawal of Russian forces from Ukraine?

We can only speculate about the reasons for US-UK total concentration on warlike and punitive measures, and refusal to join in the one sensible approach to ending the tragedy. Perhaps it is based on hope for regime change. If so, it is both criminal and foolish. Criminal because it perpetuates the vicious war and cuts off hope for ending the horrors, foolish because it is quite likely that if Putin is overthrown someone even worse will take over. That has been a consistent pattern in elimination of leadership in criminal organizations for many years, matters discussed very convincingly by Andrew Cockburn.

And at best, as you say, it would leave the problem of settlement where it stands.

Another possibility is that Washington is satisfied with how the conflict is proceeding. As we have discussed, in his criminal foolishness, Putin provided Washington with an enormous gift: firmly establishing the US-run Atlanticist framework for Europe and cutting off the option of an independent "European common home," a long-standing issue in world affairs as far back as the origin of the Cold War. I personally am reluctant to go as far as the highly knowledgeable sources we discussed earlier who conclude that Washington planned this outcome, but it's clear enough that it has eventuated. And, possibly, Washington planners see no reason to act to change what is underway.

It is worth noticing that most of the world is keeping apart from the awful spectacle underway in Europe. One telling illustration is sanctions. Political analyst John Whitbeck has produced a map of sanctions against Russia: the US and the rest of the Anglosphere, Europe and some of East Asia. None in the Global South, which is watching, bemused, as Europe reverts to its traditional pastime of mutual slaughter while relentlessly pursuing its vocation of destroying whatever else it chooses to within its reach: Yemen, Palestine, and far more. Voices in the Global South condemn Putin's brutal crime, but do not conceal the supreme hypocrisy of Western posturing about crimes that are a bare fraction of their own regular practices, right to the present.

Russia's invasion of Ukraine may very well change the global order, especially with the likely emergence of the militarization of the European Union. What does the change in Germany's Russia strategy—that is, its rearmament and the apparent end of Ostpolitik—mean for Europe and global diplomacy?

The major effect, I suspect, will be what I mentioned: more firm imposition of the US-run, NATO-based Atlanticist model and curtailing once again the repeated efforts to create a European system independent of the US, a "third force" in world affairs, as it was sometimes called. That has been a fundamental issue since the end of World War II. Putin has settled it for the time being by providing Washington with its fondest wish: a Europe so subservient that an Italian university tried to ban a series of lectures on Dostoyevsky, to take just one of many egregious examples of how Europeans are making fools of themselves.

Meanwhile, it seems likely that Russia will drift further into China's orbit, becoming even more of a declining kleptocratic raw materials producer than it is now. China is likely to persist in its programs of incorporating more and more of the world into the development-and-investment system based on the Belt and Road Initiative, the "maritime silk road" that passes through the UAE into the Middle East, and the Shanghai Cooperation Organization. The US seems intent on responding with its comparative advantage: force. Right now, that includes Biden's programs of "encirclement" of China by military bases and alliances, while perhaps even seeking to improve the US economy as long as it is framed as competing with China. Just what we are observing now.

There is a brief period in which course corrections remain possible. It may soon come to an end, as US democracy, such as it still is, continues on its self-destructive course.

Russia's invasion of Ukraine may also have dealt a severe blow to our hopes of tackling the climate crisis, at least in this decade. Do you have any comments to make on this rather bleak observation of mine?

Appropriate comments surpass my limited literary skills. The blow is not only severe, but it may also be terminal for organized human life on Earth, and for the innumerable other species that we are in the process of destroying with abandon.

In the midst of the Ukraine crisis, the IPCC released its 2022 report, by far the most dire warning it has yet produced. The report made it very clear that we must take firm measures now, with no delay, to cut back the use of fossil fuels and to move toward renewable energy. The warnings received brief notice, and then our strange species returned to devoting scarce resources to destruction and rapidly increasing its poisoning of the atmosphere, while blocking efforts for extricating itself from its suicidal path.

The fossil fuel industry can scarcely suppress its joy in the new opportunities the invasion has provided to accelerate its destruction of life on Earth. In the US, the denialist party, which has successfully blocked Biden's limited efforts to deal with the existential crisis, is likely to be back in power soon, so that it can resume the dedication of the Trump administration to destroy everything as quickly and effectively as possible.

These words might sound harsh. They are not harsh enough.

The game is not over. There still is time for radical course correction. The means are understood. If the will is there, it is possible to avert catastrophe and to move on to a much better world. The invasion of Ukraine has indeed been a severe blow to these prospects. Whether it constitutes a terminal blow or not is for us to decide.

LET'S FOCUS ON PREVENTING NUCLEAR WAR, RATHER THAN DEBATING "JUST WAR"

March 24, 2022

C. J. Polychroniou: *Noam, we are already a month into the war in Ukraine and peace talks have stalled. In fact, Putin is turning up the volume on violence as the West increases military aid to Ukraine. In a previous interview, you compared Russia's invasion of Ukraine to the Nazi invasion of Poland. Is Putin's strategy then straight out of Hitler's playbook? Does he want to occupy all of Ukraine? Is he trying to rebuild the Russian empire? Is this why peace negotiations have stalled?*

Noam Chomsky: There is very little credible information about the negotiations. Some of the information leaking out sounds mildly optimistic. There is good reason to suppose that if the US were to agree to participate seriously, with a constructive program, the possibilities for an end to the horror would be enhanced.

What a constructive program would be, at least in general outline, is no secret. The primary element is commitment to neutrality for Ukraine: no membership in a hostile military alliance, no hosting of weapons aimed at Russia (even those misleadingly called "defensive"), no military maneuvers with hostile military forces.

That would hardly be something new in world affairs, even where nothing formal exists. Everyone understands that Mexico cannot join a Chinese-run military alliance, emplace Chinese weapons aimed at the US, and carry out military maneuvers with the People's Liberation Army.

In brief, a constructive program would be about the opposite of the Joint Statement on the US-Ukraine Strategic Partnership signed by the White House on September 1, 2021. This document, which received little notice, forcefully declared that the door for Ukraine to join NATO (the North Atlantic Treaty Organization) is wide open. It also "finalized a Strategic Defense Framework that creates a foundation for the enhancement of US-Ukraine strategic defense and security cooperation" by providing Ukraine with advanced anti-tank and other weapons along with a "robust training and exercise program in keeping with Ukraine's status as a NATO Enhanced Opportunities Partner."

The statement was another purposeful exercise in poking the bear in the eye. It is another contribution to a process that NATO (meaning Washington) has been perfecting since Bill Clinton's 1998 violation of George H. W. Bush's firm pledge not to expand NATO to the East, a decision that elicited strong warnings from high-level diplomats from George Kennan, Henry Kissinger, Jack Matlock, (current CIA director) William Burns, and many others, and led Defense Secretary William Perry to come close to resigning in protest, joined by a long list of others with eyes open. That's of course in addition to the aggressive actions that struck directly at Russia's concerns (Serbia, Iraq, Libya, and lesser crimes), conducted in such a way as to maximize the humiliation.

It doesn't strain credulity to suspect that the joint statement was a factor in inducing Putin and the narrowing circle of "hard men" around him to decide to step up their annual mobilization of forces on the Ukrainian border in an effort to gain some attention to their security concerns, in this case on to direct criminal aggression—which, indeed, we can compare with the Nazi invasion of Poland (in combination with Stalin).

Neutralization of Ukraine is the main element of a constructive program, but there is more. There should be moves toward some kind of federal arrangement for Ukraine involving a degree of autonomy for the Donbas region, along the general lines of what remains of Minsk II. Again, that would be nothing new in world affairs. No two cases are identical, and no real example is anywhere near perfect, but federal structures exist in Switzerland and Belgium, among other cases—even the US to an extent. Serious diplomatic efforts might find a solution to this problem, or at least contain the flames.

And the flames are real. Estimates are that some fifteen thousand people have been killed in conflict in this region since 2014.

That leaves Crimea. On Crimea, the West has two choices. One is to recognize that the Russian annexation is simply a fact of life for now, irreversible without actions that would destroy Ukraine and possibly far more. The other is to disregard the highly likely consequences and to strike heroic gestures about how the US "will never recognize Russia's purported annexation of Crimea," as the joint statement proclaims, accompanied by many eloquent pronouncements by others who are willing to consign Ukraine to utter catastrophe while advertising their bravery.

Like it or not, those are the choices.

Does Putin want to "occupy all of Ukraine and rebuild the Russian empire"? His announced goals (mainly neutralization) are quite different, including his statement that it would be madness to try to reconstruct the old Soviet Union, but he might have had something like this in mind. If so, it's hard to imagine what he and his circle still do. For Russia to occupy Ukraine would make its experience in Afghanistan look like a picnic in the park. By now that's abundantly clear.

Putin does have the military capacity—and judging by Chechnya and other escapades, the moral capacity—to leave Ukraine in smoldering ruins. That would mean no occupation, no Russian empire, and no more Putin.

Our eyes are rightly focused on the mounting horrors of Putin's invasion of Ukraine. It would be a mistake, however, to forget that the joint statement is only one of the pleasures that the imperial mind is quietly conjuring up.

A few weeks ago, we discussed President Biden's National Defense Authorization Act, as little known as the joint statement. This brilliant document—again quoting Michael Klare—calls for "an unbroken chain of US-armed sentinel states—stretching from Japan and South Korea in the northern Pacific to Australia, the Philippines, Thailand, and Singapore in the south and India on China's eastern flank"— meant to encircle China, including Taiwan, "ominously enough."

We might ask how China feels about the fact that the US Indo-Pacific command is now reported to be planning to enhance the encirclement, doubling its spending in fiscal year 2022, in part to develop "a network of precision-strike missiles along the so-called first island chain."

For defense, of course, so the Chinese [government has] no reason for concern.

There is little doubt that Putin's aggression against Ukraine fails just war theory, and that NATO is also morally responsible for the crisis. But what about Ukraine arming civilians to fight against the invaders? Isn't this morally justified on the same grounds that resistance against the Nazis was morally justified?

Just war theory, regrettably, has about as much relevance to the real world as "humanitarian intervention," "responsibility to protect," or "defending democracy."

On the surface, it seems a virtual truism that a people in arms have the right to defend themselves against a brutal aggressor. But as always in this sad world, questions arise when we think about it a little.

Take the resistance against the Nazis. There could hardly have been a more noble cause.

One can certainly understand and sympathize with the motives of Herschel Grynszpan when he assassinated a German diplomat in 1938; or the British-trained partisans who assassinated the Nazi murderer Reinhard Heydrich in May 1942. And one can admire their courage and passion for justice, without qualification.

That's not the end, however. The first provided the Nazis with the pretext for the atrocities of *Kristallnacht* and impelled the Nazi program further toward its hideous outcomes. The second led to the shocking Lidice massacres.

Events have consequences. The innocent suffer, perhaps terribly. Such questions cannot be avoided by people with a moral bone in their bodies. The questions cannot fail to arise when we consider whether and how to arm those courageously resisting murderous aggression.

That's the least of it. In the present case, we also have to ask what risks we are willing to take of a nuclear war, which will not only spell the end of Ukraine but far beyond, to the truly unthinkable.

It is not encouraging that over a third of Americans favor "taking military action [in Ukraine] even if it risks a nuclear conflict with Russia," perhaps inspired by commentators and political leaders who should think twice before doing their Winston Churchill impersonations.

Perhaps ways can be found to provide needed arms to the defenders of Ukraine to repel the aggressors while avoiding dire consequences. But we should not delude ourselves into believing that it is a simple matter, to be settled by bold pronouncements.

Do you anticipate dramatic political developments inside Russia if the war lasts much longer or if Ukrainians resist even after formal battles have ended? After all, Russia's economy is already under siege and could end up with an economic collapse unparalleled in recent history.

I don't know enough about Russia even to hazard a guess. One person who does know enough at least to "speculate"—and only that, as he reminds us—is Anatol Lieven, whose insights have been a very useful guide all along. He regards "dramatic political developments" as highly unlikely because of the nature of the harsh kleptocracy that Putin has carefully constructed. Among the more optimistic guesses, "the most likely scenario," Lieven writes, "is a sort of semi-coup, most of which will never become apparent in public, by which Putin and his immediate associates will step down 'voluntarily' in return for guarantees of their personal immunity from arrest and their family's wealth. Who would succeed as president in these circumstances is a totally open question."

And not necessarily a pleasant question to consider.

RUSSIA'S WAR AGAINST UKRAINE HAS ACCELERATED THE DOOMSDAY CLOCK

March 30, 2022

C. J. *Polychroniou: Noam, the latest reports about the war in Ukraine indicate that Russia seems to be shifting its strategy, with an intent of partitioning the country "like North and South Korea," according to some Ukrainian officials. In the meantime, NATO decided to reinforce its eastern front, as if Russia has plans to invade Bulgaria, Romania, and Slovenia, while Washington not only continues to be mum about peace in Ukraine, but we heard Biden engage in some toxic masculinity talk against Putin in his recent visit to Poland, prompting, in turn, French president Emmanuel Macron to warn against the use of inflammatory language as he is actually trying to secure a ceasefire. In fact, even American veteran diplomat Richard Haass said that Biden's words made a dangerous situation even more dangerous. Posing this question in all sincerity, does the US ever think that conflicts can be resolved by any other means other than through intimidation and the use of continuous force?*

Noam Chomsky: There are several questions here, all important, all worth more discussion than I can try to give here. Will go through them pretty much in order.

On the current military situation, there are two radically different stories. The familiar one is provided by Ukraine's military intelligence head, General Kyrylo Budanov: Russia's attempt to overthrow the Ukrainian government has failed, so Russia is now retreating to the occupied south and east of the country, the Donbas region and the eastern Azov sea coast, planning a "Korean scenario."

The head of the Main Operational Directorate of the General Staff of the Armed Forces of the Russian Federation, Colonel General Sergey Rudskoy, tells a very different story (as of March 25): a rendition of George W. Bush's "Mission Accomplished" in Iraq, though without the dramatic trappings:

> The main goal of the "special military operation" was to defend the Donbass People's Republic from the genocidal assaults of Ukrainian Nazis over the past eight years. Since Ukraine rejected diplomacy, it was necessary to extend the operation to "demilitarization and denazification" of Ukraine, destroying military targets with great care to spare civilians. The main goals have been efficiently achieved exactly according to plan. What remains is the full "liberation of Donbass."

Two tales, same ending, which I presume is accurate.

The West, quite plausibly, adopts the former story. That is, it adopts the story that tells us that Russia is incapable of conquering cities a few miles from its border that are defended by what are limited military forces by world standards, supported by a citizen's army.

Or does the West adopt this story? Its actions indicate that it prefers the version of General Rudskoy: an incredibly powerful and efficient Russian military machine, having quickly achieved its objectives in Ukraine, is now poised to move on to invade Europe, perhaps overwhelming NATO just as efficiently. If so, it is necessary to reinforce NATO's eastern front to prevent the impending invasion by this monstrous force.

Another thought suggests itself: Could it be that Washington wishes to establish more firmly the great gift that Putin has bestowed on it by driving Europe into its grip, and is therefore intent on reinforcing an eastern front that it knows is under no threat of invasion?

So far, Washington has not strayed from the position of the joint statement that we discussed earlier. This crucially important policy statement extended Washington's welcome to Ukraine to join NATO and "finalized a Strategic Defense Framework that creates a foundation for the enhancement of US-Ukraine strategic defense and security cooperation" by providing Ukraine with advanced anti-tank and other weapons along with a "robust training and exercise program in keeping with Ukraine's status as a NATO Enhanced Opportunities Partner."

There is much learned discussion plumbing the deep recesses of Putin's twisted soul to discover why he decided to invade Ukraine. By moving on to criminal aggression, he carried a step forward the annual mobilizations on Ukraine's borders in an effort to elicit some attention to his unanswered calls to consider Russia's security concerns, which are recognized as significant by a host of top US diplomats, CIA directors, and numerous others who have warned Washington of the foolishness of ignoring these concerns.

Perhaps exploring Putin's soul is the right approach to understanding his decision in February 2022. There is, perhaps, another possibility. Perhaps he meant what he and all other Russian leaders have been saying since former President Boris Yeltsin, 25 years ago, about neutralization of Ukraine; and perhaps, even though the highly provocative joint statement has been silenced in the US, Putin might have paid attention to it and therefore decided to escalate the disregarded annual efforts to direct aggression.

A possibility, perhaps.

The press reports that "Ukraine is ready to declare neutrality, abandon its drive to join NATO and vow to not develop nuclear weapons if Russia withdraws troops and Kyiv receives security guarantee."

That raises a question: Will the US relent, and move to expedite efforts to save Ukraine further misery instead of interfering with these efforts by refusing to take part in negotiations and maintaining the position of the policy statement of last September?

The question brings us to Biden's ad-libbed call for Putin to be removed, offering Putin no escape. Biden's statement, recognized to be a virtual declaration of war that could have horrifying consequences, did cause considerable consternation worldwide, not least among his staff, who hastened to assure the world that his words didn't mean what they said. Judging by the stance of his close circle on national security issues, it's hard to be confident.

Biden has since explained that his comment was a spontaneous outburst of "moral outrage," revulsion at the crimes of the "butcher" who rules Russia. Are there some other current situations that might inspire moral outrage?

It's not hard to think of cases. One of the most terrifying is Afghanistan. Literally millions of people are facing starvation, a colossal tragedy. There is food in the markets, but lacking access to banks, people with a little money have to watch their children starve.

Why? A major reason is that Washington is refusing to release Afghanistan's funds, kept in New York banks in order to punish poor Afghans for daring to resist Washington's twenty-year war. The official pretexts are even more shameful: The US must withhold the funds from starving Afghans in case Americans want reparations for crimes of 9/11, for which Afghans bear no responsibility. Recall that the Taliban offered complete surrender, which would have meant turning over the al-Qaeda suspects. (They were only suspects at the time of the US invasion, in fact long after, as the FBI confirmed.) But the US firmly responded with the edict that "the United States is not inclined to negotiate surrenders." That was Defense Secretary Donald Rumsfeld, echoed by George W. Bush.

If there is any moral outrage about this current crime, it's hard to detect. It is far from the only case. Are there some lessons to be learned? Perhaps, but though they seem simple enough, maybe they merit a few words.

Moral outrage over Russian crimes in Ukraine is understandable and justified. The extreme selectivity in moral outrage is also understandable, but not justified. It is understandable because it is so common.

It is hard to think of a more elementary moral principle than the Golden Rule—in the Jewish tradition, the rule that "what is hateful to you, do not do to others."

There is no rule that is more elementary, or more consistently violated. That is also true for a corollary: Energy and attention should be focused on where we can do the most good. With regard to international affairs, that typically means focusing on the actions of one's own state, particularly in more or less democratic societies where citizens have some role in determining outcomes. We can deplore crimes in Myanmar [also known as Burma], but we cannot do much to alleviate the suffering and misery within Myanmar. We could do a lot to help the miserable victims who fled or were expelled, the Rohingya in Bangladesh. But we don't.

The observation generalizes. The principle is indeed elementary. To say that actual practice fails to conform to it would be a vast understatement.

It is not that we do not understand and honor the principle. We do, with true passion, when the principle is observed in the societies of official enemies: We greatly admire the Russians who are courageously defying the harsh Russian autocracy and protesting the Russian invasion. That keeps to a long tradition. We always greatly honored Soviet dissidents who condemned the crimes of their own state, and never cared at all about what they said about others, even when they applauded major US crimes. Same with Chinese and Iranian dissidents. It is only when the principle applies to ourselves that it can barely even be contemplated.

One dramatic illustration among many is the US invasion of Iraq. It can be criticized as a "strategic blunder" (according to Barack Obama) but not as what it was: unprovoked and murderous aggression, the "supreme international crime" according to the Nuremberg judgment.

Accordingly, the dramatic selectivity in moral outrage is understandable, and another outrage. In some weak form of extenuation, we can add that it is no US invention. Our predecessors as hegemonic imperial powers were no different, including Britain, arguably worse, though after centuries of disgraceful behavior there is now some beginning of reckoning.

Turning to the next question, does the US ever think that conflicts can be resolved by peaceful means? No doubt. There are examples, which deserve a closer look. We can learn a lot from them about international affairs, if we choose.

Right at this moment, we are all called upon to celebrate a remarkable example of US initiative to resolve conflict by peaceful means: the ongoing "Negev Summit" of Israel and four Arab dictatorships, which will "expand the potential for peace and conflict resolution across the region," according to Secretary of State Antony Blinken, Washington's representative at the historic meeting.

The summit brings together the most brutal and violent states within the US orbit, based on the Abraham Accords, which formalized the tacit relations between Israel, the United Arab Emirates (UAE), and Morocco, with Saudi Arabia present implicitly via its satellite, the Bahrain dictatorship. They are joined at the summit by Egypt, now suffering under the most vicious dictatorship in its ugly history, with some sixty thousand political prisoners and brutal repression. Egypt is the second-largest recipient of US military aid, after Israel. There should be no need to review the sordid record of the leading recipient, recently designated the apartheid state by Human Rights Watch and Amnesty International.

The UAE and Saudi Arabia share primary responsibility for what the UN describes as the world's worst humanitarian crisis: Yemen. The official death toll last year reached 370,000. The actual toll no one knows. The shattered country is facing mass starvation. Saudi Arabia has intensified its blockade of the sole port used for food and fuel imports. The UN is issuing extreme warnings, including the threat of imminent starvation of hundreds of thousands of children. The general warnings are echoed by US specialists, notably Bruce Riedel of the Brookings Institution, formerly the top CIA analyst on the Middle East for four presidents. He charges that the Saudi "offensive action" should be investigated as a war crime.

The Saudi and Emirati air forces cannot function without US planes, training, intelligence, spare parts. Britain is taking part in the crime, along with other Western powers, but the US is well in the lead.

The Moroccan dictatorship was also welcomed by the Trump peace initiative. In his last days in office, Donald Trump even formally recognized Morocco's annexation of Western Sahara in defiance of the UN Security Council and the International Court of Justice—

incidentally firming up Morocco's virtual monopoly of potassium, a vital and irreplaceable resource, now within US domains.

Authorizing of Morocco's criminal annexation should have come as no surprise. It followed Trump's recognition of Israel's annexation of the Syrian Golan Heights and of vastly expanded Greater Jerusalem, in both cases in violation of Security Council orders. Trump's support for violation of international law was undertaken in both cases in the splendid isolation that the US often enjoys, as in its torture of Cuba for sixty years.

These are just further illustrations of the commitment to the "rule of law" and the sanctity of sovereignty that Washington has demonstrated for seventy years in Iran, Guatemala, Brazil, Chile, Iraq, and on and on—the commitment that requires the US to extend the welcome mat to Ukraine to join NATO.

The summit that we are now celebrating is a direct outgrowth of the Abraham Accords. For implementing them, Jared Kushner has been nominated for the Nobel Peace Prize (by Harvard Law professor Alan Dershowitz).

The Abraham Accords and today's Negev Summit are by no means the first time that Washington has demonstrated its dedication to peaceful settlement of conflicts. After all, Henry Kissinger won the Nobel Peace Prize for his achievements in bringing peace to Vietnam, shortly after issuing one of the most extraordinary calls for genocide in the diplomatic record: "A massive bombing campaign in Cambodia. Anything that flies on anything that moves." The consequences were horrendous, but no matter.

Kissinger's prize brings to mind the reported proposal by an Israeli physicist that [founder of Israel's Likud party and former prime minister] Menachem Begin should be granted the physics prize. When asked why, he said, "Look, he's been granted the Peace Prize, so why not the Physics Prize?"

Sometimes the quip is unfair. Jimmy Carter surely deserved the Peace Prize that was awarded for his efforts after he left the presidency, though the award committee emphasized that while still in office, President Carter's "vital contribution to the Camp David Accords between Israel and Egypt [was] in itself a great enough achievement to qualify for the Nobel Peace Prize."

Carter's 1978 efforts were also no doubt undertaken with the best of intentions. It didn't quite turn out that way. Menachem Begin did agree to abandon Israel's project of settling the Egyptian Sinai but insisted that Palestinian rights should be excluded from the accords, and illegal settlement sharply increased under Ariel Sharon's direction, always with vital US aid and in violation of Security Council directives. And as Israeli strategic analysts quickly pointed out, removal of the Egyptian deterrent freed Israel to escalate its attacks on Lebanon, leading finally to the US-backed 1982 invasion that killed some twenty thousand Lebanese and Palestinians and destroyed much of Lebanon, with no credible pretext.

Ronald Reagan finally ordered Israel to end the assault when the bombing of the capital city of Beirut was causing international embarrassment to Washington. It of course complied but maintained its control of South Lebanon with constant atrocities against what it called "terrorist villagers" resisting the brutal occupation. It also established a vicious torture chamber in Khiam, which was kept as a memorial after Israel was forced finally to withdraw by Hezbollah guerrilla warfare. I was taken through it before it was destroyed by Israeli bombing to erase memory of the crime.

So, yes, there are some cases when the US, like other hegemonic imperial powers before it, has sought to resolve conflicts by peaceful means.

Back home, Republicans are backing up strong policies against Russia, although their "Great Leader" keeps changing his tune about Putin in order to stay in line with ongoing developments. The question here is this: Why is there still support among GOP members for Russia and Putin, especially on the far right of the political spectrum? What's motivating the far right in the US to break ranks with the Republican Party over Russia when the overwhelming majority of public opinion in the country is in support of Ukraine?

It's not just Russia and Ukraine. While Europe has condemned Prime Minister Viktor Orbán's "illiberal democracy" in Hungary, it has become the darling of much of the American right. *Fox News* and its prime broadcaster, Tucker Carlson, are in the lead, but other prominent "conservatives" are joining in with odes to the protofascist Christian nationalist regime that Orbán has imposed while shredding Hungarian freedom and democracy.

All of this reflects a conflict within the Republican Party—or to be more accurate, what remains of what was once a legitimate political party but is now ranked alongside of European parties with neofascist origins. Trump accelerated tendencies that trace back to Newt Gingrich's takeover of the party thirty years ago. And Trump is now being outflanked from the right, difficult as that was to imagine not long ago. Much of the leadership is drifting toward the Orbán model or beyond, bringing a worshipful mass base with them. I think the debate within the party over Russia and Ukraine should be considered against this background.

GOP lawmakers are intensifying efforts to ban books on race, as if slavery and racial oppression in the US are figments of one's imagination instead of historical facts. Are the pushes to ban books and suppress votes linked? Do these developments represent yet another indication that a civil war may be brewing in the US?

Book-banning is nothing new in the US and suppressing votes of the "wrong" people is as American as apple pie, to borrow the cliché. They are now returning with force as the Republican organization, soon to retake power it seems, moves toward a kind of protofascism. Some careful analysts predict civil war. At the very least, a serious internal crisis is taking shape. There has long been much talk about American decline. To the extent that it is real, the major factor is internal. If we look deeper, much of the internal social decay results from the brutal impact of the neoliberal programs of the past forty years, topics we've discussed before. It's bad enough when Hungary drifts toward Christian nationalist protofascism. When that happens in the most powerful state in world history, the implications are ominous.

Imposing harsh sanctions on countries that refuse to go along with Washington's commands is a long-established tactic on the part of the US. In fact, even scholars living in countries under sanctions are treated as undesirables. And the overall political culture in the US is not too keen at all on permitting dissident voices to be widely heard in the public arena. Do you wish to comment on these foundational features of the political culture in the United States?

This is too large a topic to take up here. And much too important for casual comment. But it's worth remembering that, once again, it is nothing new. We all recall when the august Senate changed French fries to "freedom fries" in furious reaction to France's impudent refusal to join in Washington's criminal assault on Iraq. We may see something similar soon if President Macron of France, one of the few reasonable voices in high Western circles, continues to call for moderation in words and actions and for exploring diplomatic options. The easy decline to scaremongering goes back much further, reaching comic depths when the US entered World War I and all things German instantly became anathema.

The plague you mention is not confined to US shores. To take one personal example, I recently heard from a colleague that an article of his was returned to him, unread, by a highly respected philosophy journal in England, with a notice that the article could not be considered because he is a citizen of a country under sanctions: Iran.

The sanctions are strongly opposed by Europe, but as usual, it submits to the Master, even to the extent of banning an article by an Iranian philosopher. Putin's great gift to Washington has been to intensify this subordination to power.

I can add many examples right here, some from my own personal experience, but it should not be overlooked that the malignancy spreads well beyond.

We live in dangerous times. We may recall that the Doomsday Clock abandoned minutes and shifted to seconds under Trump, and is now set at one hundred seconds to midnight—termination. The analysts who set the clock give three reasons: nuclear war, environmental destruction, and collapse of democracy and a free public sphere, which undermines the hope that informed and aroused citizens will compel their governments to overcome the dual race to disaster.

The war in Ukraine has exacerbated all three of these disastrous tendencies. The nuclear threat has sharply increased. The dire necessity of sharply reducing fossil fuel use had been reversed by adulation of the destroyers of life on Earth for saving civilization from the Russians. And democracy and a free public sphere are in ominous decline.

It is all too reminiscent of ninety years ago, though the stakes are far higher today. Then, the US responded to the crisis by leading the way to social democracy, largely under the impetus of a revived labor movement. Europe sank into fascist darkness.

What will happen now is uncertain. The one certainty is that it is up to us.

US POLICY TOWARD RUSSIA IS BLOCKING PATHS TO DE-ESCALATION IN UKRAINE

April 7, 2022

C. J. Polychroniou: *The war in Ukraine has turned Russia into a pariah state throughout Europe and North America, but Moscow continues to receive support from many countries in the Global South. The strategic relationship between Russia and China seems to be getting stronger, although both countries had identified each other as major factors for maintaining order and stability in an "emerging polycentric world" long before Putin and Xi Jinping. In fact, Russian foreign minister Sergey Lavrov said following a recent meeting with his Chinese counterpart that the two countries are working together to advance a vision of a new world order, a new "democratic world order." Is the new world order one that pits Global North and Global South countries against each other? And what do you make of the statement of Russia and China working together to promote a new "democratic world order"? To me, the idea of two autocratic states working together to promote democracy across the world sounds like a crude joke.*

Noam Chomsky: The idea that Russia and China will be working together to promote a "democratic world order" is, of course, ludicrous. They will be doing so in much the way that the US was laboring to "promote democracy" in Iraq, the goal of the invasion as President Bush announced when it became clear that the "single question"—*will Saddam* *abandon his nuclear weapons program?*—had been answered the wrong way. With rare exceptions, the intellectual class and even most scholarship leaped to attention and vigorously proclaimed the new doctrine, as I suppose is also the case today in Russia and China.

As US-run polls showed, Americans enthralled by the "noble" goals belatedly proclaimed were even joined by some Iraqis: 1 percent of those polled. Four percent thought the US invaded in order to help Iraqis. The rest concluded that if Iraq's exports had been asparagus and pickles, and the center of global petroleum production was in the South Pacific, the US wouldn't have invaded.

I don't pretend to have any expert knowledge, but from my own experience in past weeks with the Global South—press, many interviews and meetings, much personal discussion—it doesn't seem to me quite accurate to say that it is supporting Moscow, except in the sense that Moscow is getting support from the Western powers that keep paying it for petroleum products and food (probably by now the source of Russia's main export earnings).

My impression is that the Global South has sharply condemned the Russian invasion, but has asked, "What's new?" The general reaction to President Biden's harsh condemnation of Putin as a war criminal seems to be something like this: *It takes one to know one.* We agree that he is a war criminal, and as creatures of the Enlightenment, we adopt the Kantian principle of universality that is dismissed with contempt by the West, sometimes with angry charges of whataboutism.

It is, after all, not easy for people in the civilized world—increasingly, the Global South—to be impressed by the "moral outrage" of Western intellectuals who just a few years ago, when all the horrific facts were in, were enthusiastically applauding the success of the invasion of Iraq, spouting pieties about noble intentions that would have embarrassed the most abject apparatchik. And we can just imagine the reaction when they read the pious invocation of the Nuremberg judgment by the editors of the *New York Times*, who are just now coming to recognize that "to initiate a war of aggression, therefore, is not only an international crime: it is the supreme international crime, differing only from other war crimes in that it contains within itself the accumulated evil of the whole." The accumulated evil includes the instigation of ethnic conflict that has torn apart not only Iraq but the whole region, the horrors of ISIS, and much more.

Not, of course, what the editors have in mind. The supreme international crimes that they have supported for sixty years somehow escaped the Nuremberg judgment.

While there is appreciation in the Global South for the fact that at long last Western intellectuals and the political class are coming to perceive that aggressors can commit hideous crimes, they seem to feel that it is perhaps a little late, and curiously skewed, as they know from ample experience. They are also able to perceive that Westerners consumed with moral outrage over the crimes of enemies are still able to maintain their usual silence while their own leaders carry out terrible crimes right now—in Afghanistan, Yemen, Palestine, Western Sahara, and all too many other places where they could act at once, and expeditiously, to mitigate or end these crimes.

Let's turn to the "strategic relationship between Russia and China." It does indeed seem to be strengthening, though it is not much of a partnership. The corrupt Russian kleptocracy can provide raw materials and advanced weapons to the economic system that Beijing is systematically establishing through mainland Asia, reaching also to Africa and the Middle East, and by now even to US domains in Latin America. But not much more. Russia's role in this highly unequal relationship is, I think, likely to diminish further, much as Europe's international role is likely to diminish after Putin has handed Europe on a golden platter to the US-run "Atlanticist" system, a gift of substantial significance, as we've discussed before.

Can China help end the war in Ukraine? If yes, what's stopping Beijing from using its influence over Moscow for a peace agreement to be reached in Ukraine?

China could act to advance the prospects for a peaceful negotiated settlement in Ukraine. It seems that the Chinese leadership sees no advantage in doing so.

China's "information system" appears to be pretty much conforming to the Russian propaganda line. But more generally, it doesn't seem to diverge much from a fairly common stance in the Global South, illustrated graphically by the sanctions map. The states joining in sanctions against Russia are in the Anglosphere and Europe, as well as Japan, Taiwan, and South Korea. The rest of the world condemns the invasion but is mostly standing aloof.

This should not surprise us. It is nothing new. We recall well that the Iraq invasion had virtually no global support. Less familiar is the fact that the same was true of the US invasion of Afghanistan after 9/11. A few weeks after the invasion, an international Gallup poll asked the question, "Once the identity of the [9/11] terrorists is known, should the American government launch a military attack on the country or countries where the terrorists are based or should the American government seek to extradite the terrorists to stand trial?"

The wording reflects the fact that their identity was not known. Even eight months later, in his first major press conference, FBI director Robert Mueller could only affirm that al-Qaeda was suspected of the crime. If the poll had asked about actual US policy, the very limited support would doubtless have been even lower.

World opinion overwhelmingly favored diplomatic-judicial measures over military action. Opposition to invasion was particularly strong in Latin America, which has a little experience with US intervention.

The free press spared Americans knowledge of international opinion. It was therefore able to proclaim that "the opposition [to the US invasion] was mostly limited to the people who are reflexively against the American use of power."

Quite a few suffer from this malady, apparently. Global opinion today should come as no great surprise.

China's unwillingness to devote its efforts to a negotiated settlement of the Ukraine conflict deserves criticism, but it is hard to see how such criticism can properly come from Americans. After all, China is adhering to official US policy. Simply put, the policy is to "fight to the last Ukrainian for Ukrainian independence" while offering no way to save Ukraine from further tragedy. Even worse, current policy undermines such hopes by informing Putin that he has no way out: it's The Hague or proceed to destroy Ukraine.

The quote and the opinions just paraphrased are those of one of the most astute and widely respected US diplomats, Ambassador Chas Freeman, who goes on to spell out the options and to remind us of the history.

Like anyone who cares in the least about the fate of Ukrainians, Ambassador Freeman recognizes that the only alternative to Russian destruction of Ukraine—which, with their backs to the wall, Putin and his narrow circle of *siloviki* can implement—is a negotiated settlement that will be ugly, offering the aggressors an escape. He also carries the history back further than we have done in our earlier discussions, back to the Congress of Vienna of 1814, which followed the Napoleonic Wars. Klemens von Metternich and other European leaders, he observes, "had the good sense to reincorporate [defeated] France into the governing councils of Europe," overlooking its virtual conquest of Europe. That led to a century of substantial peace in Europe, which had long been the most violent part of the world. There were some wars, but nothing like what preceded. The century of peace ended with World War I.

Freeman goes on to remind us that the victors in the war did not have the good sense of their predecessors: "The victors—the United States and Britain and France—insisted on excluding Germany from a role in the affairs of Europe, as well as this newly formed Soviet Union, the result was World War II and the Cold War."

As we've discussed earlier, a leading theme throughout the Cold War was the status of Europe: Should it subordinate itself to the US within the Atlanticist-NATO framework, the US preference? Or should it become an independent "third force" along Gaullist lines, accommodating Russia within a Europe without military alliances from the Atlantic to the Urals?

The question arose starkly when the USSR collapsed, and Mikhail Gorbachev outlined the vision of a "common European home" with no military alliances from Lisbon to Vladivostok. In a limited form, the concept was revived by French president Emmanuel Macron in his recent abortive interchanges with Putin.

If there had been anyone in the Kremlin who resembled a statesman, they would have leaped at the opportunity to explore something like the Gorbachev vision. Europe has strong reasons to establish close relations with Russia, ranging from commerce to security. Whether such efforts might have succeeded, avoiding the Ukraine tragedy, we can only guess. The answer could only have been found out by trying. Instead, the hard men in Moscow turned to violence, compounding their criminal aggression with self-defeating foolishness.

The Gorbachev conception had some partial US support within the framework of the Partnership for Peace, a US initiative intended to provide a cooperative security system with a limited relation to NATO. Ambassador Freeman, who had a significant role in establishing it, describes its fate in words that are worth heeding:

> What happened in 1994, which was a midterm election year, and 1996, which was a presidential election year, was interesting. In 1994, Mr. Clinton was talking out of both sides of his mouth. He was telling the Russians that we were in no rush to add members to NATO, and that our preferred path was the Partnership for Peace. The same time he was hinting to the ethnic diasporas of Russophobic countries in Eastern Europe—and, by the way, it's easy to understand their Russophobia given their history—that, no, no, we were going to get these countries into NATO as fast as possible. And in 1996 he made that pledge explicit. [In] 1994 he got an outburst from [Boris] Yeltsin, who was then the president of the Russian Federation. [In] 1996 he got another one, and as time went on, when Mr. Putin came in, he regularly protested the enlargement of NATO in ways that disregarded Russia's self-defense interests. So, there should have been no surprise about this. For 28 years Russia has been warning that at some point it would snap, and it has, and it has done it in a very destructive way, both in terms of

its own interests and in terms of the broader prospects for peace in Europe.

None of this provides any excuse for Putin's invasion, Freeman emphasizes. But it is important to understand that "there were those people in the United States who were triumphalist about the end of the Cold War. . . . This allowed the United States to incorporate all the countries right up to Russia's borders and beyond them, beyond those borders in the Baltics, into an American sphere of influence. And, essentially, they posited a global sphere of influence for the United States modeled on the Monroe Doctrine. And that's pretty much what we have."

Russian leadership tolerated Clinton's violation of the firm US commitment to Gorbachev not to extend NATO beyond East Germany. They even tolerated George W. Bush's further provocations, and US military actions that struck directly at Russian interests, undertaken in such a way as to humiliate Russia. But Ukraine and Georgia were red lines. That was clearly understood in Washington. As Freeman continues, no Russian leader was likely to tolerate the NATO expansion into Ukraine that began after the 2014 "coup, [carried out] to prevent neutrality or a pro-Russian government in Kiev, and to replace it with a pro-American government that would bring Ukraine into our sphere. . . . So, since about 2015 the United States has been arming, training Ukrainians against Russia," effectively treating Ukraine "as an extension of NATO."

As we've discussed, that stance became explicit policy in Biden's September 2021 official statement, possibly a factor in Russia's decision to escalate to direct aggression a few months later.

Crucially, to repeat, current US policy is to "fight to the last Ukrainian" while offering no way to save Ukraine from further tragedy and in fact undermining such hopes by informing Putin that he has no way out: it's The Hague or proceed to destroy Ukraine.

China is probably relatively satisfied with the course of events. Very likely the same is true in Washington. Both have gained from the tragedy. And the euphoria among weapons and fossil fuel producers is unconcealed as they lead the way toward indescribable catastrophe, underscored in vivid terms by the Intergovernmental Panel on Climate Change report of April 4.

Turkey's position over the war in Ukraine is to maintain neutrality while acting as a mediator in the Russian-Ukrainian crisis. Can Turkey continue to maintain such a balancing act since we know that it has been supplying military assistance to Ukraine since 2019 and that it is aligned with the geostrategic vision of Washington over Ukraine?

Turkey has had an ambiguous position in global affairs for many years. It is a member of NATO, but the EU has rejected its appeals for membership on human rights grounds. In the 1990s, Turkey was indeed responsible for hideous crimes: its massive state terror against its Kurdish population, leaving tens of thousands dead, 3,500 towns and villages destroyed, a flood of hundreds of thousands of people from the devastated Kurdish regions to miserable slums in Istanbul. The crimes were mostly concealed by the "free press," perhaps because Clinton was pouring arms into Turkey, the flow escalating as atrocities mounted. Turkey became the leading recipient of US military aid (apart from Israel-Egypt, a separate category), extending a very close correlation between human rights abuses and US aid that goes far back, but somehow does not detract from its much-lauded nobility.

By 2000, Turkish state crimes were abating, and in the following years the situation greatly improved—something I was able to witness personally, with much appreciation. By 2005, under President Recep Erdoğan's increasingly harsh rule, the progress ended and reversed. That might have been in part a reaction to the continued refusal of the European Union to accept Turkish membership, ignoring the great steps forward in recent years and fortifying the sense that Europeans simply won't accept Turks into their club.

Since then, Erdoğan's rule has become far more brutal, again targeting Kurds but also attacking civil and human rights on a broad front. And he has been trying to turn Turkey into a major actor in regional affairs, with hints of a renewed Ottoman caliphate. He accepts Russian weapons over strong US objections but remains a central part of the NATO system of regional—by now global—dominance. The "balancing act" with regard to Ukraine is a case in point.

If Turkey can facilitate negotiations that will bring the Ukraine horrors to an end, that will be a most welcome development, to be applauded. We can only speculate about what the chances are while the US insists on perpetuating the conflict "to the last Ukrainian" while blocking an ugly negotiated settlement that is the alternative to destruction of Ukraine and perhaps even nuclear war.

Russian gas continues to flow to Europe although Putin had demanded that European governments pay for it in rubles. What would be the impact in the geostrategic relations between Europe and Russia if the former became independent from Russian gas?

It doesn't look likely in the near future. Europe could manage to end the use of Russian coal and oil, but gas is a different matter. That requires pipelines, which it would take years to build, or transport facilities for liquified natural gas that barely exist. But the question we should be asking I think is different. Can we ascend to the wisdom of the reactionary tyrants who provided Europe with a century of peace in Vienna in 1814? Can we move toward the Gorbachev vision of a European common home with no military alliances, a conception not too far from the US-initiated Partnership for Peace that was undermined by President Clinton? Can some resemblance to statesmanship appear in today's Russia? Such questions as these should, I think, be in the forefront of our thinking, and our active engagement in trying to influence discussion and debate, and policy choices.

Evidence of Russian war crimes is mounting. Can Putin be prosecuted for war crimes in Ukraine?

Prosecution for war crimes, in the real world, is "victor's justice." That was clear from the Nuremberg Tribunal and was not even concealed in the accompanying Tokyo Tribunal. At Nuremberg, saturation bombing of densely settled urban areas was excluded because it was a specialty of the Allies. German war criminals were exculpated if they could show that the Allies carried out the same crimes. In subsequent years, the Nuremberg principles were thrown out the window. They have only recently been discovered as a cudgel to beat official enemies.

There can be no thought of trying the US for its many horrendous crimes. An effort was once made to bring the US to justice for its war against Nicaragua. The US responded to the International Court of Justice orders to end the crimes by sharply escalating them while the press dismissed the court as a "hostile forum" as shown by its daring to convict the US (per the *New York Times*'s editors), following ample precedent.

Putin might be tried for crimes if he is overthrown within Russia and Russia can be treated as a defeated country. That is what the record indicates.

Imaginably, the world might rise to a level of civilization in which international law can be honored instead of righteously wielded against selected targets. We should never cease efforts to bring that about. In doing so, we should not succumb to the illusions fostered by the global doctrinal systems.

OUR PRIORITY ON UKRAINE SHOULD BE SAVING LIVES, NOT PUNISHING RUSSIA

April 20, 2022

C. J. Polychroniou: *Noam, Russian president Vladimir Putin said last week at a joint press conference with ally Belarusian president Alexander Lukashenko that peace talks have reached a "dead end" and that the invasion is proceeding as planned. In fact, he vowed that the war would continue until all goals that were set at the start of the invasion are completed. Does Putin not want peace in Ukraine? Is he really at war with NATO and the US? If so, particularly given how dangerous the West's policy toward Russia has been so far, what can be done now to prevent an entire country from being potentially wiped off the map?*

Noam Chomsky: Before proceeding with this discussion, I'd like to emphasize, once again, the most important point: Our prime concern should be to think through carefully what we can do to bring the criminal Russian invasion to a quick end and to save the Ukrainian victims from more horrors. There are, unfortunately, many who find heroic pronouncements to be more satisfying than this necessary task. Not a novelty in history, regrettably. As always, we should keep the prime issue clearly in mind, and act accordingly.

Turning to your comment, the final question is by far the most important one; I'll return to the earlier ones.

There are, basically, two ways for this war to end: a negotiated

241

diplomatic settlement or destruction of one or the other side, either quickly or in prolonged agony. It won't be Russia that is destroyed. Uncontroversially, Russia has the capacity to obliterate Ukraine, and if Putin and his cohort are driven to the wall, in desperation they might use this capacity. That surely should be the expectation of those who portray Putin as a "madman" immersed in delusions of romantic nationalism and wild global aspirations.

That's clearly an experiment that no one wants to undertake—at least no one who has the slightest concern for Ukrainians.

The qualification is unfortunately necessary. There are respected voices in the mainstream who simultaneously hold two views: (1) Putin is indeed a "deranged madman" who is capable of anything and might lash out wildly in revenge if backed to the wall; (2) "Ukraine must win. That is the only acceptable outcome." We can help Ukraine defeat Russia, they say, by providing advanced military equipment and training, and backing Putin to the wall.

Those two positions can only be simultaneously held by people who care so little about the fate of Ukrainians that they are willing to try an experiment to see whether the "deranged madman" will slink away in defeat or will use the overwhelming force at his command to obliterate Ukraine. Either way, the advocates of these two views win. If Putin quietly accepts defeat, they win. If he obliterates Ukraine, they win: It will justify far harsher measures to punish Russia.

It is of no little interest that such willingness to play games with the lives and fate of Ukrainians receives high praise, and is even considered a noble and courageous stance. Perhaps other words might come to mind.

Putting aside the qualification—unfortunately necessary in this strange culture—the answer to the question posed seems clear enough: engage in serious diplomatic efforts to end the conflict. Of course, that's not the response for those whose prime goal is to punish Russia—to fight Russia to the last Ukrainian, as Ambassador Chas Freeman describes current US policy, matters we have discussed.

The basic framework for a diplomatic settlement has long been understood and has been reiterated by Ukrainian president Volodymyr

Zelenskyy. First, neutralization of Ukraine, providing it with a status rather like Mexico or Austria. Second, putting off the matter of Crimea. Third, arrangements for a high level of autonomy for Donbas, perhaps within a federal arrangement, preferably to be settled in terms of an internationally run referendum.

Official US policy continues to reject all of this. High administration officials don't just concede that "prior to the Russian invasion of Ukraine, the United States made no effort to address one of Vladimir Putin's most often stated top security concerns—the possibility of Ukraine's membership into NATO." They praise themselves for having taken this position, which may well have been a factor in impelling Putin to criminal aggression. And the US continues to maintain this position now, thus standing in the way of a negotiated settlement along the lines Zelenskyy outlined, whatever the cost to Ukrainians.

Can a settlement along those general lines still be achieved, as seemed likely before the Russian invasion? There is only one way to find out: to try. Ambassador Freeman is far from alone among informed Western analysts in chastising the US government for having "been absent [from diplomatic efforts] and, at worst, implicitly opposed" to them with its actions and rhetoric. That, he continues, is "the opposite of statecraft and diplomacy" and a bitter blow to Ukrainians by prolonging the conflict. Other respected analysts, such as Anatol Lieven, generally agree, recognizing that at the very least, "the US has done nothing to facilitate diplomacy."

Regrettably, rational voices, however respected, are at the margins of discussion, leaving the floor to those who want to punish Russia—to the last Ukrainian.

At the press conference, Putin did appear to be joining the US in preferring "the opposite of statecraft and diplomacy," though his remarks do not close off these options. If peace talks are now at a "dead end," that doesn't mean that they cannot be resumed, at best with committed participation of the great powers, China and the US.

China is rightly condemned for its unwillingness to facilitate "statecraft and diplomacy." The US as usual is exempt from criticism in US mainstream media and journals (though not completely), except for not providing more weapons to prolong the conflict or using other measures to punish Russians, the dominant concern, it appears.

One measure the US could use is proposed from the halls of Harvard Law School, at the supposed liberal extreme of opinion. Professor emeritus Laurence Tribe and law student Jeremy Lewin propose that President Joe Biden should follow the precedent set by George W. Bush in 2003, when he seized "Iraqi funds sitting in American banks, allocating the proceeds to aid the Iraqi people and to compensate victims of terrorism."

Did President Bush do something else in 2003 "to aid the Iraqi people"? That annoying question would be raised only by those guilty of the sin of "whataboutism," one of the recent devices designed to bar any attention to our own actions and their consequences for today.

The authors recognize that there are some problems in freezing funds that have been kept for security in New York banks. They bring up the freezing of Afghanistan's funds by the Biden administration, which was "controversial, owing mostly to unsettled questions regarding court attachment of assets and allocating claims among dueling plaintiffs . . . suits filed by the relatives of those killed or wounded on 9/11."

Unmentioned, perhaps not controversial, is the plight of Afghan mothers watching their children starve because they cannot access their bank accounts to buy food in the markets, and more generally the fate of millions of Afghans facing starvation.

Further comment bearing on President Bush's 2003 efforts "to aid the Iraqi people" is provided, inadvertently, by the leading foreign policy analyst of the *New York Times*, Thomas Friedman in his headline, "How Do We Deal with a Superpower Led by a War Criminal?"

Who could imagine that a superpower could be led by a war criminal in this enlightened day and age? A difficult dilemma to face, even to contemplate, in a country of pristine innocence like ours.

Is it any wonder that the more civilized part of the world, mostly the Global South, contemplates the spectacle unfolding here with astonishment and disbelief?

Returning to the press conference, Putin did say that the invasion was proceeding as planned and would continue until the initial goals are achieved. If the consensus of Western military analysts and political elites is anywhere near accurate, that is Putin's way of acknowledging that the initial goals of quickly conquering Kyiv and installing a puppet government had to be abandoned because of fierce and courageous Ukrainian resistance, exposing the Russian military as a paper tiger incapable even of conquering cities a few miles from its border that are defended by a mostly citizens' army.

The consensus of experts then draws a further conclusion: The US and Europe must devote even greater resources to protecting themselves from the next onslaught of this rapacious military monster who is poised to launch an attack to overwhelm NATO and the US.

The logic is overwhelming.

According to the consensus, Russia is now revising its abandoned plans and concentrating on a major assault in the Donbas region, where some fifteen thousand people are reported to have been killed since the Maidan uprising in 2014. By whom? It should not be hard to determine with many Organization for Security and Co-operation in Europe (OSCE) observers on the ground.

It seems to me to go too far to conclude that Putin is aiming for war with NATO and the US, that is, mutual annihilation. I think he wants peace—on his terms. (What monster doesn't?) What these terms are we can only discover by trying to find out, through "statecraft and diplomacy." We cannot find out by refusing to engage in this option, refusing even to contemplate or discuss it. We cannot find out by carrying forward the official policy announced last September and reinforced in November, matters that we have discussed repeatedly: the official US policy on Ukraine that is withheld from Americans by the "free press" but surely studied very carefully by Russian intelligence, which has access to the White House website.

Returning to the essential point, we should be doing what we can to bring the criminal aggression to an end and doing so in a way that will save Ukrainians from further suffering and even possible obliteration if Putin and his circle are driven to the wall with no way out. That calls for a popular movement that will press the US to reverse its official policy and to join in diplomacy and statecraft.

Punitive measures (sanctions, military support for Ukraine) might be justified if they contribute to this end, not if designed to punish Russians while prolonging the agony and threatening Ukraine with destruction, with unspeakable ramifications beyond.

There are unconfirmed reports that Russia has used chemical weapons in the Ukrainian city that has been perhaps most brutally attacked—namely Mariupol. In turn, the UK's government rushed to announce rather boldly that "all options are on table" if these reports are correct. Indeed, NATO secretary-general Jens Stoltenberg has already stated that such development would "totally change the nature of the conflict." What does "all options on table" mean, and could it possibly include that scenario that the Ukraine war might go nuclear?

The phrase "all options are on the table" is normal in what passes for statecraft in the US and UK—all in direct violation of the UN Charter (and if anyone were to care, the US Constitution). We don't know what might be in the minds of those who regularly issue these declarations. Perhaps they mean what the words say: that the US is prepared to resort to nuclear weapons, thus very likely destroying itself along with much of life on Earth (though beetles and bacteria may proliferate). Maybe that is tolerable in their minds if it at least punishes Russians, who, we are told, are such an irremediable curse that the only solution may be "permanent Russian isolation" or even "Russia *delenda est.*"

It is, to be sure, appropriate to be much concerned about use of chemical weapons, even when unconfirmed. At the risk of more whataboutism, we should also be concerned about the well-confirmed reports of deformed fetuses in Saigon hospitals right now, among the terrible results of the chemical warfare unleashed by the Kennedy administration to destroy crops and forests, a core part of the program to "protect" the rural population who were supporting the Viet Cong, as Washington knew well. We should be concerned enough to do something to alleviate the consequences of these terrible programs.

If Russia might have used or be contemplating the use of chemical weapons, it is definitely a matter of deep concern.

There are also claims that thousands of Ukrainians have been forcefully deported from Mariupol to remote parts of Russia, evoking dark memories of the Soviet mass deportations under Stalin. Kremlin officials have rejected such claims as "lies" but have openly talked about relocating civilians trapped in Mariupol. If reports of forced civilian deportations from Mariupol to Russia are proven true, what would be the purpose of such reprehensible actions, and wouldn't they add to the list of Putin's war crimes?

They surely would add to the list, already quite long. And, fortunately, we will know a lot about these crimes. There already are extensive investigations of Russian war crimes underway, and despite technical difficulties, they will proceed.

That, too, is normal. When enemies carry out crimes, a major industry is mobilized to reveal every tiny detail. As should be done. War crimes should not be concealed and forgotten.

Regrettably, that is the near-universal practice in the US. A few of the myriad examples have just been alluded to. But the fact that today's global hegemon adopts the reprehensible practices of its predecessors still leaves us free to expose the crimes of today's official enemies, a task that should be undertaken, and surely will be in this case. Others outside of the reach of the US propaganda system will be appalled by the hypocrisy, but that's no reason not to welcome the highly selective exposure of war crimes.

Those with some perverse interest in looking at ourselves can learn some lessons from the way atrocities are handled when exposed. The most notable case is the My Lai massacre, finally recognized after freelance reporter Seymour Hersh exposed the crime *to the West*. In South Vietnam, it had long been known but did not arouse much attention. The Quaker medical center in Quang Ngai didn't even bother reporting it because such crimes were so common. In fact, the official US government investigation found another one like it at the nearby village of My Khe.

The My Lai massacre could be absorbed within the propaganda system by restricting the blame to GIs in the field who didn't know who was going to shoot at them next. Exempt were—and are—those who sent them on these mass murder expeditions. Furthermore, the focus on one of the many crimes on the ground served to conceal the fact that they were the merest footnote to a huge bombing campaign of slaughter and destruction directed from air-conditioned offices, mostly suppressed by the media, though Edward Herman and I were able to write about it in 1979, making use of detailed studies provided to us by *Newsweek* correspondent Kevin Buckley, who had investigated the crime along with his colleague Alex Shimkin but was unable to publish more than fragments.

Short of such cases, which are rare, US crimes are not examined and little is known about them. An old story among the very powerful.

It's not easy to understand what is in the back of the minds of war criminals like Putin—or those who don't exist, according to the canon as preached by *New York Times* pundits who are aghast at the discovery that war criminals exist—among official enemies.

Finland and Sweden seem to be warming up to the idea of joining NATO. In the event of such development, Russia has threatened to deploy nuclear weapons and hypersonic missiles in the Baltic region. Does it make sense for neutral countries to join NATO? Do they really have reasons to be concerned about their own security?

Let's return to the overwhelming consensus of Western military analysts and political elites: The Russian military is so weak and incompetent that it couldn't conquer cities near its border that are defended mostly by a citizen's army. So, therefore, those with overwhelming military power must tremble in their boots about their security in the face of this awesome military power, on the march.

One can understand why this conception should be a favorite in the offices of Lockheed Martin and other military contractors in the world's leading arms exporter, relishing the new prospects for expanding their bulging coffers. The fact that it is accepted in much wider circles, and also guides policy, again perhaps merits some thought.

Russia does have advanced weapons, which can destroy (though evidently not conquer), so the Ukraine experience is held to indicate.

For Finland and Sweden, abandoning neutrality and joining NATO might enhance the likelihood of their use. Since the security argument is not easy to take seriously, that seems to be the most likely consequence of their joining NATO.

It's also worth recognizing that Finland and Sweden are already fairly well integrated into the NATO command system, just as was happening with Ukraine from 2014, solidified further with the official US government policy statements of last September and November and the refusal of the Biden administration "to address one of Vladimir Putin's most often stated top security concerns—the possibility of Ukraine's membership into NATO"—on the eve of the invasion.

PROPAGANDA WARS ARE RAGING AS RUSSIA'S WAR ON UKRAINE EXPANDS

April 28, 2022

C. J. Polychroniou: *Wartime propaganda has become in the modern world a powerful weapon in garnering public support for war and providing a moral justification for it, usually by highlighting the "evil" nature of the enemy. It's also used in order to break down the will of the enemy forces to fight. In the case of Russia's invasion of Ukraine, Kremlin propaganda seems so far to be working inside Russia and dominating Chinese social media, but it looks like Ukraine is winning the information war in the global arena, especially in the West. Do you agree with this assessment? Any significant lies or war myths around the Russia-Ukraine conflict worth pointing out?*

Noam Chomsky: Wartime propaganda has been a powerful weapon for a long time, I suspect as far back as we can trace the historical record. And often a weapon with long-term consequences, which merit attention and thought.

Just to keep to modern times, in 1898, the US battleship *Maine* sank in Havana harbor, probably from an internal explosion. The Hearst press succeeded in arousing a wave of popular hysteria about the evil nature of Spain. That provided the needed background for an invasion of Cuba that is called here "the liberation of Cuba." Or, as it should be called, the prevention of Cuba's self-liberation from

Spain, turning Cuba into a virtual US colony. So it remained until 1959, when Cuba was indeed liberated, and the US, almost at once, undertook a vicious campaign of terror and sanctions to end Cuba's "successful defiance" of the 150-year-old US policy of dominating the hemisphere, as the State Department explained fifty years ago.

Whipping up war myths can have long-term consequences.

A few years later, in 1916, Woodrow Wilson was elected president with the slogan "Peace without Victory." That was quickly transmuted to Victory without Peace. A flood of war myths quickly turned a pacifist population to one consumed with hatred for all things German. The propaganda at first emanated from the British Ministry of Information; we know what that means. American intellectuals of the liberal [John] Dewey circle lapped it up enthusiastically, declaring themselves to be the leaders of the campaign to liberate the world. For the first time in history, they soberly explained, war was not initiated by military or political elites, but by the thoughtful intellectuals— them—who had carefully studied the situation and, after careful deliberation, rationally determined the right course of action: to enter the war, to bring liberty and freedom to the world, and to end the Hun atrocities concocted by the British Ministry of Information.

One consequence of the very effective Hate Germany campaigns was imposition of a victor's peace, with harsh treatment of defeated Germany. Some strongly objected, notably John Maynard Keynes. They were ignored. That gave us Hitler.

In a previous interview, we discussed how Ambassador Chas Freeman compared the postwar Hate Germany settlement with a triumph of statesmanship (not by nice people): The Congress of Vienna, 1815. The congress sought to establish a European order after Napoleon's attempt to conquer Europe had been overcome. Judiciously, the congress incorporated defeated France. That led to a century of relative peace in Europe.

There are some lessons.

Not to be outdone by the British, President Wilson established his own propaganda agency, the Committee on Public Information (Creel Committee), which performed its own services.

These exercises also had a long-term effect. Among the members of the committee were Walter Lippmann, who went on to become the leading public intellectual of the twentieth century, and Edward Bernays, who became a prime founder of the modern public relations industry, the world's major propaganda agency, dedicated to undermining markets by creating uninformed consumers making irrational choices—the opposite of what one learns about markets in Econ 101. By stimulating rampant consumerism, the industry is also driving the world to disaster, another topic.

Both Lippmann and Bernays credited the Creel Committee for demonstrating the power of propaganda in "manufacturing consent" (Lippmann) and "engineering of consent" (Bernays). This "new art in the practice of democracy," Lippmann explained, could be used to keep the "ignorant and meddlesome outsiders"—the general public—passive and obedient while the self-designated "responsible men" will attend to important matters, free from the "trampling and roar of a bewildered herd." Bernays expressed similar views. They were not alone.

Lippmann and Bernays were Wilson-Roosevelt-Kennedy liberals. The conception of democracy they elaborated was quite in accord with dominant liberal conceptions, then and since.

The ideas extend broadly to the more free societies, where "unpopular ideas can be suppressed without the use of force," as George Orwell put the matter in his (unpublished) introduction to *Animal Farm* on "literary censorship" in England.

So it continues. Particularly in the more free societies, where means of state violence have been constrained by popular activism, it is of great importance to devise methods of manufacturing consent, and to ensure that they are internalized, becoming as invisible as the air we breathe, particularly in articulate educated circles. Imposing war myths is a regular feature of these enterprises.

It often works, quite spectacularly. In today's Russia, according to reports, a large majority accept the doctrine that in Ukraine, Russia is defending itself against a Nazi onslaught reminiscent of World War II, when Ukraine was, in fact, collaborating in the aggression that came close to destroying Russia while exacting a horrific toll.

The propaganda is as nonsensical as war myths generally, but like others, it relies on shreds of truth, and has, it seems, been effective domestically in manufacturing consent.

We cannot really be sure because of the rigid censorship now in force, a hallmark of US political culture from far back: the "bewildered herd" must be protected from the "wrong ideas." Accordingly, Americans must be "protected" from propaganda which, we are told, is so ludicrous that only the most fully brainwashed could possibly keep from laughing.

According to this view, to punish Vladimir Putin, all material emanating from Russia must be rigorously barred from American ears. That includes the work of outstanding US journalists and political commentators, like Chris Hedges, whose long record of courageous journalism includes his service as the *New York Times* Middle East and Balkans bureau chief, and astute and perceptive commentary since. Americans must be protected from his evil influence, because his reports appear on RT. They have now been expunged. Americans are "saved" from reading them.

Take that, Mr. Putin.

As we would expect in a free society, it is possible, with some effort, to learn something about Russia's official position on the war—or as Russia calls it, "special military operation." For example, via India, where Foreign Minister Sergey Lavrov had a long interview with *India Today TV* on April 19.

We constantly witness instructive effects of this rigid indoctrination. One is that it is de rigueur to refer to Putin's criminal aggression in Ukraine as his "unprovoked invasion of Ukraine." A Google search for this phrase finds "about 2,430,000 results" (in 0.42 seconds).

Out of curiosity, we might search for "unprovoked invasion of Iraq." The search yields "about 11,700 results" (in 0.35 seconds)—apparently from antiwar sources, a brief search suggests.

The example is interesting not only in itself, but because of its sharp reversal of the facts. The Iraq War was totally unprovoked: Dick Cheney and Donald Rumsfeld had to struggle hard, even to resort to torture, to try to find some particle of evidence to tie Saddam Hussein to al-Qaeda. The famous disappearing weapons of mass destruction wouldn't have been a provocation for aggression even if there had been some reason to believe that they existed.

In contrast, the Russian invasion of Ukraine was most definitely provoked—though in today's frantic political climate, it is necessary to add the truism that provocation provides no justification for the invasion.

A host of high-level US diplomats and policy analysts have been warning Washington for thirty years that it was reckless and needlessly provocative to ignore Russia's security concerns, particularly its red lines: no NATO membership for Georgia and Ukraine, in Russia's geostrategic heartland.

In full understanding of what it was doing, since 2014, NATO (meaning basically the US), has "provided significant support [to Ukraine] with equipment, with training, tens of thousands of Ukrainian soldiers have been trained, and then when we saw the intelligence indicating a highly likely invasion Allies stepped up last autumn and this winter," before the invasion, according to NATO secretary-general Jens Stoltenberg.

The US commitment to integrate Ukraine within the NATO command was also stepped up in fall 2021 with the official policy statements we have already discussed—kept from the bewildered herd by the "free press," but surely read carefully by Russian intelligence. Russian intelligence did not have to be informed that "prior to the Russian invasion of Ukraine, the United States made no effort to address one of Vladimir Putin's most often stated top security concerns—the possibility of Ukraine's membership into NATO," as the State Department conceded, with little notice here.

Without going into any further details, Putin's invasion of Ukraine was clearly provoked, while the US invasion of Iraq was clearly unprovoked. That is exactly the opposite of standard commentary and reporting. But it is also exactly the norm of wartime propaganda, not just in the US, though it is more instructive to observe the process in free societies.

Many feel that it is wrong to bring up such matters, even a form of pro-Putin propaganda: we should, rather, focus laser-like on Russia's ongoing crimes. Contrary to their beliefs, that stand does not help Ukrainians. It harms them. If we are barred, by dictate, from learning about ourselves, we will not be able to develop policies that will benefit others, Ukrainians among them. That seems elementary.

Further analysis yields many other instructive examples. We discussed Harvard law professor Laurence Tribe's praise for President George W. Bush's decision in 2003 to "aid the Iraqi people" by seizing "Iraqi funds sitting in American banks"—and, incidentally, invading and destroying the country, too unimportant to mention. More fully, the funds were seized "to aid the Iraqi people and to compensate victims of terrorism," for which the Iraqi people bore no responsibility.

We didn't go on to ask how the Iraqi people were to be aided. It is a fair guess that it is not compensation for US pre-invasion "genocide" in Iraq.

"Genocide" is not my term. Rather, it is the term used by the distinguished international diplomats who administered the "Oil-for-Food program," the soft side of President Bill Clinton's sanctions (technically, via the UN). The first, Denis Halliday, resigned in protest because he regarded the sanctions as "genocidal." He was replaced by Hans von Sponeck, who not only resigned in protest with the same charge but also wrote a very important book providing extensive details of the shocking torture of Iraqis by Clinton's sanctions, *A Different Kind of War*.

Americans are not entirely protected from such unpleasant revelations. Though von Sponeck's book was never reviewed, as far as I can determine, it can be purchased from Amazon by anyone who has happened to hear about it. And the small publisher that released the English edition was even able to collect two blurbs: from John Pilger and me, suitably remote from the mainstream.

There is, of course, a flood of commentary about "genocide." By the standards used, the US and its allies are guilty of the charge over and over, but voluntary censorship prevents any acknowledgment of this, just as it protects Americans from international Gallup polls showing that the US is regarded as by far the greatest threat to world peace, or that world public opinion overwhelmingly opposed the US invasion of Afghanistan (also "unprovoked," if we pay attention), and other improper information.

I don't think there are "significant lies" in war reporting. The US media are generally doing a highly creditable job in reporting Russian crimes in Ukraine. That's valuable, just as it's valuable that international investigations are underway in preparation for possible war crimes trials.

That pattern is also normal. We are very scrupulous in unearthing details about crimes of others. There are, to be sure, sometimes fabrications, sometimes reaching the level of comedy, matters that the late Edward Herman and I documented in extensive detail. But when enemy crimes can be observed directly, on the ground, journalists typically do a fine job reporting and exposing them. And they are explored further in scholarship and extensive investigations.

As we've discussed, on the very rare occasions when US crimes are so blatant that they can't be dismissed or ignored, they may also be reported, but in such a way as to conceal the far greater crimes to which they are a small footnote. The My Lai massacre, for example.

On Ukraine winning the information war, the qualification "in the West" is accurate. The US has always been enthusiastic and rigorous in exposing crimes of its enemies, and in the current case, Europe is going along. But outside of US-Europe, the picture is more ambiguous. In the Global South, the home of most of the world's population, the invasion is denounced but the US propaganda framework is not uncritically adopted, a fact that has led to considerable puzzlement here as to why they are "out of step."

That's quite normal too. The traditional victims of brutal violence and repression often see the world rather differently from those who are used to holding the whip.

Even in Australia, there's a measure of insubordination. In the international affairs journal *Arena*, editor Simon Cooper reviews and deplores the rigid censorship and intolerance of even mild dissent in US liberal media. He concludes, reasonably enough, that "this means it is almost impossible within mainstream opinion to simultaneously acknowledge Putin's insupportable actions *and* forge a path out of the war that does not involve escalation, and the further destruction of Ukraine."

No help to suffering Ukrainians, of course.

That's also nothing new. That has been a dominant pattern for a long time, notably during World War I. There were a few who didn't simply conform to the orthodoxy established after Wilson joined the war. The country's leading labor leader, Eugene Debs, was jailed for daring to suggest to workers that they should think for themselves. He was so detested by the liberal Wilson administration that he was excluded from Wilson's postwar amnesty. In the liberal Deweyite intellectual circles, there were also some who were disobedient. The most famous was Randolph Bourne. He was not imprisoned but was barred from liberal journals so that he could not spread his subversive message that "war is the health of the state."

I should mention that a few years later, much to his credit, Dewey himself sharply reversed his stand.

It is understandable that liberals should be particularly excited when there is an opportunity to condemn enemy crimes. For once, they are on the side of power. The crimes are real, and they can march in the parade that is rightly condemning them and be praised for their (quite proper) conformity. That is very tempting for those who sometimes, even if timidly, condemn crimes for which we share responsibility and are therefore castigated for adherence to elementary moral principles.

Has the spread of social media made it more or less difficult to get an accurate picture of political reality?

Hard to say. Particularly hard for me to say because I avoid social media and only have limited information. My impression is that it is a mixed story.

Social media provide opportunities to hear a variety of perspectives and analyses, and to find information that is often unavailable in the mainstream. On the other hand, it is not clear how well these opportunities are exploited. There has been a good deal of commentary—confirmed by my own limited experience—arguing that many tend to gravitate to self-reinforcing bubbles, hearing little beyond their own beliefs and attitudes, and worse, entrenching these more firmly and in more intense and extreme forms.

That aside, the basic news sources remain pretty much as they were: the mainstream press, which has reporters and bureaus on the ground. The internet offers opportunities to sample a much wider range of such media, but my impression, again, is that these opportunities are little used.

One harmful consequence of the rapid proliferation of social media is the sharp decline of mainstream media. Not long ago, there were many fine local media in the US. Mostly gone. Few even have Washington bureaus, let alone elsewhere, as many did not long ago. During Ronald Reagan's Central America wars, which reached extremes of sadism, some of the finest reporting was done by reporters of the *Boston Globe*, some close personal friends. That has all virtually disappeared.

The basic reason is advertiser reliance, one of the curses of the capitalist system. The founding fathers had a different vision. They favored a truly independent press and fostered it. The Post Office was largely established for this purpose, providing cheap access to an independent press.

In keeping with the fact that it is to an unusual extent a business-run society, the US is also unusual in that it has virtually no public media: nothing like the BBC, for example. Efforts to develop public service media—first in radio, later in TV—were beaten back by intense business lobbying.

There's excellent scholarly work on this topic, which extends also to serious activist initiatives to overcome these serious infringements on democracy, particularly by Robert McChesney and Victor Pickard.

Nearly 35 years ago, you and Edward Herman published Manufacturing Consent: The Political Economy of the Mass Media. *The book introduced the "propaganda model" of communication, which operates through five filters: ownership, advertising, the media elite, flak, and the common enemy. Has the digital age changed the "propaganda model"? Does it still work?*

Unfortunately, Edward—the prime author—is no longer with us. Sorely missed. I think he would agree with me that the digital age hasn't changed much, beyond what I just described. What survives of mainstream media in a largely business-run society still remains the main source of information and is subject to the same kinds of pressures as before.

There have been important changes apart from what I briefly mentioned. Much like other institutions, even including the corporate sector, the media have been influenced by the civilizing effects of the popular movements of the '60s and their aftermath. It is quite illuminating to see what passed for appropriate commentary and reporting in earlier years. Many journalists have themselves gone through these liberating experiences.

Naturally, there is a huge backlash, including passionate denunciations of "woke" culture that recognizes that there are human beings with rights apart from white Christian males. Since Nixon's "Southern Strategy," the GOP leadership has understood that since they cannot possibly win votes on their economic policies of service to great wealth and corporate power, they must try to direct attention to "cultural issues": the false idea of a "Great Replacement," or guns, or indeed anything to obscure the fact that we're working hard to stab you in the back. Donald Trump was a master of this technique, sometimes called the "thief, thief" technique: when you're caught with your hand in someone's pocket, shout "Thief, thief!" and point somewhere else.

Despite these efforts, the media have improved in this regard, reflecting changes in the general society. That's by no means unimportant.

What do you make of "whataboutism," which is stirring up quite a controversy these days on account of the ongoing war in Ukraine?

Here again there's a long history. In the early postwar period [World War II], independent thought could be silenced by charges of comsymp: you're an apologist for Stalin's crimes. It's sometimes condemned as McCarthyism, but that was only the vulgar tip of the iceberg. What is now denounced as "cancel culture" was rampant and remained so.

That technique lost some of its power as the country began to awaken from dogmatic slumber in the '60s. In the early '80s, Jeane Kirkpatrick, a major Reaganite foreign policy intellectual, devised another technique: moral equivalence. If you reveal and criticize the atrocities that she was supporting in the Reagan administration, you're guilty of "moral equivalence." You're claiming that Reagan is no different than Stalin or Hitler. That served for a time to subdue dissent from the party line.

Whataboutism is a new variant, hardly different from its predecessors.

For the true totalitarian mentality, none of this is enough. GOP leaders are working hard to cleanse the schools of anything that is "divisive" or that causes "discomfort." That includes virtually all of history apart from patriotic slogans approved by Trump's 1776 Commission, or whatever will be devised by GOP leaders when they take command and are in a position to impose stricter discipline. We see many signs of it today, and there's every reason to expect more to come.

It's important to remember how rigid doctrinal controls have been in the US—perhaps a reflection of the fact that it is a very free society by comparative standards, hence posing problems to the doctrinal managers, who must be ever alert to signs of deviation.

By now, after many years, it's possible to utter the word "socialist," meaning moderately social democrat. In that respect, the US has finally broken out of the company of totalitarian dictatorships. Go back sixty years and even the words "capitalism" and "imperialism" were too radical to voice. Students for a Democratic Society president Paul Potter, in 1965, summoned the courage to "name the system" in his presidential address, but couldn't manage to produce the words.

There were some breakthroughs in the '60s, a matter of deep concern to American liberals, who warned of a "crisis of democracy" as too many sectors of the population tried to enter the political arena to defend their rights. They counseled more "moderation in democracy," a return to passivity and obedience, and they condemned the institutions responsible for "indoctrination of the young" for failing to perform their duties.

The doors have been opened more widely since, which only calls for more urgent measures to impose discipline.

If GOP authoritarians are able to destroy democracy sufficiently to establish permanent rule by a white supremacist Christian nationalist caste subservient to extreme wealth and private power, we are likely to enjoy the antics of such figures as Florida governor Ron DeSantis, who banned 40 percent of children's math texts in Florida because of "references to Critical Race Theory (CRT), inclusions of Common Core, and the unsolicited addition of Social Emotional Learning (SEL) in mathematics," according to the official directive. Under pressure, the state released some terrifying examples, such as an educational objective that "students build proficiency with social awareness as they practice with empathizing with classmates."

If the country as a whole ascends to the heights of GOP aspirations, it will be unnecessary to resort to such devices as "moral equivalence" and "whataboutism" to stifle independent thought.

One final question. A UK judge has formally approved Julian Assange's extradition to the US despite deep concerns that such a move would put him at risk of "serious human rights violations," as Agnès Callamard, former UN special rapporteur on extrajudicial, summary, or arbitrary executions, had warned a couple of years ago. In the event that Assange is indeed extradited to the US, which is pretty close to certain now, he faces up to 175 years in prison for releasing public information about the wars in Iraq and Afghanistan. Can you comment on the case of Julian Assange, the law used to prosecute him, what his persecution says about freedom of speech and the state of US democracy?

Assange has been held for years under conditions that amount to torture. That's fairly evident to anyone who was able to visit him (I was, once) and was confirmed by the UN special rapporteur on torture [and other cruel, inhuman, or degrading treatment or punishment] Nils Melzer in May 2019.

A few days later, Assange was indicted by the Trump administration under the Espionage Act of 1917, the same act that President Wilson employed to imprison Eugene Debs (among other state crimes committed using the act).

Legalistic shenanigans aside, the basic reasons for the torture and indictment of Assange are that he committed a cardinal sin: he released to the public information about US crimes that the government, of course, would prefer to see concealed. That is particularly offensive to authoritarian extremists like Trump and Mike Pompeo, who initiated the proceedings under the Espionage Act.

Their concerns are understandable. They were explained years ago by the professor of the Science of Government at Harvard, Samuel Huntington. He observed that "power remains strong when it remains in the dark; exposed to the sunlight it begins to evaporate."

That is a crucial principle of statecraft. It extends to private power as well. That is why manufacture/engineering of consent is a prime concern of systems of power, state and private.

This is no novel insight. In one of the first works in what is now called political science, 350 years ago, his "First Principles of Government," David Hume wrote that

> nothing appears more surprising to those, who consider human affairs with a philosophical eye, than the easiness with which the many are governed by the few; and the implicit submission, with which men resign their own sentiments and passions to those of their rulers. When we enquire by what means this wonder is effected, we shall find, that, as Force is always on the side of the governed, the governors have nothing to support them but opinion. It is therefore, on opinion only that government is founded; and this maxim extends to the most despotic and most military governments, as well as to the most free and most popular.

Force is indeed on the side of the governed, particularly in the more free societies. And they'd better not realize it, or the structures of illegitimate authority will crumble, state and private.

These ideas have been developed over the years, importantly by Antonio Gramsci. The Mussolini dictatorship understood well the threat he posed. When he was imprisoned, the prosecutor announced that "we must prevent this brain from functioning for 20 years."

We have advanced considerably since fascist Italy. The Trump-Pompeo indictment seeks to silence Assange for 175 years, and the US and UK governments have already imposed years of torture on the criminal who dared to expose power to the sunlight.

US IS PRIORITIZING ITS JOCKEYING WITH RUSSIA, NOT UKRAINIANS' LIVES

May 4, 2022

C. J. Polychroniou: *After months of fighting, it's obvious that the invasion is not going according to the Kremlin's plans, hopes, and expectations. NATO figures have claimed that Russian forces have already suffered as many deaths as they did during the entire duration of the Afghan war, and the position of the Zelenskyy government now seems to be "peace with victory." Obviously, the West's support for Ukraine is key to what's happening on the ground, both militarily and in terms of diplomatic solutions. Indeed, there is no clear path to peace, and the Kremlin has stated that it is not seeking to end the war by May 9 (known as Victory Day, which marks the Soviets' role in defeating Nazi Germany). Don't Ukrainians have the right to fight to death before surrendering any territory to Russia, if they choose to do so?*

Noam Chomsky: To my knowledge, no one has suggested that Ukrainians don't have that right. Islamic Jihad also has the abstract right to fight to the death before surrendering any territory to Israel. I wouldn't recommend it, but it's their right.

Do Ukrainians want that? Perhaps now in the midst of a devastating war, but not in the recent past.

President Zelenskyy was elected in 2019 with an overwhelming mandate for peace. He immediately moved to carry it out, with great courage. He had to confront violent right-wing militias who threatened to kill him if he tried to reach a peaceful settlement along the lines of the Minsk II formula. Historian of Russia Stephen Cohen points out that if Zelenskyy had been backed by the US, he could have persisted, perhaps solving the problem with no horrendous invasion. The US refused, preferring its policy of integrating Ukraine within NATO. Washington continued to dismiss Russia's red lines and the warnings of a host of top-level US diplomats and government advisers as it has been doing since Clinton's abrogation of Bush's firm and unambiguous promise to Gorbachev that in return for German reunification within NATO, NATO would not expand one inch beyond Germany.

Zelenskyy also sensibly proposed putting the very different Crimea issue on a back burner, to be addressed later, after the war ends.

Minsk II would have meant some kind of federal arrangement, with considerable autonomy for the Donbas region, optimally in a manner to be determined by an internationally supervised referendum. Prospects have, of course, diminished after the Russian invasion. How much we don't know. There is only one way to find out: to agree to facilitate diplomacy instead of undermining it, as the US continues to do.

It's true that "the West's support for Ukraine is key to what's happening on the ground, both militarily and in terms of diplomatic solutions," though I would suggest a slight rephrasing: The West's support for Ukraine is key to what's happening on the ground, both militarily and in terms of undermining instead of facilitating diplomatic solutions that might end the horror.

Trump has accused the Biden administration of "unmitigated failure" including Ukraine. What do you make of his calls for Ukraine and Russia to end the war? Has he turned into a statesman while out of office?

Trump's call, to which you refer, is worth quoting: "It doesn't make sense that Russia and Ukraine aren't sitting down and working out some kind of an agreement. If they don't do it soon, there will be nothing left but death, destruction, and carnage. This is a war that never should have happened, but it did. The solution can never be as good as it would have been before the shooting started, but there is a solution, and it should be figured out now—not later—when everyone will be DEAD!"

He was of course castigated and denounced as a Putin-lover, a fool, or worse. Along with Corbyn in England, with comments to the same effect that I quoted, Trump is the only figure I've found in high places who has taken this very sensible position. I see no credible reason to conceal the fact.

Of course, there is a torrent of denunciations of Putin for failure to negotiate seriously. Trump's comment, however, is not restricted to the official enemy but applies generally, including what's unmentionable: US actions (and inaction).

Congress, including congressional Democrats, are acting as if they prefer the exhortation by Democratic chair of the House Permanent Select Committee of Intelligence Adam Schiff that we have to aid Ukraine "so that we can fight Russia over there, and we don't have to fight Russia here."

Schiff's warning is nothing new. It is reminiscent of Reagan's calling a national emergency because the Nicaraguan army is only two days, marching time from Harlingen, Texas, about to overwhelm us. Or LBJ's plaintive plea that we have to stop them in Vietnam or they will "sweep over the United States and take what we have."

That's been the permanent plight of the US, constantly threatened with annihilation. Best to stop *them* over *there*.

The US has been a leading provider of security assistance to Ukraine since 2014. And last week, President Biden asked Congress to approve $33 billion to Ukraine, which is more than double what Washington has already committed since the start of the war. Isn't it therefore safe to conclude that Washington has a lot riding on the way the war ends in Ukraine?

Since the relevant facts are virtually unspeakable here, it's worth reviewing them.

Since the Maidan uprising in 2014, NATO (meaning basically the US) has "provided significant support with equipment, with training, tens of thousands of Ukrainian soldiers have been trained, and then when we saw the intelligence indicating a highly likely invasion, Allies stepped up last autumn and this winter," before the invasion (NATO secretary-general Jens Stoltenberg).

I've already mentioned Washington's refusal to back newly elected president Zelenskyy when his courageous effort to implement his mandate to pursue peace was blocked by right-wing militias, and the US refused to back him, preferring to continue its policy of integrating Ukraine into NATO, dismissing Russia's red lines.

As we've discussed earlier, that commitment was stepped up with the official US policy statement of September 2021 calling for sending more advanced military equipment to Ukraine while continuing "our robust training and exercise program in keeping with Ukraine's status as a NATO Enhanced Opportunities Partner." The policy was given further formal status in the November 10 US-Ukraine Charter on Strategic Partnership signed by Secretary of State Antony Blinken.

The State Department has acknowledged that "prior to the Russian invasion of Ukraine, the United States made no effort to address one of Vladimir Putin's most often stated top security concerns—the possibility of Ukraine's membership into NATO."

So, matters continued after Putin's criminal aggression. Once again, what happened has been reviewed accurately by Anatol Lieven:

> A US strategy of using the war in Ukraine to weaken Russia is also of course completely incompatible with the search for a ceasefire and even a provisional peace settlement. It would require Washington to oppose any such settlement and to keep the war going. And indeed, when in late March the Ukrainian government put forward a very reasonable set of peace proposals, the lack of public US support for them was extremely striking.
>
> Apart from anything else, a Ukrainian treaty of neutrality (as proposed by President Zelensky) is an absolutely inescapable part of any settlement—but weakening Russia involves maintaining Ukraine as a de facto US ally. US strategy

as indicated by [Defense Secretary] Lloyd Austin would risk Washington becoming involved in backing Ukrainian nationalist hardliners against President Zelensky himself.

With this in mind, we can turn to the question. The answer seems plain: judging by US actions and formal pronouncements, it is "safe to conclude that Washington has a lot riding on the way the war ends in Ukraine." More specifically, it is fair to conclude that in order to "weaken Russia," the US is dedicated to the grotesque experiment that we have discussed earlier; avoid any way of ending the conflict through diplomacy and see whether Putin will slink away quietly in defeat or will use the capacity, which of course he has, to destroy Ukraine and set the stage for terminal war.

We learn a lot about the reigning culture from the fact that the grotesque experiment is considered highly praiseworthy, and that any effort to question it is either relegated to the margins or bitterly castigated with an impressive flow of lies and deceit.

TO TACKLE CLIMATE, OUR MORALITY
MUST CATCH UP WITH OUR INTELLIGENCE

May 11, 2022

C. J. Polychroniou: *Noam, the war in Ukraine is causing unimaginable human suffering, but it is also having global economic consequences and is terrible news for the fight against global warming. Indeed, as a result of rising energy costs and concerns about energy security, decarbonization efforts have taken a back seat. In the US, the Biden administration has embraced the Republican slogan "Drill, baby, drill," Europe is set on building new gas pipelines and import facilities, and China plans to boost coal production capacity. Can you comment on the implications of these unfortunate developments and explain why short-term thinking continues to prevail among world leaders even at a time when humanity could be on the brink of an existential threat?*

Noam Chomsky: The last question is not new. In one or another form, it has arisen throughout history.

Take one case that has been extensively studied: Why did political leaders go to war in 1914, supremely confident of their own righteousness? And why did the most prominent intellectuals in every warring country line up with passionate enthusiasm in support of their own state—apart from a handful of dissidents, the most prominent of whom were jailed (Bertrand Russell, Eugene Debs, Rosa Luxemburg, and Karl Liebknecht)? It wasn't a terminal crisis, but it was serious enough.

The pattern goes far back in history. And it continues with little change after August 6, 1945, when we learned that human intelligence had risen to the level where it soon would be able to exterminate everything.

Observing the pattern closely, over the years, a basic conclusion seems to me to emerge clearly: whatever is driving policy, it is not security—at least, security of the population. That is at best a marginal concern. That holds for existential threats as well. We have to look elsewhere.

A good starting point, I think, is what seems to me to be the best-established principle of international relations theory: Adam Smith's observation that the "masters of mankind"—in his day the merchants and manufacturers of England—are the "principal architects of [state] policy." They use their power to ensure that their own interests "are most peculiarly attended to" no matter how "grievous" the effects on others, including the people of England, but most brutally the victims of the "savage injustice of the Europeans." His particular target was British savagery in India, then in its early stages, already horrifying enough.

Nothing much changes when the crises become existential. Short-term interests prevail. The logic is clear in competitive systems, like unregulated markets. Those who do not play the game are soon out of it. Competition among the "principal architects of policy" in the state system has somewhat similar properties, but we should bear in mind that security of the population is far from a guiding principle, as the record shows all too clearly.

You are quite right about the horrific impact of the criminal Russian invasion of Ukraine. Discussion in the US and Europe focuses on the suffering in Ukraine itself, quite reasonably, while also applauding our policy of accelerating the misery, not so reasonably. I'll return to that.

The policy of escalating the war in Ukraine, instead of trying to take steps to end it, has a horrific impact far beyond Ukraine. As widely reported, Ukraine and Russia are major food exporters. The war has cut off food supplies to populations in desperate need, particularly in Africa and Asia.

Take just one example, the world's worst humanitarian crisis according to the UN: Yemen. Over 2 million children face imminent starvation, the World Food Program reports. Almost 100 percent of cereal [is imported] "with Russia and Ukraine accounting for the largest share of wheat and wheat products (42%)," in addition to re-exported flour and processed wheat from the same region.

The crisis extends far beyond. Let's try to be honest about it: perpetuation of the war is, simply, a program of mass murder throughout much of the Global South.

That's the least of it. There are discussions in purportedly serious journals about how the US can win a nuclear war with Russia. Such discussions verge on criminal insanity. And, unfortunately, US-NATO policies provide many possible scenarios for quick termination of human society. To take just one, Putin has so far refrained from attacking the supply lines sending heavy weapons to Ukraine. It won't be a great surprise if that restraint ends, bringing Russia and NATO close to direct conflict, with an easy path to tit-for-tat escalation that could well lead to a quick goodbye.

More likely, in fact, highly probable, is slower death through poisoning of the planet. The most recent IPCC report made it crystal clear that if there is to be any hope for a livable world, we must stop using fossil fuels right now, proceeding steadily until they are soon eliminated. As you point out, the effect of the ongoing war is to end the far-too-limited initiatives underway, indeed to reverse them and to accelerate the race to suicide.

There is, naturally, great joy in the executive offices of the corporations dedicated to destroying human life on Earth. Now they are not only freed from constraints and from the carping of annoying environmentalists, but they are lauded for saving the civilization that they are now encouraged to destroy even more expeditiously. Arms producers share their euphoria about the opportunities offered by the continuing conflict. They are now encouraged to waste scarce resources that are desperately needed for humane and constructive purposes. And like their partners in mass destruction, the fossil fuel corporations, they are raking in taxpayer dollars.

What could be better, or from a different perspective, more insane? We would do well to recall President Dwight D. Eisenhower's words in his "Cross of Iron" speech in 1953:

> Every gun that is made, every warship launched, every rocket fired signifies, in the final sense, a theft from those who hunger and are not fed, those who are cold and are not clothed. This world in arms is not spending money alone. It is spending the sweat of its laborers, the genius of its scientists, the hopes of its children. The cost of one modern heavy bomber is this: a modern brick school in more than 30 cities. It is two electric power plants, each serving a town of 60,000 population. It is two fine, fully equipped hospitals. It is some fifty miles of concrete pavement. We pay for a single fighter with a half-million bushels of wheat. We pay for a single destroyer with new homes that could have housed more than 8,000 people. . . . This is not a way of life at all, in any true sense. Under the cloud of threatening war, it is humanity hanging from a cross of iron.

These words could hardly be more appropriate today.

Let's return to why "world leaders" pursue this mad course. First, let's see if we can find any who deserve the appellation, except in irony.

If there were any, they would be devoting themselves to bringing the conflict to an end in the only way possible: by diplomacy and statecraft. The general outlines of a political settlement have long been understood. We have discussed them before and have also documented the dedication of the US (with NATO in tow) to undermine the possibility of a diplomatic settlement, quite openly, and with pride. There should be no need to review the dismal record again.

A common refrain is that "Mad Vlad" is so insane, and so immersed in wild dreams of reconstructing an empire and maybe conquering the world, that there's no point even listening to what Russians are saying—that is, if you can evade US censorship and find some snippets on Indian state TV or Middle East media. And there is surely no need to contemplate diplomatic engagement with such a creature. Therefore, let's not even explore the only possibility for ending the horror and just continue to escalate it, no matter what the consequences for Ukrainians and the world.

Western leaders, and much of the political class, are now consumed with two major ideas: The first is that Russian military force is so overwhelming that it may soon seek to conquer Western Europe, or even beyond. Thus, we have to "fight Russia over there" (with Ukrainian bodies) so that "we don't have to fight Russia here" in Washington, DC, or so we are warned by House Permanent Select Committee on Intelligence chair Adam Schiff, a Democrat.

The second is that Russian military force has been shown to be a paper tiger, so incompetent and frail, and so poorly led, that it can't conquer cities a few kilometers from its border defended largely by a citizens' army.

The latter thought is the object of much gloating. The former inspires terror in our hearts.

Orwell defined "doublethink" as the capacity to hold two contradictory ideas in mind and to believe them both, a malady only imaginable in ultra-totalitarian states.

Adopting the first idea, we must arm ourselves to the teeth to protect ourselves from the demonic plans of the paper tiger, even though Russian military spending is a fraction of NATO's, even excluding the US. Those suffering memory loss will be delighted that Germany has finally gotten the word, and may soon surpass Russia in military spending. Now Putin will have to think twice before conquering Western Europe.

To repeat the obvious, the war in Ukraine can end with a diplomatic settlement, or with the defeat of one side, either quickly or in prolonged agony. Diplomacy, by definition, is a give-and-take affair. Each side must accept it. It follows that in a diplomatic settlement, Putin must be offered some escape hatch.

We either accept the first option, or we reject it. That at least is not controversial. If we reject it, we are choosing the second option. Since that is the near-universal preference in Western discourse, and continues to be US policy. Let's consider what it entails.

The answer is straightforward: the decision to reject diplomacy means that we will engage in an experiment to see whether the irrational mad dog will slink away quietly in total defeat, or whether he will use the means that he certainly has to destroy Ukraine and set the stage for terminal war.

And while conducting this grotesque experiment with the lives of Ukrainians, we will ensure that millions starve from the food crisis, we will toy with the possibility of nuclear war, and we will race on enthusiastically to destroying the environment that sustains life.

It is of course conceivable that Putin will just surrender, and that he'll refrain from using the forces at his command. And perhaps we can simply laugh off the prospects of resort to nuclear weapons. Conceivable, but what kind of person would be willing to take that gamble?

The answer is: Western leaders, quite explicitly, along with the political class. That has been obvious for years, even stated officially. And to make sure that all understand, the position was forcefully reiterated in April at the first monthly meeting of the "Contact Group," which includes NATO and partner countries. The meeting was not held at NATO headquarters in Brussels, Belgium. Rather, all pretenses were dropped, and it was held at the US Ramstein Air Base in Germany; technically German territory, but in the real world belonging to the US.

Defense Secretary Lloyd Austin opened the meeting by declaring that "Ukraine clearly believes it can win and so does everyone here." Therefore, the assembled dignitaries should have no hesitation in pouring advanced weapons into Ukraine and persisting in the other programs, proudly announced, to bring Ukraine effectively within the NATO system. In their wisdom, the attending dignitaries and their leader guarantee that Putin will not react in ways they all know he can.

The record of military planning for many years, in fact, centuries, indicates that "everyone here" may indeed hold these remarkable beliefs. Whether they do or not, they are, clearly, willing to carry out the experiment with the lives of Ukrainians and the future of life on Earth.

Since we are assured on this high authority that Russia will passively observe all of this with no reaction, we can take further steps to "integrate Ukraine into NATO de facto," in accord with the goals of the Ukrainian defense ministry, establishing "full compatibility of the Ukrainian army with the armies of NATO countries"—thereby also guaranteeing that no diplomatic settlement can be reached with any Russian government, unless Russia is somehow turned into a US satellite.

Current US policy calls for a long war to "weaken Russia" and ensure its total defeat. The policy is very similar to the Afghan model of the 1980s, which is, in fact, now explicitly advocated in high places; by former secretary of state Hillary Clinton, for example.

Since that is close to current US policy, even a working model, it is worthwhile to look at what actually happened in Afghanistan in the '80s when Russia invaded. Fortunately, we now have a detailed and authoritative account by Diego Cordovez, who directed the successful UN programs that ended the war, and the distinguished journalist and scholar Selig Harrison, who has extensive experience in the region.

The Cordovez-Harrison analysis completely overthrows the received version. They demonstrate that the war was ended by careful UN-run diplomacy, not by military force. Soviet military forces were fully capable of continuing the war. The US policy of mobilizing and funding the most extremist radical Islamists to fight the Russians amounted to "fighting to the last Afghan," they conclude, in a proxy war to weaken the Soviet Union. "The United States did its best to prevent the emergence of a U.N. role," that is, the careful diplomatic efforts that ended the war.

US policy apparently delayed the Russian withdrawal that had been contemplated from shortly after the invasion—which, they show, had limited objectives, with no resemblance to the awesome goals of world conquest that were conjured up in US propaganda. "The Soviet invasion was clearly not the first step in an expansionist master plan of a united leadership," Harrison writes, confirming the conclusions of historian David Gibbs based on released Soviet archives.

The chief CIA officer in Islamabad, who ran the operations directly, put the main point simply: the goal was to kill Russian soldiers—to give Russia their Vietnam, as proclaimed by high US officials, revealing the colossal inability to understand anything about Indochina that was the hallmark of US policy for decades of slaughter and destruction.

Cordovez-Harrison wrote that the US government "was divided from the start between 'bleeders,' who wanted to keep Soviet forces pinned down in Afghanistan and thus to avenge Vietnam, and 'dealers,' who wanted to compel their withdrawal through a combination of diplomacy and military pressure." It's a distinction that shows up very often. The bleeders usually win, causing immense damage. For "the decider," to borrow W. Bush's self-description, it is safer to look tough than to appear to be too soft.

Afghanistan is a case in point. In the Carter administration, Secretary of State Cyrus Vance was a dealer, who suggested far-reaching compromises that would have almost certainly prevented, or at least sharply curtailed, what was intended to be a limited intervention. National Security Adviser Zbigniew Brzezinski was the bleeder, intent on avenging Vietnam, whatever that meant in his confused worldview, and killing Russians, something he understood very well, and relished.

Brzezinski prevailed. He convinced Carter to send arms to the opposition that was seeking to overthrow the pro-Russian government, anticipating that the Russians would be drawn into a Vietnam-style quagmire. When it happened, he could barely contain his delight. When asked later whether he had any regrets, he dismissed the question as ridiculous. His success in drawing Russia into the Afghan trap, he claimed, was responsible for the collapse of the Soviet empire and ending the Cold War—mostly nonsense. And who cares if it harmed "some agitated Muslims," like the million cadavers, putting aside such incidentals as the devastation of Afghanistan, and the rise of radical Islam.

The Afghan analogy is being publicly advocated today, and more importantly, is being implemented in policy.

The dealer-bleeder distinction is nothing new in foreign policy circles. A famous example from the early days of the Cold War is the conflict between George Kennan (a dealer) and Paul Nitze (a bleeder), won by Nitze, laying the basis for many years of brutality and near destruction. Cordovez-Harrison explicitly endorse Kennan's approach, with ample evidence.

An example close to Vance-Brzezinski is the conflict between Secretary of State William Rogers (a dealer) and National Security Adviser Henry Kissinger (a bleeder) over Middle East policy in the Richard Nixon years. Rogers proposed reasonable diplomatic solutions to the Israel-Arab conflict. Kissinger, whose ignorance of the region was monumental, insisted on confrontation, leading to the 1973 war, a close call for Israel with a serious threat of nuclear war.

These conflicts are perennial, almost. Today there are only bleeders in high places. They have gone as far as to enact a huge Lend-Lease Act for Ukraine, passed almost unanimously. The terminology is designed to evoke the memory of the enormous Lend-Lease program that brought the US into the European war (as intended) and linked the European and Asian conflicts into a World War (unintended). "Lend Lease tied together the separate struggles in Europe and Asia to create by the end of 1941 what we properly call World War II," writes historian Adam Tooze. Is that what we want in today's quite different circumstances?

If that is what we want, as seems to be the case, let us at least reflect on what it entails. That is important enough to repeat.

It entails that we reject out of hand the kind of diplomatic initiatives that in reality ended the Russian invasion of Afghanistan, despite US efforts to impede them. We therefore undertake an experiment to see whether integration of Ukraine into NATO, total defeat of Russia in Ukraine, and further moves to "weaken Russia," will be observed passively by the Russian leadership, or whether they will resort to the means of violence they unquestionably possess to devastate Ukraine and set the stage for possible general war.

Meanwhile, by extending the conflict instead of seeking to end it, we impose severe costs on Ukrainians, drive millions of people to death by starvation, hurtle the burning planet even more rapidly to the sixth mass extinction, and—if we are lucky—escape terminal war.

No problem, the government and political class tell us. The experiment carries no risk because the Russian leadership is sure to accept all of this with equanimity, passing quietly into the ash heap of history. As for the "collateral damage," they can join the ranks of Brzezinski's "agitated Muslims." To borrow the phrase made famous by Madeleine Albright: "This is a very hard choice, but the price—we think the price is worth it."

Let's at least have the honesty to recognize what we are doing, eyes open.

Global emissions rose to a record high in 2021, so the world went back to a "business-as-usual" approach once the worst of the COVID-19 pandemic subsided—for now. How hardwired is human behavior? Are we capable of having moral duties toward future people?

It is a deep question, the most important question we can contemplate. The answer is unknown. It may be helpful to think about it in a broader context.

Consider Enrico Fermi's famous paradox: In simple words, where are they? A distinguished astrophysicist, Fermi knew that there are a huge number of planets within the reach of potential contact that have the conditions to sustain life and higher intelligence. But with the most assiduous search, we can find no trace of their existence. So where are they?

One response that has been seriously proposed, and cannot be dismissed, is that higher intelligence has developed innumerable times, but has proven to be lethal: it discovered the means for self-annihilation but did not develop the moral capacity to prevent it. Perhaps that is even an inherent feature of what we call "higher intelligence."

We are now engaged in an experiment to determine whether this grim principle holds of modern humans, a very recent arrival on Earth, some 200,000 to 300,000 years ago, a flick of an eye in evolutionary time. There is not much time to find the answer—or more precisely, to determine the answer, as we will do, one way or the other. That is unavoidable. We will either act to show that our moral capacity reaches as far as to control our technical capacity to destroy, or that it does not.

An extraterrestrial observer, if there were one, would unfortunately conclude that the gap is too immense to prevent species suicide, and with it the sixth mass extinction. But it could be mistaken. That decision is in our hands.

There is a rough measure of the gap between capacity to destroy and capacity to contain that death wish: the Doomsday Clock of the Bulletin of Atomic Scientists. The distance of the hands from midnight can be regarded as an indication of the gap. In 1953, when the US and Soviet Union exploded thermonuclear weapons, the minute hand was set to two minutes to midnight. It did not reach that point again until Donald Trump's term in office. In his last year, the analysts abandoned minutes and switched to seconds: 100 seconds to midnight, where the clock now stands. Next January it will be set again. It's not hard to make a case that the second hand should move closer to midnight.

The grim question arose with brilliant clarity on August 6, 1945. That day provided two lessons: (1) human intelligence, in its glory, was approaching the capacity to destroy everything, an achievement reached in 1953; and (2) human moral capacity lagged far behind. Few even cared, as people of my age will remember very well. Viewing the hideous experiment to which we are enthusiastically committed today, and what it entails, it is hard to see improvement, to put it mildly.

That doesn't answer the question. We know far too little to answer it. We can only observe closely the one case of "higher intelligence" that we know of, and ask what it suggests about the answer.

Far more importantly, we can act to determine the answer. It is within our power to bring about the answer that we all hope for, but there is no time to waste.

THE SUPREME COURT IS WIELDING ILLEGITIMATE AUTHORITY IN THE US

May 20, 2022

C. J. Polychroniou: *Noam, over the past couple of decades, we've been witnessing a surge of illegitimate authority. And I am not thinking so much about the increasing influence of transnational corporations on democratic processes as about decisions made by a handful of appointed or elected individuals that affect the lives of millions of people. For example, a few people sitting at the Supreme Court were appointed for life by presidents that lost the popular vote, and they often enough issue decisions that go against the majority of voters' preferences. Another example is members of the US Congress who block bills aimed at the improvement of the economic well-being of citizens and the protection of the environment, choosing instead to introduce legislation catered to the interests of powerful lobby groups. Can you comment about this most despairing state of affairs in the US political landscape?*

Noam Chomsky: The Supreme Court has traditionally been a reactionary institution. There is some deviation, but it's rare. The Warren Court's major decisions greatly enhanced freedom and basic rights, but not in isolation: There were popular movements, primarily African American but joined by others to a degree, which made it possible for the Warren Court's rulings to be implemented. Today's reactionary Roberts Court is reverting to the norm with its dedicated efforts to reverse this deviation.

And it can do so thanks in large measure to the conniving and deceit of the leading anti-democratic figure in the Republican organization—no longer an authentic political party: Mitch McConnell.

All of this is, or should be, well known. I'll return to a few comments about it.

Less well known is how far back this goes. Some of the story is familiar, but not all. It's familiar that the enormous power of the Supreme Court traces back to Justice John Marshall's decision in *Marbury v. Madison* to make the judiciary the arbiter of the meaning of the law, powers going well beyond what is granted in the Constitution. His appointment by John Adams, and his own immediate appointments and decisions, were designed to undercut the newly elected Jefferson administration.

Shades of McConnell.

Marshall's opinions had a major impact in shaping the constitutional order as it, in fact, is interpreted. His imprint on the court is unmatched.

All of that is again well known.

Much less well known are the assumptions that lie behind Marshall's major decisions. In fact, these have only recently been revealed in legal scholarship by the important work of Paul Finkelman, who did the first systematic study of Marshall's rulings on a central element of American history: slavery, which is likely to be expunged from history curricula if Republicans regain power and can implement their totalitarian initiatives to determine what cannot be taught in schools.

Finkelman explores "Chief Justice John Marshall's personal and political commitment to slavery, as a lifelong buyer and seller of human beings, and his deep hostility to the presence of free blacks in America." He then proceeds to show that in his judicial rulings, Marshall "always supported slaveowners when blacks claimed to be free. Similarly, he consistently failed to enforce the federal prohibitions on American participation in the African slave trade or, after 1808, the absolute prohibition on bringing new slaves into the United States." As Finkelman points out, Marshall's harsh and brutal rulings were "consistent with his lifelong personal and political support for slavery."

Apart from the immediate impact on the lives of those treated as less than human in his day and throughout American history, Marshall was no ordinary justice. It is an understatement to say that he is "perhaps the Supreme Court's most influential chief justice."

This is not the place to review the long and often sordid history of the court. It's enough to remember that it hardly accords with the patriotic slogans we are enjoined to chant by the new totalitarians in Washington.

As for Congress, the story is mixed. One constant feature is service to the rich and powerful, relying on means of the kind you mention. Popular activism has sometimes proved to be an effective counterforce, with major effects on civilizing the country. The New Deal period from the '30s through the '60s is the most recent case. Though the business classes worked hard to whittle New Deal measures away, they retained strong political support, including from the last authentic conservative president, Dwight Eisenhower. In his view, "Should any political party attempt to abolish social security, unemployment insurance, and eliminate labor laws and farm programs, you would not hear of that party again in our political history. There is a tiny splinter group, of course, that believes you can do these things. . . . [But] their number is negligible and they are stupid."

Eisenhower's attitudes illustrate how far his party has declined in recent years, meanwhile defaming the term "conservatism."

One current illustration of the drift of the party to the far right is its love affair with the racist "illiberal democracy" of Viktor Orbán's Hungary. It is not confined to Tucker Carlson and the like but goes far beyond. As one illustration, the American Conservative Union "convenes in Budapest next month [June] to celebrate a European leader accused of undermining democracy and individual rights." Justly accused, but Orbán regards it as praise, not accusation, and today's "conservatives" appear to agree.

Eisenhower's prognosis was wrong. The "splinter group"—which unfortunately was far from that—was not merely waiting in the wings. It was gnawing away at measures to benefit the public, often effectively. By the late Carter years, its influence was strongly felt. The Democrats had by then pretty much abandoned any authentic concern with working people, becoming increasingly a party of affluent professionals.

Reagan opened the doors wide to those whom Eisenhower had bitterly condemned, launching the powerful neoliberal assault on the general population of the past forty years, which is still vigorously underway. This is not the place to review its impact once again. It is encapsulated in the Rand Corporation study that we have discussed, which found that these programs have "transferred" close to $50 trillion from the middle and working classes to the ultrarich in forty years, a pretty impressive feat of highway robbery.

Today's Republican organization can barely control its enthusiasm at the prospect of carrying the assault further, concealed with cynical populist slogans.

All of this is transpiring before our eyes, quite openly. The congressional GOP virtually goose-steps in obedience to McConnell's explicit and public orders, reprised from the Obama years. There is one and only one legislative priority: regain power. That means ensuring that the country is ungovernable, and that any legislation that might benefit the general population must be blocked. Then failure to achieve anything can be blamed on Democrats—a few of whom participate in the sham.

The most striking current example is the Build Back Better program, a quite respectable initiative that would have greatly helped the population when it left Bernie Sanders's desk. Whittled away step-by-step under the McConnell principle, now not even shreds remain.

Meanwhile, the GOP leadership established their red lines: (1) defund the IRS, so that it cannot interfere with the massive tax cheating by the prime GOP constituency, the very rich; (2) don't touch the one legislative achievement of the Trump years, what Joseph Stiglitz called "the Donor Relief Act of 2017," a massive giveaway to the very rich and corporate sector, stabbing everyone else in the back. This giveaway to the rich also hurt the right's own voters, whom the GOP has labored to keep in line since Nixon by diverting attention from its actual programs to "cultural issues" that appeal to Christian nationalists, white supremacists, Evangelicals, avid gun lovers, and segments of the working class devastated by neoliberal programs and long abandoned by the Democrats.

The court has played its role in reviving the ugliest elements of the history we are instructed to suppress. Probably the most egregious decision of the Roberts Court was to dismantle the Voting Rights Act on ridiculous grounds (*Shelby*), offering the South the means to restore Jim Crow. *Citizens United* extended the Buckley doctrine that money is speech—very convenient for the very rich particularly—to giving virtually free rein to those sectors in a position to buy elections.

Next on the chopping block is *Roe v. Wade*. The effects will be extreme. A right regarded by most women, and others, as solidly established is to be wiped out. That's almost unprecedented. Undermining of the right of Black people to vote by the *Shelby* decision is a partial precedent.

Justice Alito's leaked draft is based primarily on the principle that court decisions should give primacy to what is "deeply rooted in this Nation's history and tradition." And he is quite right that women's rights do not satisfy this condition. The founders adopted British common law, which held that a woman is property, owned by her father, ownership transferred to her husband. One early argument for denying the vote to women was that it would be unfair to unmarried men, since a married man would have two votes, his own and his "property's." (The infamous three-fifth's human provision granted that right to slaveowners.) It wasn't until 1975 that the Supreme Court granted full personhood to women, granting them the right to serve on federal juries as "peers."

This ultra-reactionary judicial doctrine is, like others, quite flexible. One illustration is Antonin Scalia's *Heller* decision, which reversed a century of precedent and established personal gun ownership as Holy Writ. In his very learned opinion, Scalia succeeded in ignoring all of the rich "history and tradition" that lies behind the decree that "a well-regulated Militia, being necessary to the security of a free State, the right of the people to keep and bear Arms, shall not be infringed."

The history and tradition are hardly a secret, from the founders through the nineteenth century, though of course they have no relevance to American history since: (1) the Brits are coming; (2) militias are needed to attack, expel, and exterminate the Indigenous nations once the British constraint on expansion was removed, arguably the primary reason for the revolution—though later they were displaced by a more efficient killing machine, the US Cavalry; (3) slaves had to be controlled by force, a threat that was becoming severe with slave revolts in the Caribbean and the South; (4) before the constitutional system was firmly established, there was concern that the British model might be imposed (as Alexander Hamilton had suggested) and might lead to a tyranny that would have to be resisted by popular forces.

None of this "history and tradition" had any relevance by the twentieth century, at least in semi-rational circles. But it was surely there in history and tradition, not just *there* but a central part of the history that is scheduled for cancellation as the GOP marches down-ward. All of this proceeds with the help of the reactionary judiciary that has been constructed carefully by McConnell and allies, with the goal of imposing a barrier to anything like the deviation of Eisenhower for a long time.

Michael Waldman, president of the Brennan Center for Justice and a specialist on the Second Amendment, observes that since Scalia reversed long-standing precedent by ignoring history and tradition, the court has had little to say about the gun issue, much to the discomfiture of the extreme right on the court. But that, Waldman suggests, may be about to change. The court is considering a case that might overturn a 1913 New York law that restricts carrying a concealed weapon in public places. From Alito's comments in oral argument, and Thomas's well-known positions, Waldman suspects that the 1913 ruling may be overturned. We'll then enjoy a world in which concealed weapons are everywhere.

It's worth remembering that today's frenzied gun culture is largely the creation of the public relations industry, in fact one of its first great triumphs, a revealing history explored in depth by Pamela Haag in *The Gunning of America: Business and the Making of American Gun Culture*.

Guns were indeed used for definite purposes, those just described. And individual farmers could use an old musket to scare away critters attacking cattle. For them a gun was a tool, like a shovel. Arms manufacturers were meanwhile developing advanced weapons, but for armies, not the public, which had little interest in them.

By the late nineteenth century, a problem was arising. After the Civil War, the domestic market largely collapsed for advanced armaments. Peace in Europe undermined another market. The US Army was not engaged in major wars. The nascent PR industry was enlisted to the cause. It concocted an exciting image of a Wild West that never existed, with brave cowboys and sheriffs fast on the draw, and the rest of the familiar fantasies, later exploited by Hollywood and TV. The subtext was that your son is dying to have a Winchester rifle so that he can be a real man, and his sister must have a little pink pistol. It worked, brilliantly, as many of us can attest from childhood memories, if not beyond.

The mythology was later expanded as part of the awesome GOP propaganda campaign to divert attention away from their actual policies and commitments. Scalia's radical departure from "history and tradition" then turned the Second Amendment into the only part of the Constitution that is worshipped fervently, that is even known by much of the population.

What are the boundaries of political authority? Why is there a surge of illegitimate authority in today's "democracies"? And how should concerned citizens disobey illegitimate decisions made by politicos and the Supreme Court?

Class war never ceases. One participant, the business classes—the "masters of mankind" in Adam Smith's phrase—is constantly engaged in the conflict, with no little passion in a country like the US that has an unusually high level of business class consciousness. As Smith pointed out 250 years ago, they strive to control state policy and employ it for their own interests, commonly succeeding, though with occasional partial setbacks. If their victims are beaten down or retire from the struggle, they win enormous victories for themselves. We have just experienced that during the neoliberal regression, which undermined democracy along with the huge robbery. That's a basic factor in the surge of "illegit-imate authority" in today's declining democracies, and in the pervasive anger, resentment, and distrust of authority.

There is, of course, a lot to say about why and how this stunning victory was achieved, but that goes beyond the bounds of this discus-sion. We should, however, be aware of the fraudulence of standard shibboleths like "letting the market reign" and other phrases that barely count as caricatures.

The "boundaries" of this triumph of illegitimate authority can only be set by an engaged public, just as happened in the '30s and at other periods of history when the "masters" were somewhat tamed. There are no general answers to questions about appropriate mea-sures. There are general guidelines and aspirations, but tactical deci-sions depend on circumstances. And they are not to be disparaged as "merely tactical." Those are the decisions on which people's lives depend—in the present era, even survival.

Surveys reveal that an overwhelming majority of Americans want to see major changes to the country's political system. How can we fix the US political system? What rules, for instance, need to be changed?

I don't feel confident about what the majority want. Furthermore, what people want is shaped by the range of options they perceive. These, in turn, are largely structured by the reigning institutions, which are in substantial measure in the hands of the "masters of mankind."

For example, today the options are "get a job or starve," so getting a job is perceived to be one of the highest goals in life. In the early days of the Industrial Revolution, Americans regarded "getting a job" as an intolerable attack on human rights and dignity. They understood that it meant subordinating yourself to a master for most of your waking hours. And they had alternatives in mind. The slogan of the Knights of Labor, the first great labor organization, was that "those who work in the mills should own them." Anything less than that was intolerable.

Meanwhile, farmers in what was then mostly an agrarian coun-try sought to create a "cooperative commonwealth" in which farmers would work together, free from the Northern bankers and market managers. That's the authentic populist movement, which began to establish contacts with the Knights. Their efforts were crushed by state and private violence, another defeat of radical democracy. And "what people want" then changed, as the options they could envision reduced.

The task of organizers and activists is first of all to break the fetters of ideological control and to help people understand that there are ways of looking at the world that are different from those constructed by the masters and their ideological institutions. That will enable changes in what people want. Then come the crucial questions of what should be changed, and how.

The climate crisis is intensifying. To take just a few random examples, heat waves are shattering records across major sections of the United States, and a recent report on France's drought shows that climate change is "spiraling out of control." Unsurprisingly, climate protests worldwide have become more common and more aggressive. Do disruptive climate protests help or hinder the acceleration of a sustainable transition?

Here we face difficult questions of tactics, which as always are of critical importance. What kinds of tactics will bring more people to become actively engaged in fending off the sixth extinction, and saving human society from the imminent disaster to which the masters are driving it? And what tactical choices will undermine this essential goal by alienating people? There's no algorithm, no general answer. It has to be thought through carefully. There will be different answers in different places and times.

We cannot stress often enough, or intensely enough, how critical this matter is. We are hurtling to disaster at a terrifying rate, sharply accelerated by recent events. The Russian invasion of Ukraine had an enormously consequential effect on fossil fuel production, which will soon destroy us if not curbed. The war reversed the limited steps to avert the catastrophe. If that is permitted to continue, we are doomed.

Is there a reason to suspect that the next stage of economic development, based perhaps on a green revolution, will actually have greater legitimacy and be more democratic than the present socioeconomic order?

A prior question is whether there will be a next stage of economic development. Or, in fact, a next stage of human history at all aside from *sauve qui peut*: Grab what you can for yourself and maybe escape the destruction and chaos by hitching a ride on Elon Musk's last spaceship to Mars.

The next stage will be either that, or it will be a green revolution, a real one: no greenwashing, none of the fakery in which the fossil fuel and financial industries are highly skilled. We know what has to be done and can be done, feasibly. The means are available. What is in question is the will and commitment.

If we can make it that far, there are lots of reasons to expect that an authentic green revolution can lead to a much more humane social order, and a much better life.

Our choice, and not much time to delay.

WE MUST INSIST THAT NUCLEAR WARFARE IS AN UNTHINKABLE POLICY

June 2, 2022

C. J. Polychroniou: *After months of fighting, there is still very little hope of peace in Ukraine. Russia is now refocusing its efforts on taking control of the east and south of the country with the likely intent of incorporating them into the Russian Federation, while the West has signaled that it will step up military support for Ukraine. In the light of these developments, Ukrainian officials have ruled out a ceasefire or concessions to Moscow, although President Volodymyr Zelenskyy also went on record saying that only diplomacy can end the war. Don't these two positions cancel each other out? Doesn't a mutually acceptable agreement for a war to end always contain concessions? Indeed, back in March, the Ukrainian government had signaled its intention that it was willing to make big concessions for the war to end. So, what's going on? Could it be that neither side is fully invested in peace?*

Noam Chomsky: I'll come back to the questions, but we should carefully consider the stakes. They are very high. They go far beyond Ukraine, desperate and tragic as the situation is there. Anyone with a moral bone in their body will want to think through the issues carefully, without heroic posturing.

Let's consider what is at stake.

First, of course, is Putin's invasion of Ukraine, a crime (to repeat once again) that can be compared to the US invasion of Iraq or the

Hitler-Stalin invasion of Poland, the kind of crimes against peace for which Nazi war criminals were hanged—though only the defeated are subject to punishment in what we call "civilization." In Ukraine itself, there will be a terrible toll as long as the war persists.

There are broader consequences, which are truly colossal. That's no exaggeration.

One is that tens of millions of people in Asia, Africa, and the Middle East are literally facing starvation as the war proceeds, cutting off desperately needed agricultural supplies from the Black Sea region, the primary supplier for many countries, including some already facing utter disaster, like Yemen. Will return to how that is being handled.

A second is the growing threat of terminal nuclear war. It is all too easy to construct plausible scenarios that lead to a rapid climb up the escalation ladder. To take one, right now the US is sending advanced anti-ship missiles to Ukraine. The flagship of the Russian fleet has already been sunk. Suppose more of the fleet is attacked. How does Russia then react? And what follows?

To mention another scenario, so far Russia has refrained from attacking the supply lines used to ship heavy armaments to Ukraine. Suppose it does so, placing it in direct confrontation with NATO— meaning the US. We can leave the rest to the imagination.

Other proposals are circulating that would very likely lead to nuclear war—which means the end, for all of us, facts that do not seem to be properly understood. One is the widely voiced call for a no-fly zone, which means attacking anti-aircraft installations inside Russia. The extreme danger of such proposals is understood by some, notably the Pentagon, which so far has been able to veto the most dangerous proposals. For how long in the prevailing mood?

These are horrendous prospects. Prospects: what might happen. When we look at what actually is happening, it gets worse. The Ukraine invasion has reversed the much-too-limited efforts to address global warming—which will soon become global frying. Prior to the invasion, some steps were being taken to avert catastrophe. Now that has all been thrown into reverse. If that continues, we're done.

One day, the IPCC issues another severe warning that if we are to survive, we must start right now to reduce use of fossil fuels. Right now, no delay. The next day, President Biden announces vast new expansion of fossil fuel production.

Biden's call to increase fossil fuel production is sheer political theater. It has nothing to do with today's fuel prices and inflation, as claimed. It will be years before the poisons reach the market—years that could be spent on moving the world rapidly to renewable energy. That's perfectly feasible, but barely discussed in the mainstream. There's no need to comment here. The topic has recently been expertly analyzed by economist Robert Pollin in another of his essential contributions to understanding this critical issue of survival and acting on that understanding.

It is crystal clear that settling the Ukraine crisis is of extraordinary significance, not just for Ukraine itself but because of the calamitous consequences beyond if the war persists.

What then can we do to facilitate ending the tragedy? Let's begin with virtual truism. The war can end in one of two ways: either there will be a diplomatic settlement, or one side will capitulate. The horror will go on unless it ends with a diplomatic settlement or capitulation.

That at least should be beyond discussion.

A diplomatic settlement differs from capitulation in one crucial respect: each side accepts it as tolerable. That's true by definition, so it is beyond discussion.

Proceeding, a diplomatic settlement must offer Putin some kind of escape hatch—what is now disdainfully called an "off-ramp" or "appeasement" by those who prefer to prolong the war.

That much is understood even by the most dedicated Russia-haters, at least those who can entertain some thought in their minds beyond punishing the reviled enemy. One prominent example is the distinguished foreign policy scholar Graham Allison of Harvard University's Kennedy School of Government, who also has long direct experience in military affairs. Five years ago, he instructed us that it was then clear that Russia as a whole is a "demonic" society and "deserves to be strangled." Today he adds that few can doubt that

Putin is a "demon," radically unlike any US leader, who at worst only make mistakes, in his view.

Yet even Allison argues that we must contain our righteous anger and bring the war to a quick end by diplomatic means. The reason is that if the mad demon "is forced to choose between losing and escalating the level of violence and destruction, then, if he's a rational actor, he's going to choose the latter"—and we may all be dead, not just Ukrainians.

Putin is a rational actor, Allison argues. And if he is not, all discussion is useless because he can destroy Ukraine and maybe even blow up the world at any moment—an eventuality we cannot prevent by any means that won't destroy us all.

Proceeding with truism, to oppose or even act to delay a diplomatic settlement is to call for prolonging the war with its grim consequences for Ukraine and beyond. This stand constitutes a ghastly experiment: let's see whether Putin will slink away quietly in total defeat, or whether he will prolong the war with all its horrors, or even use the weapons that he indisputably has to devastate Ukraine and to set the stage for terminal war.

All of this seems obvious enough. Or it should, but not in the current climate of hysteria, where such near truisms elicit a great flood of utterly irrational reactions: *The monster Putin won't agree; it's appeasement; what about Munich; we have to establish our own red lines and keep to them whatever the monster says;* etc.

There is no need to dignify such outpourings with a response. They all amount to saying: let's not try, and instead undertake the ghastly experiment.

The ghastly experiment is operative US policy, and is supported by a wide range of opinion, always with noble rhetoric about how we must stand up for principle and not permit crime to go unpunished. When we hear this from strong supporters of US crimes, as we commonly do, we can dismiss it as sheer cynicism, the Western counterpart to the most vulgar apparatchiks of the Soviet years, eager to eloquently denounce Western crimes, fully supportive of their own. We also hear it from opponents of US crimes, from people who surely do not want to carry out the ghastly experiment that they are advocating. Here other issues arise: the rising tide of irrationality that is undermining any hope for serious discourse—a necessity if Ukraine is to be spared indescribable tragedy, and even if the human experiment is to persist much longer.

If we can escape cynicism and irrationality, the humane choice for the US and the West is straightforward: seek to facilitate a diplomatic settlement, or at least don't undermine the option.

On this matter, official Western opinion is split. France, Germany, and Italy have been calling for negotiations to establish a ceasefire and move toward a diplomatic settlement. The US and Britain, the West's two warrior states, object. Their position is that the war must proceed: the ghastly experiment.

The longstanding US policy of undermining diplomacy, which we have reviewed in detail in earlier discussions, was presented in sharper form a few weeks ago at a meeting of NATO powers and others organized by Washington at the US airbase in Ramstein, Germany. The US issued the marching orders: the war must be continued so as to harm Russia. That is the widely advocated "Afghan model" that we have discussed: in the words of the definitive scholarly study of the topic, it is the policy of "fighting Russia to the last Afghan" while seeking to delay Russian withdrawal and to undermine the UN diplomatic efforts that finally brought the tragedy to an end.

Explaining US-NATO goals at Ramstein, Defense Secretary Lloyd Austin said that "we want to see Russia weakened to the degree that it can't do the kinds of things that it has done in invading Ukraine."

Let's think about it. How do we ensure that Russia can never again invade another country? We put aside here the unthinkable question of whether reshaping US policy might contribute to this end, for example, examining Washington's openly declared refusal to consider any Russian security concerns and many other actions that we have discussed.

To achieve the announced goal, it seems that we must at least reenact something like the Versailles Treaty, which sought to ensure that Germany would not be able to go to war again.

But Versailles did not go far enough, as was soon made clear. It follows that the new version being planned must "strangle the demon" in ways that go beyond the Versailles effort to control the Huns. Perhaps something like the Morgenthau Plan.

That is the logic of the pronouncements. Even if we don't take the words seriously and give them a limited interpretation, the policy entails prolonging the war, whatever the consequences are for Ukrainians and the "collateral damage" beyond: mass starvation, possible terminal war, continued destruction of the environment that sustains life.

Narrower questions of a similar sort arise with regard to the blockade, with its lethal effects in the Global South. Right now, Ukrainian ports are blockaded by the Russian Navy, preventing desperately needed exports. What can be done about it?

As always, there are two directions to explore: military or diplomatic. "War-war or jaw-jaw" in the phrase attributed to Churchill, who assigned priority to the latter.

War-war is official US policy: send advanced anti-ship missiles to force Russia to stop blockade of ports. Beyond the Russian flagship, more can be sunk. Will the Russians observe quietly? Maybe. How would the US react in similar circumstances? We can put that aside.

Another possibility, proposed by the *Wall Street Journal* editors, is "to use warships to escort merchant ships out of the Black Sea." The editors assure us that it would conform to international law, and that Russians will stop at nothing. So, if they react, we can proclaim proudly that we upheld international law as all goes up in flames.

The editors observe that there are precedents: "The U.S. has marshalled allies for such a mission twice in recent decades. In the late 1980s the U.S. reflagged and protected Kuwaiti oil tankers as they sailed out of the Persian Gulf during the Iran-Iraq tanker war."

That is correct, though there is a small oversight. The US did indeed intervene directly to provide crucial support for Reagan's good friend Saddam Hussein in his invasion of Iran. That was after supporting Saddam's chemical warfare that killed hundreds of thousands of Iranians, and even charging Iran for Saddam's massacre of Kurds with chemical warfare. Iran was the demon of the day. A fine precedent.

Those are options for ending the blockade, keeping to convention by restricting attention to force rather than possible peaceful steps.

Are there any? One cannot know without thinking about them, looking at what is transpiring, and trying. It may be of relevance that Russia did propose something of the sort, though in our increasingly totalitarian culture, it can be reported only at the extreme margins. Quoting from a libertarian website:

> Russian Deputy Foreign Minister Andrey Rudenko . . . [argued] his country is not solely responsible for the burgeoning food emergency while pointing to Western sanctions blocking the export of grain and fertilizers.
>
> "You have to not only appeal to the Russian Federation but also look deeply at the whole complex of reasons that caused the current food crisis. [Sanctions] interfere with normal free trade, encompassing food products including wheat, fertilizers and others," Russian Deputy Foreign Minister Andrey Rudenko said.

Is it worth considering? Not in our culture, which automatically reaches for the revolver.

The reflexive preference for violence, and its grim consequences, have not been overlooked abroad. That's common in the Global South, which has ample experience with Western practice, but even among allies. The editor of the Australian international affairs journal *Arena* deplores the rigid censorship and intolerance of even mild dissent in US media, concluding that "this means it is almost impossible within mainstream opinion to simultaneously acknowledge Putin's insupportable actions *and* forge a path out of the war that does not involve escalation, and the further destruction of Ukraine."

Quite correct. And unless we can escape this self-imposed trap, we are likely to march on to annihilation. It is all reminiscent of the early days of World War I when the great powers enthusiastically undertook a self-destructive war, but this time with incomparably more severe consequences lurking not far in the distance.

I've said nothing about what Ukrainians should do, for the simple and sufficient reason that it's not our business. If they opt for the ghastly experiment, that's their right. It's also their right to request weapons to defend themselves from murderous aggression.

Here we return to what is our business: ourselves. How should we respond to these requests? I'll repeat in a moment my personal belief, but here, too, a little honesty wouldn't hurt. There are many ringing declarations upholding the sacred principle that victims of criminal assault must be supported in their just demand for weapons to defend themselves. It is easy to show that those who issue them don't believe a word of what they are saying, and in fact, almost always, strongly support providing weapons and crucial diplomatic support to the aggressor. To take just the most obvious case, where are the calls to provide Palestinians with weapons to defend themselves from half a century of brutal criminal occupation in violation of Security Council orders and international law—or even to withdraw the decisive US support for these crimes?

One can, of course, read the reports of US-backed settler-IDF atrocities in the Israeli press, in the daily columns of the great journalist Gideon Levy. And we can read the withering reports by another honorable Israeli journalist, Amira Hass, reviewing the bitter condemnations of the ecological damage caused by the "demonic" Russians in Ukraine, which somehow miss the Israeli attack on Gaza last May, when "Israeli shells ignited hundreds of tons of pesticides, seeds, fertilizers, other chemicals, nylon and plastic sheeting, and plastic piping in a warehouse in the northern Gaza town of Beit Lahia." The shelling ignited fifty tons of hazardous substances, with lethal effects on the shattered population, which is living in conditions of bare survival, international agencies report, after decades of US-backed Israeli sadism. It is "chemical warfare by indirect means," the highly reputable Palestinian legal research and activism agency al-Haq reports, after extensive investigation.

None of this, and vastly more, inspires any word in the mainstream about ending huge US support for the murderous occupier, or, of course, for any means of defense.

But enough of such outrageous "whataboutism," otherwise known as elementary honesty, and a common theme outside of our tightly controlled doctrinal system. How should the principle apply in the unique case of Ukraine, where the US for once opposes aggression? My own view, to repeat, is that the Ukrainian request for weapons should be honored, with caution to bar shipments that will escalate the criminal assault, punishing Ukrainians even more, with potential cataclysmic effects beyond.

If the war in Ukraine can be ended through diplomacy, a peace deal could take many forms. The diplomatic solution advanced by many experts is the one based on a Ukrainian treaty of neutrality while Russia drops its objections to Ukraine's membership in the EU, although the road to membership will inevitably be very long. However, there is one scenario which is rarely discussed, yet this is where things could be headed. This is Graham Allison's "Korean scenario," where Ukraine is divided into two parts without a formal treaty. Do you regard this as a likely or possible scenario?

It is one of a number of possible very ugly outcomes. Speculation seems to me rather idle. Better, I think, to devote our energy to thinking of constructive ways to overcome the developing tragedies—which, again, go far beyond Ukraine.

We might even envision a broader framework, something like the "common European home" with no military alliances proposed by Mikhail Gorbachev as an appropriate framework of world order after the collapse of the Soviet Union. Or we might pick up some of the early wording of the Partnership for Peace, initiated by Washington in the same years, as when President Clinton in 1994 assured Boris Yeltsin that "the broader, higher goal [is] European security, unity and integration—a goal I know you share."

These promising prospects for peaceful integration were soon undercut, however, by Clinton's plans for NATO expansion, over strong Russian objections, long preceding Putin.

Such hopes can be revived, to the great benefit of Europe, Russia, and world peace generally. They might have been revived by Putin had he pursued Macron's tentative initiatives toward accommodation instead of foolishly choosing criminal aggression. But they are not necessarily dead.

It's useful to recall some history. For centuries, Europe was the most vicious place on earth. For French and Germans, the highest goal in life was to slaughter one another. As recently as my childhood, it seemed unimaginable that it could ever end. A few years later, it did end, and they have since been close allies, pursuing common goals in a radical reversal of a long history of brutal conflict. Diplomatic successes need not be impossible to achieve.

It is now a commonplace that the world has entered a new Cold War. In fact, even the once-unthinkable scenario of using nuclear weapons in warfare is no longer taboo talk. Have we entered an era of confrontation between Russia and the West, a geostrategic and political rivalry reminiscent of the Cold War?

Nuclear warfare had better become taboo talk, and unthinkable policy. We should be working hard to restore the arms-control regime that was virtually dismantled by Bush II and Trump, who didn't have quite enough time to complete the job but came close. Biden was able to rescue the last major relic, New START, just days before its expiration.

The arms-control regime should then be extended, looking forward to the day when the nuclear powers will join the UN Treaty on Prohibition of Nuclear Weapons, now in force.

Other measures can be taken to alleviate the threat, among them implementing nuclear-weapons-free-zones (NWFZs). They exist in much the world, but are blocked by US insistence on maintaining nuclear weapons facilities within them. The most important would be a NWFZ in the Middle East. That would end the alleged Iranian nuclear threat and eliminate any thin pretext for the criminal US-Israeli bombings, assassinations, and sabotage in Iran. That crucial advance in world peace is, however, blocked by the US alone.

The reason is not obscure: it would interfere with Washington's protection of Israel's huge nuclear arsenal. That has to be kept in the dark. If exposed, US law would come into play, threatening Washington's extraordinary support for Israel's illegal occupation and constant crimes—another topic that is unmentionable in polite society.

All steps should be taken to remove the scourge of nuclear weapons from the earth, before they destroy all of us.

In the world system that is taking shape, the confrontation with Russia is something of a sideshow. Putin has handed Washington a marvelous gift by turning Europe into a virtual US vassal, cutting off the prospects that Europe might become an independent "third force" in international affairs. A consequence is that the fading Russian kleptocracy, with its huge stock of natural resources, is being incorporated into the Chinese-dominated zone. This growing system of development and loans stretches over Central Asia and reaches to the Middle East through the UAE and Maritime Silk Road, with tentacles stretching to Africa and even to Washington's "little region over here," as FDR's secretary of war Henry Stimson described Latin America while calling for dismantling of all regional associations except for our own.

It is the "China threat" that is the centerpiece of US strategy. The threat is enhanced if resource-rich Russia is incorporated as a junior partner.

The US is now vigorously reacting to what it calls "Chinese aggression," such as devoting state resources to developing advanced technology and internal repression. The reaction, initiated by Trump, has been carried forward by Biden's policy of "encirclement" based on a ring of "sentinel states" off the coast of China. These are armed with advanced weapons, recently upgraded to high-precision weapons, aimed at China. The "defense" is backed by a fleet of invulnerable nuclear submarines that can destroy not just China but the world many times over. Since that is not good enough, they are now being replaced as part of the enormous Trump-Biden military expansion.

The stern US reaction is understandable. "China, unlike Russia, is the only country powerful enough to challenge U.S. dominance on the world stage," Secretary of State Antony Blinken announced in describing this intolerable threat to world order (a.k.a. US dominance).

While we talk of "isolating Russia," if not "strangling" this "demonic" society, most of the world is keeping its ties open to Russia and to the China-dominated global system. It is also watching, bemused, as the US destroys itself from within.

Meanwhile, the US is developing new alliances, which will presumably strengthen in November if the GOP takes over Congress and manages to gain long-term control of the political system through its quite open efforts to undermine political democracy.

One such alliance is being firmed up right now with the racist, self-declared "illiberal democracy" of Hungary, which has crushed free speech and independent cultural and political institutions and is worshipped by leading figures of the GOP from Trump to media star Tucker Carlson. Steps toward that goal were taken a few days ago at the conference of far-right elements in Europe that met in Budapest, where the star attraction was the Conservative Political Action Conference, a core element of the Republican Party.

The alliance between the US and the European extreme right has a natural ally in the Abraham alliance forged by Trump and Jared Kushner. This widely hailed alliance formalized the tacit relations between Israel and the most reactionary states of the MENA (Middle East–North Africa) region. Israel and Hungary already have close relations, based on shared racist values and a sense of grievance for being shunned by more liberal elements in Europe. Another natural partner is today's India, where Prime Minister Modi is shattering Indian secular democracy and establishing a Hindu ethnocracy, bitterly repressing the Muslim population, and extending India's domains with his brutal occupation of Kashmir.

The US is already virtually alone in recognizing the two existing illegal MENA occupations in violation of Security Council orders: Israel's annexation of the Syrian Golan Heights and of vastly expanded Greater Jerusalem, and Morocco's annexation of Western Sahara to extend its near monopoly of irreplaceable phosphate reserves. With the GOP in power, the US might complete the picture by recognizing Hindu India's violent takeover of Kashmir.

A new global order is taking shape, but the US-Russia confrontation is not its central element.

Speaking of a new Cold War, I must say I am in utter disbelief by the delirious reaction on the part of so many in the US to analyses seeking to provide background to Russia's invasion of Ukraine, and the same is true in connection with voices calling for diplomacy to end the war. They conflate explanation and justification and willfully ignore historical facts, such as the decision of the US to expand NATO eastward without consideration to Russia's security concerns. And it isn't as if this decision was greeted at the time with approval by leading diplomats and foreign affairs experts. Former US envoy to the Soviet Union Jack F. Matlock Jr. and former secretary of state Henry Kissinger warned against NATO expansion and Ukraine's inclusion. George Kennan's reaction to the Senate's 1998 ratification of NATO eastward expansion up to the borders of Russia was even more blunt: "I think it is the beginning of a new cold war. . . . I think the Russians will gradually react quite adversely. . . . I think it is a tragic mistake. There was no reason for this whatsoever. . . . Of course there is going to be a bad reaction from Russia, and then [the NATO expanders] will say that we always told you that is how the Russians are—but this is just wrong."

Were these top US diplomats Russian pawns, as is often said today of anyone offering background information why Russia has invaded Ukraine? I'd like to have your thoughts on this matter.

You can add others who delivered stern warnings to Washington that it was reckless and needlessly provocative to ignore Russia's announced security concerns, including current CIA director William Burns and his predecessor Stansfield Turner, even hawks like Paul Nitze, in fact, almost the whole of the diplomatic corps who had any deep knowledge of Russia. Those warnings were particularly strong with regard to Russia's concerns, well before Putin and including every Russian leader, over incorporation into NATO of Georgia and Ukraine. These are Russia's geostrategic heartland as is evident by a look at a topographic map and recent history, Operation Barbarossa.

Are they all Russian pawns? I suppose that can be claimed in today's climate of frenzied irrationality, a danger to ourselves and the world.

It's useful to have a look at chapters of history that are far enough back so that we can consider them with some degree of detachment.

An obvious choice, as mentioned earlier, is the First World War. It is now recognized that it was a terrible war of futility and stupidity in which none of the agents had a tenable stand.

That's now. Not at the time. As the great powers of the day stumbled into war, the educated classes in each proclaimed the nobility of the cause of their own state. A famous manifesto of prominent German intellectuals appealed to the West to support the land of Kant, Goethe, Beethoven, and other leading figures of civilization. Their counterparts in France and Britain did the same, as did the most distinguished American intellectuals when Woodrow Wilson joined the war shortly after having won the 1916 election on a platform of Peace without Victory.

Not everyone took part in the celebration of the grandeur of their own state. In England, Bertrand Russell dared to question the party line; in Germany, he was joined by Rosa Luxemburg and Karl Liebknecht; in the US, by Eugene Debs. All were imprisoned. Some, like Randolph Bourne in the US, escaped that fate. Bourne was only barred from all liberal journals.

This pattern is not a departure from the historical norm. It pretty much is the norm, regrettably.

The World War I experience did provide important lessons. That was recognized very quickly. Two highly influential examples are Walter Lippmann and Edward Bernays. Lippmann went on to become a most prominent US twentieth-century public intellectual. Bernays became one of the founders and intellectual leaders of the huge public relations industry, the world's major propaganda agency, devoted to undermining markets by creating uninformed consumers who will make irrational choices and to fostering the unbridled consumerism that ranks alongside the fossil fuel industries as a threat to survival.

Lippmann and Bernays were Wilson-Roosevelt-Kennedy liberals. They were also members of the propaganda agency established by President Wilson to convert a pacifist population to raging anti-German fanatics, the Creel Committee on Public Information, a properly Orwellian title. Both were highly impressed by its success in "manufacture of consent" (Lippmann), "engineering of consent" (Bernays). They recognized this to be a "new art in the practice of democracy," a means to ensure that the "bewildered herd"—the general population—can be "put in their place" as mere "spectators," and will not intrude into domains where they do not belong: policy decisions. These must be reserved for the "intelligent minority," "the technocratic and policy-oriented intellectuals" in the Camelot version.

That is pretty much reigning liberal democratic theory, which Lippmann and Bernays helped forge. The conceptions are by no means new. They trace back to the early democratic revolutions of the seventeenth and eighteenth centuries in England and then its US colony. They were invigorated by the World War I experience.

But while the masses may be controlled with "necessary illusions" and "emotionally potent oversimplifications" (in the words of Reinhold Niebuhr, venerated as the "theologian of the liberal establishment"), there is another problem: the "value-oriented intellectuals" who dare to raise questions about US policy that go beyond tactical decisions. They can no longer be jailed, as during World War I, so those in power now seek to expel them from the public domain in other ways.

OVERTURN OF *ROE* SHOWS HOW EXTREME AN OUTLIER THE US HAS BECOME

June 30, 2022

C. J. Polychroniou: *Noam, as gun massacres continue to plague US society, the question that naturally pops into mind is this: Why is the US government so uniquely bad among developed countries at tackling issues in general that affect people's lives? Indeed, it is not just gun violence that makes the US an outlier. It is also a big outlier when it comes to health, income inequality, and the environment. In fact, the US in an outlier with regard to its overall mode of economic, political, and social organization.*

Noam Chomsky: We can begin by taking note of an important date in US history: June 23, 2022. On that date, the senior justice of the Supreme Court, Clarence Thomas, issued a decision solemnly pronouncing his country completely unhinged, a threat to itself and the world.

Those were not, of course, Justice Thomas's words, speaking for the usual 6–3 majority of the reactionary Roberts Court, but they capture their import: in the United States, people may carry a concealed weapon for "self-defense," with no further justification. In no functioning society have people been living in such terror of their fellow citizens that they need guns for self-defense if they're taking a walk with their dogs or going to pick up their children at their (properly barricaded) nursery school.

A true sign of the famous American exceptionalism.

Even apart from the lunacy proclaimed from on high on that historic date, the United States is a highly unusual society, in many ways. The most important are the most general. In your words, "its overall mode of economic, political, and social organization." That merits a few comments.

The basic nature of the modern state capitalist world, including every more or less developed society, was well enough described 250 years ago by Adam Smith in *Wealth of Nations* and in the Madisonian framework of the Constitution of what was soon to become the most powerful state in world history.

In Smith's words, the "masters of mankind" are those with economic power—in his day, the merchants and manufacturers of England. They are the "principal architects" of government policy, which they shape to ensure that their own interests are "most peculiarly attended to," however "grievous" the effects on others, including the people of England but more severely those subject to its "savage injustice" abroad. To the extent that they can, in every age they pursue their "vile maxim": "All for ourselves, nothing for other people."

In the Madisonian constitutional framework, power was to be in the hands of "the wealth of the nation," men (women were property, not persons) who recognize the rights of property owners and the need to "protect the minority of the opulent against the majority." The basic principle was captured succinctly by the first chief justice of the Supreme Court, John Jay: "Those who own the country ought to govern it." His current successors understand that very well, to an unusual extent.

Madison's doctrine differed from Smith's description of the world in some important respects. In his book *The Sacred Fire of Liberty*, Madison scholar Lance Banning writes that Madison "was—to depths that we today are barely able to imagine—an eighteenth-century gentleman of honor." He expected that those granted power would act as an "enlightened Statesman" and "benevolent philosopher," "pure and noble," "men of intelligence, patriotism, property and independent circumstances . . . whose wisdom may best discern the true interests of their country, and whose patriotism and love of justice will be least likely to sacrifice it to temporary or partial considerations."

His illusions were soon shattered.

In very recent years, the reigning doctrine in the courts has been a variety of "originalism" that would have judges view the world from the perspective of a group of wealthy white male slaveowners, who were indeed reasonably enlightened—by the standards of the eighteenth century.

A more rational version of "originalism" was ridiculed seventy years ago by Justice Robert Jackson: "Just what our forefathers did envision, or would have envisioned had they foreseen modern conditions, must be divined from materials almost as enigmatic as the dreams Joseph was called upon to interpret for Pharaoh." That is a saner version than the Bork-Scalia-Alito et al. current version because of the highlighted phrase.

The contortions about "originalism" are of no slight interest. There's no space to go into it here, but there are a few matters that deserve attention, just keeping to the most dedicated adherents to the doctrine—not the saner version ridiculed by Justice Jackson, but the very recent and now prevailing doctrine, which Jackson presumably would have regarded as too absurd even to discuss.

One issue has to do with the role of historical tradition. In Alito's decision overturning *Roe v. Wade*, he stresses the importance of relying on historical tradition in determining whether rights are implied in the Constitution (and amendments). He points out, correctly, that the treatment of women historically gives little basis for according them rights.

In plain words, the history in law and practice is grotesque.

In his decision allowing people to carry concealed weapons to defend themselves in the hideous country he takes the US to be, Thomas also referred to the importance of historical tradition, but he had little to say about it and the actual history undermines his allusions.

In the very important 2008 *Heller* decision, overturning a century of precedent and establishing his new version of the Second Amendment as Holy Writ, Justice Scalia explicitly ignored the entire historical tradition, including the reasons why the framers called for a well-organized militia. The actual tradition, from the beginning, shows that the Second Amendment was largely an anachronism by the twentieth century.

Even putting aside the problem of interpreting Pharoah's dreams, the recently established originalist doctrine appears to be rather flexible, though there are some uniform features, as we have seen again in the past few days: The doctrine can be adapted to yield deeply reactionary outcomes that infringe radically on essential human rights.

Justice Thomas emphasized that consistent thread in his concurring opinion in Alito's decision overturning *Roe v. Wade*. He wrote that "in future cases, we should reconsider all of this Court's substantive due process precedents, including *Griswold, Lawrence,* and *Obergefell*." These are the cases in which the court upheld the right to privacy in personal life, specifically the right to contraception, same-sex sexual relations and same-sex marriage. As Justice Kennedy put it in his majority opinion in *Lawrence*, what is at stake is the right of people "to engage in their [private] conduct without intervention of the government."

Thomas agreed with Alito that his majority opinion overturning *Roe v. Wade* did not in itself reach as far as Thomas's projections, which have a good record of being later affirmed. We will soon see.

These issues are of great importance today, as the court is arrogating to itself extraordinary authority to determine how society must function, a form of judicial supremacy that not only has little constitutional basis but should not be tolerated in a democratic society.

The long-term McConnell strategy of packing the courts is casting its dark shadow over American society, not to speak of the prospects for survival.

Turning to the broader social context, one critical feature of the United States is the unusual power of the masters of mankind, by now multinational corporations and financial institutions. It is of great significance that the masters include the wide-ranging energy system: fossil fuel producers, banks and other financial institutions, and corporate law firms who devise legal strategies to ensure that the interests of their paymasters "are most peculiarly attended to." Their interests are further safeguarded by NATO, the self-described "defensive alliance," which, when not rampaging somewhere, must fulfill its general post–Cold War mission: "to guard pipelines that transport oil and gas that is directed for the West," and more generally to protect sea routes used by tankers and other "crucial infrastructure" of the energy system (NATO secretary-general Jaap de Hoop Scheffer, 2007).

There have been many changes in the past 250 years, of course, but these basic principles hold steady. And with consequences of overwhelming importance, right now.

We need not review the evidence showing that we are at a unique moment in history. Decisions that must be made right now will determine the course of future history, if there is to be any. There is a narrow window in which we must implement the quite feasible measures to avert cataclysmic destruction of the environment. The masters of mankind in the world's most powerful state have been hard at work to close that window, and to ensure that their exorbitant short-term profit and power will remain untouched as the world goes up in flames.

That may sound overdramatic, too apocalyptic. Perhaps it does sound that way, but unfortunately it is true and not overstated. It is also no secret. We can gain some insight into the process in the lead story in the *New York Times* a few days ago. Energy and environment correspondent Coral Davenport reports the near consummation of the longtime campaign of the fossil fuel industry and its minions in Washington to prevent the government from instituting regulations that would impede its primary goal of profit (with ensuing cataclysm), relying on the Roberts Court to give its imprimatur.

We can dismiss the legalistic chicanery and the comical professions of high principle. The facts are plain and simple. The success of the project of destroying organized human life on Earth in the near future is a testimony to the unusual power of the masters of mankind in the US.

The project is more ambitious than protection of the immediate interests of the energy system. The Supreme Court will soon deal with the case of *West Virginia v. EPA*, which has to do with "the federal government's authority to reduce carbon dioxide from power plants—pollution that is dangerously heating the planet." But that's only a start, Davenport reports.

Other cases are wending their way through the courts, exploring various legal strategies to achieve the longer-term goal: to prevent the EPA and other regulatory agencies from enacting measures that are not explicitly legislated. That means just about all measures, since Congress cannot possibly reach decisions on the specific contingencies that arise, or even inquire into them. To do so requires the kind of intensive expert analysis by regulatory agencies and interaction with the public that the project of the masters seeks to ban. The project translates into carte blanche for private power to do as it wishes. In spirit, this is an extension of the reigning extremist version of originalism and has the same result of favoring the interests of the masters and consigning the rest to deserved oblivion.

It is worth looking into the sources of this unusual power of "those who own the country," which manifests itself in many ways. One factor is that as the native scourge was eliminated, the conquered territories were viewed as a kind of "blank slate," with no existing framework of feudal structures. The feudal system, with all its horrors, did assign people some kind of place, however awful, with some rights.

Starting from fresh in a conquered country, individual settlers were on their own. They did have ways to benefit, many at least. The conquered country offered unparalleled advantages: rich resources, vast territory, incomparable security. And like other societies, the US has been blessed with an intellectual class that is eager to extol its real or imagined virtues while suppressing inconvenient reality.

To be sure, for the truly totalitarian mind that is never enough, as we see in current GOP initiatives to suppress books and teaching that might be "divisive" or cause discomfort to (white) students—that is, all of history, everywhere.

The masters are highly organized and have many institutions devoted to their needs, apart from the state that they largely control: trade associations, chambers of commerce, the Business Roundtable, American Legislative Exchange Council (ALEC), many others.

When Thatcher and other neoliberal ideologues preach that there is no society, only individuals subject to the market, they understand well that the rich and privileged are exempt.

The efforts of the masters to atomize the rest are pursued with true passion. The traps of mass consumerism are one mode. Another is harsh suppression of labor organizing, the primary means of self-defense during the industrial era. In keeping with the unusually powerful role of the masters, the US has an unusually violent labor history, adopting new modalities during the Reagan-Clinton imposition of the neoliberal programs that have torn society to shreds, not only in the US. The independent farmers of the genuine Populist movement of the late nineteenth century and their dream of a "cooperative commonwealth" met the same fate.

We should not, however, discount the successes. The nineteenth century struggles to create an independent labor movement based on the principle that "those who work in the mills should own them," and to link it with the powerful Populist movement, were crushed, but not without a residue.

The struggles continued, with significant successes. Those years also saw the rise of mass education, a major contribution to democracy with the US far in the lead—hence, not surprisingly, a target of the neoliberal assault on rights and democracy. The militant labor movement of the 1930s, rising from the ashes of Wilsonian suppression, led America to social democracy while Europe was succumbing to fascism—processes now being reversed under neoliberal assault. The popular movements of the 1960s forged the way to the establishment of freedom of speech as a substantial right, to an extent unparalleled elsewhere, along with civilizing the society over a broad range. The achievements have been targeted by the neoliberal reaction, but not destroyed.

The struggle never ends.

The US is unusual in other ways. It is, of course, a settler-colonial society like all of the Anglosphere, the offshoots of Britain, which was the most democratic society of the day, and also most powerful and violent. These features carried over in complex ways to the daughter societies. Despite the efforts of the framers to contain the threat of democracy, popular pressures expanded it, sufficiently so that the great statesmen of Europe, like Kissinger's hero [Klemens von] Metternich, were deeply concerned about "the pernicious doctrines of republicanism and popular self-rule" spread by "the apostles of sedition" in the liberated colonies, an early version of the "domino theory" that is a ubiquitous feature of imperial domination. King George III was also concerned that the American Revolution might lead to erosion of empire, as it did.

The US has been by far the wealthiest and most powerful state of the Anglosphere, surpassing Britain itself, which was reduced to a "junior partner" of its former colony as the British Foreign Office lamented after World War II when the US took the mantle of global hegemony, displacing Britain and virtually eliminating France. US history reflects that power. It's hard to find another society that has been almost continuously at war—almost always aggressive war—since its founding.

A major—arguably *the* major—reason for the revolution was to overturn the British Royal Proclamation of 1763 that prevented the colonists from attacking the Indigenous nations beyond the Appalachian Mountains. The colonists had other ideas in mind, including notorious land speculators like the founder of the country, George Washington, known to the Iroquois as "the town destroyer."

The brutality of the conquests was hardly a secret. The first US secretary of war, General Henry Knox, described what his countrymen were doing as "the utter extirpation of all the Indians in most populous parts of the Union" by means "more destructive to the Indian natives than the conduct of the conquerors of Mexico and Peru." It was soon to become far worse, though not without efforts to conceal it, beginning with Jefferson's infamous passage in the Declaration of Independence denouncing King George for unleashing "the merciless Indian savages" against the peaceful colonists, who wanted only their "utter extirpation."

On the side, the US picked up half of Mexico in what President/ General U. S. Grant called one of the most "wicked wars" of aggression in history, greatly regretting his participation in the crime as a junior officer.

The task was viciously consummated by the end of the nineteenth century. By then the US was turning to other exercises of violence and subversion too familiar to recount, to the present moment.

All of this has its impact on the prevailing culture. In the light of history, it becomes a little less shocking to see that even after the Uvalde massacre, almost half of Republican voters, mostly from rural traditional white Christian sectors, think that we must accept such horrors as the price of freedom.

The gun culture has other roots, of course, some of which we have discussed. There is much more, some brought out in an incisive report by journalist and political analyst Chris Hedges, based partly on his own experience growing up in the rural America that has been crushed by neoliberal globalization, leaving guns as the last residue for men of some illusion of dignity and social role.

We should add that it is still possible to access Hedges's outstanding work. Most of it was in regular programs on RT [America], which is now canceled under the suffocating censorship designed to protect Americans from any awareness of what Russian leaders may be saying or thinking. Some fragments are permitted, those that can be twisted to show that Putin intends to conquer the world. Those versions receive triumphant exposure, but not, say, the regular negotiation offers, which, while not acceptable, might provide an opening for a diplomatic settlement of the kind that the US government has been dedicated to undermine.

It's been repeatedly said that the US political system is broken and observers decry political polarization in today's Congress. In what sense can we speak of a broken political system when the elites seem to have a strong grip on the policy agenda?

We can put the matter somewhat differently. A political system is broken insofar as the policy agenda is largely in the hands of some sector of power, typically "those who own the country" and therefore have the right to govern it to ensure that their own interests are properly attended to and that the minority of the opulent are well protected.

One effect of the neoliberal assault on the social order has been to amplify the grip of the masters over the political agenda, a natural consequence of the concentration of unaccountable economic power, which is, indeed, impressive. A rough measure is given by the Rand Corporation study that we have discussed earlier, which found that since Reagan opened to doors to highway robbery, almost $50 trillion has been "transferred" from the working and middle classes to the super-rich. That has proceeded alongside of the tendency toward monopolization that results from deregulation, spurred further by the highly protectionist measures of the "free trade agreements" of the Clinton years.

Harvard economists Anna Stansbury and Lawrence Summers attribute the sharp concentration of wealth in the past forty years primarily to the assault on labor, initiated by Reagan (and Thatcher in the UK), carried forward in Clintonite neoliberal globalization. In their words, "Declining unionization, increasingly demanding and empowered shareholders, decreasing real minimum wages, reduced worker protections, and the increases in outsourcing domestically and abroad have disempowered workers with profound consequences for the labor market and the broader economy"—and as an immediate consequence, a stronger grip by the masters on the policy agenda.

The decline of functioning democracy is not limited to the US. The impact on the social order of forty years of bitter class war—the operative meaning of "neoliberalism"—is starker in the US because of the relative weakness of the social protections that are the norm elsewhere, even such elementary matters as maternal care, found everywhere apart from the US and a few Pacific islands. The most dramatic of these social failures is the scandalous privatized health system, with almost twice the costs of comparable societies and some of the worst general outcomes. (The rich are spared.)

Specific illustrations are startling. One recent study found that the "fragmented and inefficient" US health care system was responsible for 212,000 COVID deaths in 2020 alone, along with over $105 billion in extra medical expenses in addition to the nearly $440 billion of extra expenses in normal years, all avoidable with universal health care.

These deficiencies go back many years, despite the very substantial improvements of the New Deal policies that have been under neoliberal attack. The pandemic has brought to light starkly the lethal nature of the business model that has been imposed during these destructive years. The outcome is aptly described by political economist Thomas Ferguson:

> The pandemic shined a terrible, unforgiving light on how fragile a globalized world really is. "Just in time" production, off-shoring, transnational supply chains, and the hollowing-out of firms as they degraded workers into external contractors with lower wages and fewer benefits produced fatally brittle social systems. As the pandemic spread and transnational supply chains broke down, the cumulative impact of more than a generation of steady government cuts in taxes, safety nets, education, and—above all—health care became overwhelming. Virtually every country became paralyzed for a while. In the United States, the United Kingdom, and many developing countries, I think we will eventually recognize that the pandemic actually broke their social systems. As pandemic relief fades from memory and the gruesome toll of delayed deaths, long Covid, substance abuse, and mental health problems climbs higher and higher, the true dimensions of the havoc the pandemic wrought, not least on the US labor force, will stand out more clearly.

Ideologues whose arrogance far exceeds their understanding have played a very dangerous game with the international social order for the past forty years, not for the first time in human history. Those who gave the orders—the masters of mankind—may exult about their short-term gains, but they, too, will rue the havoc they have wrought.

The polarization you mention is very real, but the term is somewhat misleading. The Republican Party has been going off the rails ever since Newt Gingrich took control of Congress in the Clinton years. A decade ago, political analysts Thomas Mann and Norman Ornstein of the American Enterprise Institute observed that the growing polarization is "asymmetric." The Democrats have not shifted greatly, but "the Republican Party has become a radical insurgency—ideologically extreme, scornful of facts and compromise, and dismissive of the legitimacy of its political opposition."

By then, Mitch McConnell, the real evil genius of the radical insurgency, had firm grasp of the reins. The course to destruction of democracy took a further leap forward under Trump and has since reached a quite astonishing level.

The Texas Republican Party, which is at or near the radical extreme of the GOP, has just called virtually for secession. Its June 2022 convention determined that Biden "was not legitimately elected," so Texas is free to ignore decisions of the federal government. Going further, the Texas Republican Party condemns homosexuality as an "abnormal lifestyle choice," calls for schools to teach that life begins at birth, and roundly condemns any restriction on guns, arguing that those under twenty-one are "most likely to need to defend themselves" and may need to quickly buy guns "in emergencies such as riots," while claiming that red flag laws violate the due process rights of people who haven't been convicted of a crime.

Texas may be leading the radical insurgency, but not by much. Some 70 percent of Republicans hold that the 2020 election was stolen and that Trump is the legitimate president. Half of Republicans believe that "top Democrats are involved in elite child sex-trafficking rings."

A large majority think that "the Democratic Party is trying to replace the current electorate with voters from poorer countries around the world," and there are other fantasies that would be hard to believe in a normal country.

That's the Republican voting base, after half a century of refinement of the Nixon "Southern Strategy." The leading idea is to divert attention of voters from GOP dedication to the reinforcement of the vile maxim to "cultural issues" that can be exploited to make political capital of the justified resentment and anger elicited by the policies being instituted, the class war of the neoliberal years.

Admiration of this achievement of the masters is somewhat tempered by the fact that the new GOP was pushing an open door. By the

1970s, the Democrats had pretty much abandoned concern for working people and the poor, openly becoming a party of affluent professionals and Wall Street: the Clintonite party managers and the kind of people who attended Obama's lavish parties.

There is, then, polarization. The Republican leadership became a radical insurgency while across the aisle the leadership found their own more moderate ways to join the class war.

That's the leadership. The public, as usual, has not been silent. On the Democratic side, there has been a revival of New Deal–style social democracy, sometimes beyond, invigorated by the impressive work of Bernie Sanders. On the Republican side it has, unfortunately, descended to a form of Trump worship, reminiscent to an extent of the Hitler worship of ninety years ago.

A new report from researchers at Yale and Columbia Universities shows that the US has fallen behind on climate goals, thanks to four years of Trump in power. Yet, the Biden administration itself is falling quite short on the climate crisis. With that in mind, and given the nature of the US political system, how do we move forward in the fight against global warming?

This is the most important issue of all, for reasons it should be unnecessary to review. To repeat, there are still opportunities to save us from our folly, but the window is not wide, and it is rapidly closing.

The Trump years were an utter catastrophe for the world. Furthermore, the GOP became a denialist party well before Trump, ever since the Koch energy conglomerate brought a quick end to its brief recognition of reality under McCain. The last Republican primary was in 2016, before the Republican Party was taken over by Trump. The candidates were the cream of the crop of the GOP. At the time they were not only all opposed to Trump but were scandalized by him.

Uniformly, the candidates said that what is happening is not happening, with two exceptions. Jeb Bush said that maybe it is, but it doesn't matter. Ohio governor John Kasich was alone in saying that of course global warming is happening, and humans have a significant role. He was praised for that, but mistakenly, because of what he added. Yes, the climate is being destroyed, but we in Ohio will continue to produce and use coal freely and will not apologize for it.

That's the GOP before Trump took it over. It's the GOP that is likely to be running the most powerful state in history very soon.

Under activist pressure, Biden adopted a climate program that was inadequate given the severity of the crisis but was a long step beyond anything that had preceded, and if implemented, would have had some positive effects and granted some time to move beyond. McConnell obstructionism put an end to that, with the help of a few right-wing Democrats, primarily coal baron Joe Manchin, the leading congressional recipient of fossil fuel funding.

More generally, all of the positive Biden programs, mostly crafted by Sanders, met the same fate. Discussion of this tragedy for the country mostly focuses on the few Democrat collaborators, but the real story is GOP obstruction. Quite unfairly, Biden is criticized for the failure to implement his program. Yes, he could have done more, but the blame falls on the radical insurgency.

The political factions dedicated to destroying organized life on Earth—not an exaggeration—are only apparently "the principle architects of policy." Behind them are the masters of mankind. The Koch conglomerate intervention was a vulgar illustration. The processes are more pervasive.

One major program is reaching a dread consummation, as discussed earlier. It received a shot in the arm from the increase in gasoline prices, the major contributor to inflation, accelerated by Putin's criminal invasion of Ukraine. The euphoria in the executive offices of the fossil fuel companies is matched only in the offices of weapons producers. They no longer have to face the annoyance of fending off environmental activists. They are now praised for pouring poisons into the atmosphere and urged to do more, accelerating the march to destruction.

In a sane world the reaction would be different. We would seize the opportunity to move more rapidly to sustainable energy to save coming generations from a miserable fate. The temporary problem of inflation is severe, and can be overcome for those suffering from it by fiscal measures, and beyond. Options reach as far as turning the fossil fuel producers into a public utility. Robert Pollin has shown that they could literally be purchased by the government for a fraction of the sums that the Treasury Department poured into compensating financial institutions for losses during the early stages of the pandemic.

That's hardly unprecedented. Second World War measures came close to that in practice. That was, of course, total war, but today's crisis is even more severe, far more so in fact.

There are recent precedents. In 2009, the US auto industry was on the verge of collapse. The Obama administration virtually nationalized it, paid off its losses, and returned it to the former ownership (with some new faces) so that it could continue with what it had been doing before.

There was another possible choice, had there been popular backing: Turn the industry to a new task. Instead of creating traffic jams and poisoning the atmosphere, produce what the country needs— efficient mass public transportation based on renewable energy, a better life for all and for the future. And a different ownership was imaginable: perhaps the workforce and community, something resembling democracy. There are many options. We are not limited to those that cater to the existing energy system and the grim fate that it is designing for the human species, quite consciously, with meticulous planning.

INDEX

ABOUT HAYMARKET BOOKS

Haymarket Books is a radical, independent, nonprofit book publisher based in Chicago. Our mission is to publish books that contribute to struggles for social and economic justice. We strive to make our books a vibrant and organic part of social movements and the education and development of a critical, engaged, and internationalist Left.

We take inspiration and courage from our namesakes, the Haymarket Martyrs, who gave their lives fighting for a better world. Their 1886 struggle for the eight-hour day—which gave us May Day, the international workers' holiday—reminds workers around the world that ordinary people can organize and struggle for their own liberation. These struggles—against oppression, exploitation, environmental devastation, and war—continue today across the globe.

Since our founding in 2001, Haymarket has published more than nine hundred titles. Radically independent, we seek to drive a wedge into the risk-averse world of corporate book publishing. Our authors include Angela Y. Davis, Arundhati Roy, Keeanga-Yamahtta Taylor, Eve L. Ewing, Aja Monet, Mariame Kaba, Naomi Klein, Rebecca Solnit, Olúfẹ́mi O. Táíwò, Mohammed El-Kurd, José Olivarez, Noam Chomsky, Winona LaDuke, Robyn Maynard, Leanne Betasamosake Simpson, Howard Zinn, Mike Davis, Marc Lamont Hill, Dave Zirin, Astra Taylor, and Amy Goodman, among many other leading writers of our time. We are also the trade publishers of the acclaimed Historical Materialism Book Series.

Haymarket also manages a vibrant community organizing and event space in Chicago, Haymarket House, the popular Haymarket Books Live event series and podcast, and the annual Socialism Conference.

ALSO AVAILABLE FROM HAYMARKET BOOKS

ABOUT THE AUTHORS

Noam Chomsky is Institute Professor (emeritus) in the Department of Linguistics and Philosophy at the Massachusetts Institute of Technology and Laureate Professor of Linguistics and Agnese Nelms Haury Chair in the Program in Environment and Social Justice at the University of Arizona. His work is widely credited with having revolutionized the field of modern linguistics. Chomsky is the author of numerous bestselling political works, which have been translated into scores of languages. Recent books include *What Kind of Creatures Are We?*, as well as *Optimism Over Despair, Notes on Resistance,* and *Chronicles of Dissent.*

C. J. Polychroniou is a political economist/political scientist who has taught and worked in universities and research centers in Europe and the United States. His main research interests are in European economic integration, globalization, the political economy of the United States, and the deconstruction of neoliberalism's politico-economic project. He is a regular contributor to *Truthout* as well as a member of *Truthout's* Public Intellectual Project. He has published several books, and his articles have appeared in a variety of journals, magazines, newspapers, and popular news websites. Many of his publications have been translated into several foreign languages, including Croatian, French, Greek, Italian, Portuguese, Spanish, and Turkish. He lives in Conshohocken, Pennsylvania.